GAME, SET, MATCH: WINNING THE NEGOTIATIONS GAME

By Henry S. Kramer

2001

ALM Publishing
New York, New York

Cover Design: *Eileen Guida*
Interior Page Design & Production: *Amparo Graf*

Library of Congress Cataloging-in-Publication Data

Kramer, Henry S., 1941-
   Game, set, match : winning the negotiations game / by Henry S. Kramer.
      p.cm.
   ISBN 0-9705970-2-9
   1. Negotiation in business. I. Title.

HD58.6 .K73 2001
658.4'052--dc21   00-067673

PREFACE AND ACKNOWLEDGEMENTS

T here are a number of excellent books on negotiations, so why another one? This book is the direct result of a request from the students in my 1999 negotiations simulation program at Cornell University's New York State School of Industrial & Labor Relations. My students asked for a written practical guide containing those "tips, tricks, and traps" used by professional negotiators that we discussed during the course. We found no pre-existing work that took that form and covered all aspects of bargaining.

There are many excellent negotiating texts which provide sound theory for the face to face portion of negotiations, but most omit how to go about the intensive planning and preparation processes often necessary for a successful negotiation. This led to my decision to create this book both as a step by step, "nuts and bolts," approach on how to conduct all types of face to face bargaining and as a desk reference tool for use in negotiations planning. Because in the real world people move naturally through the bargaining process in chronological order, the most useful arrangement of the materials seemed to be to track negotiations on a time line from inception to follow through.

Since all of us negotiate many times in our lives, this book is written for the broadest possible audience. Certainly there are differences in the negotiations skills used in personal, commercial, and labor negotiations, so feel free to pick and choose which topics are relevant to the negotiation at hand. You may want to read it from cover to cover or, if you are an experienced negotiator, to use it as a desk reference tool to consult during bargaining. Because of the book's desk reference aspects, a very limited amount of material has been repeated in different chapters, although usually with a relevant orientation and perspective. I have tried to keep repetition to a minimum.

My purpose is to help you **win** when you negotiate, that is to gain the greatest practical advantage for yourself or your side. While I recognize and encourage "mutual gains" and "win-win" bargaining, my thrust is on achievement of your own goals as your primary mission, always within the context of ethical behavior. To help you win, I've chosen to reveal many of the professional secrets that have made me a successful negotiator over the years, techniques used to negotiate large scale change in the work place. Now that my secrets are public, it will probably be far more difficult for me to use them myself.

People often learn from examples, so the book contains many hypothetical (and a few real) examples to illustrate points. Many of the names used in the examples may sound familiar. Any similarity to persons, living or dead, is purely coincidental. Quotations from famous people and the choice of names in the examples have been used to make a serious subject more entertaining. When legal issues are discussed in the text, they are necessarily dealt with through generalizations. Since actual cases often turn on the facts and the law is changeable, a caveat is in order. This book must never be used as a substitute for the services of competent legal counsel.

No book of this type could have been put together without the assistance and support of a variety of people. Special thanks are due to my wife, Judy, who not only was extremely patient with me while the chapters were written, but who also read each of them several times and made useful suggestions for changes. At American Law Media, my editor, Steven J. Katz, Esq., was, as always, a particular asset. Thanks are due to Ms. Sara Diamond, Esq. and Ms. Caroline

Sorokoff, Esq., who patiently played a role as we negotiated, yes negotiated, the acquisition of this book. Finally, I'd like to express my appreciation to the several people who read the manuscript in advance and made comments: Mr. Brian Gershengorn, Mr. Matt Varble, and Ms. Maureen Robson, from my Cornell class of 1999, my Cornell class of the year 2000 who have been the first to put the book to work, and New York City entrepreneur Mr. Ed Chan.

It's time to play Game, Set, Match. Good luck and may you win game, set, and match.

Henry S. Kramer
Ithaca, New York
2000

TABLE OF CONTENTS

CHAPTER 3 **LEGAL, NEGOTIATIONS MANAGEMENT ISSUES, AND ETHICS**

CHAPTER 4   GETTING GOOD DATA

CHAPTER 5   **COSTING YOUR PLAN AND THE OTHER
SIDE'S PROPOSALS**

CHAPTER 12 THE MID-NEGOTIATION PROCESS

CHAPTER 13 THE END GAME AND CLOCK MANAGEMENT

CHAPTER 14   FOLLOWING UP ON YOUR RESULTS

CHAPTER 1

UNDERSTANDING THE NEGOTIATIONS GAME

THE GAME WE ALL PLAY

Game, Set, Match. "Many if not all life situations can be viewed as games if 'game' is interpreted broadly enough. . . . The subject could just as easily be called negotiation theory as game theory." [John Allen Paulos] Negotiations are almost as unavoidable in life as death and taxes. You probably bargain more often than you realize, so developing good skills in the negotiations game is a valuable life asset when you buy a car, purchase or sell your home, try to negotiate a raise at work, settle a litigation, arrange a commercial deal, seek a variance from local government, or negotiate a labor agreement. Whatever the type of negotiation, whether or not the other side thinks of itself as "winning," you will want to conclude your negotiations game with the satisfaction that comes from achieving your goals. As that eternal loser of baseball games, Charlie Brown, once said, "Winning isn't everything, but losing isn't anything."

How often do people really negotiate? Let's look at one person's experience. Assume you are Jon, a very successful marketing manager at Nerds Unlimited, a moderately sized high tech company. Last January, during your vacation, you were in Istanbul. There you haggled with an old trader (whose years of practice and knowledge of his subject made him a superb negotiator) over the purchase of your very first fine Turkish rug. When you returned home, you were promoted and transferred from the Boston regional office to the corporate headquarters campus in Palo Alto, California. After meeting with Executive Vice President Dilbert and Human Resources Director Catbert, you accepted their offer of a five percent salary increase for your new and vastly increased responsibilities.

The transfer left you with real estate and housing problems. In March, you sold your old house in Cambridge, rented temporary quarters near Stanford University, and decided to custom build your dream home. You signed a realtor contract with a commission schedule and worked out a selling price on your old house. The realtor wanted a quick sale (and commission) and pressed you to set a low price to "move this property quickly." You signed a lease in Palo Alto for temporary housing, haggled over the monthly rent and deposit, and executed a "buyer's agent" contract with the California realtor who located a lot for you and suggested a builder. In April, you worked out a construction agreement for the new Palo Alto house with a progress payment arrangement, at a price of six hundred thousand dollars. You met with bank officers to get the best possible deal on a construction mortgage, settling for a six and a half percent adjustable rate loan.

With your housing resolved, you decided to buy the little red convertible you'd always coveted. You worked out a leasing deal with a car dealer's sales representative, obtaining an eight thousand dollar trade-in price on your old car, some thrown in items, and lease financing. The lease you signed cost you $350 a month, plus fifteen cents for each mile over ten thousand a year, and carried an interest rate of eight percent. In July, you sat down with your company's chief financial officer to resolve a budget for your marketing department. The department ended up with a two percent increase over previous year figures. During August, you spent several days as part of a task force meeting with the union that represents the clerical employees at the Palo Alto corporate park site and reached a new five year contract, without a strike.

In your personal life, you began your efforts to get the Palo Alto planning board to grant historical status to a unique property. In October you joined a church and began working to get the minister of your former church in Cambridge selected as the new minister in Palo Alto.

You have been busy. All the described activities have something in common. In each and every one of these instances, you were using your skills in the negotiations game. Your family and colleagues correctly congratulated you for having done fairly well. But, perhaps your score would have been better if you'd applied a few of the techniques used by experienced negotiators. How could you have increased your score? You could have driven a better bargain on the Turkish rug if you'd had more information about the value of these rugs. At work, your company was prepared to give you up to a ten percent salary increase. They were delighted when you asked for eight percent and even more pleased when you settled for five percent. You paid the real estate agent in Cambridge a seven percent commission. However, a number of fine agents were accepting work at a commission of six percent. Your realtor, anxious to get a quick sale and a quick commission, convinced you to accept a price on your old home which was $20,000 lower than its fair market value. The buyer of your Cambridge house and the seller of your new land in Palo Alto each gained bargaining advantage because you openly stated that you wanted to move rapidly in completing your relocation. The building contract for your new custom house was four percent over your builder's bottom line (on this big ticket item it cost you an extra $24,000). Adjustable rate mortgages were available at a first year rate of five and three quarters percent instead of six and a half percent, costing you many thousands over the life of the loan. Because you did not invest the time to explore alternatives, you also paid ten percent more than you should have for temporary housing.

In talking with a friend who leases a car similar to yours, you learned that your car leasing deal could have been better. The monthly payments are too high, the trade-in value for your old car was too low, you didn't get enough included miles per year for your use pattern, and the quoted interest rate hid certain costs. Like most people, you were intimidated by the car dealer who gave you the "deal of your life," but only after getting the "approval of the new car lease manager." Your friend later told you the dealership has no such position.

The chief financial officer of your company had an additional percent available for your department budget. You accepted her statement that "there isn't any more." Later, you found out that most other departments got the additional percent. A fellow manager then told you, "unlike Boston, only the persistent very squeaky wheel gets greased at Palo Alto headquarters."

Perhaps your most serious scoring lapse came in labor contract negotiations. There, you were faced with an international union representative who makes his living in day-to-day collective bargaining. The union squeezed one and a half percent more out of you in wages than was necessary for settlement in each year of a five year contract covering one hundred people. This will cost your company about a million extra dollars.

Your political and church related negotiations suffered from a lack of knowledge of the history and traditions of the relevant organizations. Those who knew these things better reached a compromise with you that gave you only a small portion of your objectives.

So, did you fail? No, although you clearly could have played better if you had improved your negotiating skills. Don't be too critical of yourself. In baseball, a hitter who bats three hundred fails to get a hit seven times out of ten, and yet may still be regarded as a star. But, the rare hitter who can regularly post an average in the high three hundreds or the extraordinary four hundred hitter is transformed into a super star. The point here is that although you did well in your various negotiations, you could have done considerably better had you known the secrets of professional negotiators. Armed with these secrets it is possible to achieve greater success. Armed with them, you will do better and find the process more interesting, satisfying, and acceptable.

At one time or another, almost all of us play the negotiations game. Some negotiations are outwardly friendly, while others are openly confrontational. Even seemingly friendly negotiations contain a core that is at least partially adversarial. Some negotiations are simple, some are quite complex with large stakes. But, it is almost impossible to avoid situations in which we have things we need to attain and when we must bargain with others in order to achieve them at a price we are willing to pay. Negotiating is as ancient art. A colleague of mine had a cartoon on his wall which featured two very pretty senoritas standing outside a cantina each holding up three fingers, while two mounted caballeros signaled two fingers. The caption read, "The origins of collective bargaining." One thing is guaranteed. Unless you are a complete hermit, you will not go through life without having to negotiate.

Some common examples of negotiation or bargaining relationships include:

- Auto purchaser or lessor and sales representative;
- Buyer, seller, and brokers for real estate;
- Sales representative and purchasing agent;
- Attorneys discussing settlement of a case;
- Accountants, attorneys, and individuals with IRS representatives at audits;
- Labor relations manager and union representative;

- Politicians working out a compromise; and,
- Zoning appeal meetings.

This book is designed to provide you with some practical, down-to-earth, tips, tricks, and traps related to the bargaining game. Not all of these tips will apply to any given negotiation. Simple negotiations require less complex techniques and less time and effort than complex ones. If you are facing complex negotiations, your investment of time in learning how professionals negotiate and how to either beat them at their own game, or at least hold your own, is likely to yield large dividends. In commercial negotiations, the value of the package you are negotiating will usually far outweigh the salaries of all the negotiators and the cost of their support services.

The book is laced with examples that allow you to relate the application of negotiating skills to the real world and which demonstrate the costs and opportunities of using negotiating skills. Some of the examples relate to personal life, some to commerce, and some to labor relations. The basic skills used in each of these types of negotiations are essentially the same, although there is variation in the legal rules for conducting them. While the negotiating skills described here could be extended to domestic situations, the thrust of this book is about the world of work and volunteer type work equivalents such as churches and politics, as they relate to dealings between adults.

Some people will never enjoy negotiating. Despite years of experience, even professional negotiators don't always enjoy the negotiating process. This happens when the stakes are high and critical information is unobtainable. Negotiating in the dark is very difficult. Some negotiations, such as those with automobile dealers, leave people frustrated because the dealers know so much more about the situation than the customers, even those customers who do some research.

Can you walk away from most negotiations? Certainly, but there are relationships in which negotiations are part of an ongoing process which cannot be terminated. Labor negotiations are a classic example of "shotgun weddings." Apart from rare union decertifications, an established union-management relationship cannot simply be ended by some easy form of "industrial divorce." The parties to a private sector labor negotiation must reach agreement or risk a disruptive labor dispute. If you take excessive advantage of temporary negotiating power, at least in the perception of the other side, the ensuing negotiations may be very difficult. Some commercial partnerships are also too expensive or difficult to dissolve. However, when you are in a commercial negotiation which is not going well, you may resolve the difficulty by breaking off the negotiations and finding a new potential partner. In commercial matters, you may even negotiate simultaneously with multiple parties.

One of the most difficult negotiation concepts for the Cornell University students in my collective bargaining simulation classes is that negotiations are not conducted in a vacuum. Negotiators must juggle a complex range of dynamic factors. At a minimum, successful commercial and labor negotiations necessitate bringing to bear a knowledge of the other side and of the applicable economics, law, politics, and public relations. Negotiations take place in a fluid, dynamic environment in which day-to-day events potentially change the relative power positions of both sides.

Suppose that you are selling widgets in a market in which there is a critical shortage of widgets. You are negotiating with an original equipment manufacturer who seriously needs to buy a large quantity of widgets and has turned to you because you appear to be the only organization that is able to meet its needs. Yesterday morning, you were in the happy position of being able to demand a significant premium for manufacturing your widgets. But, late yesterday, the entire market for widgets changed and collapsed as one of your competitors announced a new process that would shortly flood the market with an abundance of cheap widgets. The other side's bargaining power increased dramatically while yours diminished significantly. Yesterday you were piloting a yacht, today you have a canoe with only a small paddle. Your entire negotiating strategy will have to change. Now, imagine that two weeks later, the other company admits that there are serious flaws in its new process and that it will be at least two years before they are able to begin widget production. Once again, the balance of negotiating power will shift. While most shifts aren't this dramatic, changes do occur.

If you know as much as possible about the negotiations game, you will feel more confident when you find yourself in the negotiating process. Unlike people in many other cultures, in the United States we do not routinely bargain for consumer goods. We buy a few houses and several cars over a lifetime. But, at work, we have to negotiate constantly with customers, clients, suppliers, other internal functions, peers, superiors, and subordinates, although we may not tend to think of these dealings as negotiations.

Some things about negotiations, including bluffing, may make you uncomfortable. People often bluff during negotiations.

Ben McCay is the Executive Assistant District Attorney in the County of Old York. McCay holds a conference in his office with Victor Violent, who has been indicted for second degree murder, and Violent's criminal defense attorney, Penny Mason. McCay offers a plea deal at manslaughter one, saying, "You know our case is very strong. We have an eye witness who puts you squarely at the crime site"(which is true). But, McCay knows that the witness is both inarticulate and seedy and that the district attorney's office would prefer to keep him off the stand but cannot make a good case without him. Accordingly, McCay has been authorized to go as low as manslaughter two to settle the matter. Mason, who hates to go to trial unless she has a surprise up her sleeve which will guarantee a last minute win, suggests the district attorney accept a plea of manslaughter two. McCay counters with manslaughter one with a sentencing recommendation and Mason and Violent accept. Criminal defense pleas are classic examples of negotiations between attorneys. Bluff is anything but unknown in these negotiations.

You may find it difficult personally or ethically to take a position you know you cannot hold in order to see if the other side will blink first. At times, you may have to take a personal or professional risk to achieve the outcome you want. Sometimes the risk will turn against you. You may find it difficult to look someone in the eye and say "we won't do that," when you know very well that you may and, if pressed, you will. For truly professional negotiators, all outward negotiating table behavior is the result of conscious thought, not the expression of true or internal emotions. This means "being on stage" and demonstrating enormous self control. Because of this, negotiations may be stressful and take a physical and emotional toll on professional negotiators. You may resent the amount of work necessary to have sufficient information to negotiate on a level playing field. You may even hate negotiations, but you won't be able to avoid them entirely. On the other hand, when you have a good plan, sufficient information, and a lot of leverage, negotiations can be fun and provide a real sense of accomplishment when you achieve your goals.

At its heart, the negotiation game is adversarial, no matter how sugar-coated we try to make it. People cooperate because their interests seem to coincide, at least on a given point. Perhaps the classic example is the World War II alliance of the United States and Great Britain with the Soviet Union. For a time, these strange Allies' aims and interests converged on one overwhelmingly important objective, the defeat of Hitler's Third Reich. Once that objective was met, our unnatural "alliance" with the Soviets turned into the Cold War, for the enemy of my enemy is not necessarily my friend. Rarely will any two people or two organizations have identical overall long term objectives.

Many people find confrontation difficult and seek out a cooperative model as a way of avoiding the outward manifestations of conflict. The model of cooperation for many in United States labor-management relations is the relationship between the big three auto makers and the United Auto Workers Union. Yet, when push comes to shove, the goal of the UAW is fixed by its legal obligation to protect represented employees' collective interests (for which a union is not to be faulted), even at the cost of the auto makers' other stakeholders, such as stockholders and suppliers. That this model has not become prevalent in the United States may reflect the more realistically adversarial view that most employers have of the role of organized labor unions.

That negotiations are adversarial still leaves open the door for both sides to come away from the table with the feeling that they both have achieved some success. The negotiations game requires compromise and will result in settlement only when the final package falls within both sides' acceptable limits. Particularly in long term relationships, a feeling on the part of both sides that they have "won" the negotiations game is critical, not only for the deal itself but for willing and cooperative implementation.

Not all negotiations can or do result in agreements or settlements. Indeed, settlements require what may be termed a "settlement window." This window is an area of overlap in which both sides' fundamental objectives, their "must haves," share common ground. If you enter a negotiation on the basis that you will settle for no less than receiving one hundred dollars per widget (or settle a litigation for no less than one million dollars) or you will walk away from the deal, and the other side will pay no more than ninety dollars per widget (or nine hundred thousand dollars to settle) or it will walk away from the deal, and these positions are completely firm, no deal can be reached, despite the best negotiating skills in the world.

On the opposite end of the spectrum, no negotiating skill whatever is necessary if your instructions are "pay them whatever it takes to get the merchandise." Under these circumstances, anyone can settle and the settlement itself represents no achievement for the negotiator. Someone was once introduced to me as an experienced labor contract negotiator. He had been chief spokesman in dozens and dozens of negotiations. When he described his achievements he said, "I never had a strike." But, his instructions had always been to settle at whatever cost it took to avoid a strike and he had never been required to win anything apart from that in return. Under those circumstances, a trained negotiator was hardly necessary. Any competent adult could do the job on those terms.

Another frustration will often be never knowing how well you actually did in a negotiation game compared to the maximum achievable. An auto sales representative is never going to tell you, "Oh, by the way, you could have bought that car for two hundred dollars less. Have a nice day." If you have driven an excellent deal, you may never know it. Conversely, you may have been taken to the cleaners and you may never find out. You may discover the facts only if someone tactlessly says, "I bought the exact same car with the same options and trade-in price from the same sales representative at about the same time you did for two hundred dollars less than you paid." If you need clear feedback, you are not likely to get it in connection with negotiating. Another example of this lack of information problem occurs when a passenger encounters the airlines "yield management" system for setting air fares. It may be that no two people on the plane paid the same fare. While some of the airlines have web sites where you can offer your own price, you will forever be at a disadvantage because the airline always has more information about what it will take to secure a seat than you do.

The negotiations game is "process driven." The more you understand the process and utilize it in pursuing your objectives, the better you will do. This means being introspective at times. You will need to be able to step back from the table and see yourself and your negotiating team as others see them. It also means crafting the other side's perceptions of you and your team in the way most favorable to achieving your objectives.

This book is organized to follow the flow of a complex negotiation from the planning and objective-setting strategy phase into the tactical day-to-day practical techniques professional negotiators use. Negotiations themselves, once begun, may be divided conveniently into three phases much like a chess match. There is an opening game, a mid game, and an end game. The techniques used in each phase are somewhat different.

This book is about "winning" the negotiations game. Winning means that you have achieved more and done better in negotiations than you would have accomplished without training and without developed insights into the negotiating process. Negotiating skill cannot change market forces but it can permit you to do as well as possible in the real world. It is usually helpful to develop negotiations in such a way that the other side *perceives* that it too has won a victory. However, this book is about winning for yourself, as a primary objective. Giving the other guy a victory is a fine secondary objective but it should never obscure that you are in negotiations to do the best possible thing for yourself or your organization.

In a business context, negotiating skills are very valuable. Many commercial and labor relations transactions involve fairly large sums of money, in which even the variation in terms won by a good negotiator in a single negotiation may well reach six or seven figures and equal or exceed the negotiator's yearly salary and cost to the organization for one or more years. A good negotiator can be a real contributor to the bottom line. In personal life, houses and cars tend to be our principle big ticket purchases. Here we deal not in hundreds but in thousands or tens of thousands of dollars over time. The investment of time, effort and cost it takes to become a better negotiator for big ticket items should pay for itself many times over.

OVERALL OBJECTIVE (MISSION)

"[A mission is] the task, together with the purpose, that clearly indicates the action to be taken and the reason therefore" [Department of Defense] For negotiations of any sort, the difference between success and failure is planning. If you don't have a plan (whether or not it is written) you are truly likely to end up where you don't want to be, having achieved only a small fraction, if any, of your objectives.

In negotiations, one can view the initial process of goal setting in three phases. The first phase is to know your core goals or, in other words, your mission. The second phase is to develop a strategic view of what your detailed objectives are and their level of priority. The third phase is to have a tactical plan for day-to-day activities to actually carry out your strategic plans.

James C. Burris (Lt. Col. Ret.), the former Vice President of Human Resources of BASF Wyandotte Corporation (who taught leadership at West Point and who commanded a battalion in Vietnam), in common with many former military people, counseled those who worked for him that projects should start with a mission statement. That advice is well taken. Your approach to any negotiation would wisely start off with a defined mission statement, approved as necessary by the authorities in your organization.

In order to give those executing them the necessary strategic and tactical freedom of action, negotiation missions should usually be stated only in broad terms. From the mission statement, the negotiator or the negotiating team can move on to an analysis to determine the objectives necessary to carry out the mission and assign tasks to various team members. For example, General Eisenhower's mission in the European Theater in World War II was simply defined as "to enter the continent of Europe, and in conjunction with the other United Nations, undertake operations aimed at the heart of Germany and the destruction of her armed forces." There was no definition of "heart" or of the "other United Nations," leaving Eisenhower room to define a strategy and wiggle room to include or exclude the Soviets from Allied planning.

The mission statement for a commercial agreement might read, for example, "to secure a reliable sole source supplier for widgets at the Thomas City plant for the next five years at a cost not to exceed budgetary estimates." An example of a mission statement for a labor contract might read, "to obtain at least a three year agreement, if possible without a labor dispute, within budget, which secures management's current rights and secures new operating flexibilities in return for economic concessions." Note that in both these examples, only the essentials are spelled out. The details are left to the negotiators and the organization's internal processes for approval.

For individuals negotiating for their own interests or for accountants and attorneys negotiating for clients, a formal mission statement may well be omitted. The negotiator should nevertheless have a clearly defined overall objective and when serving a client should secure the client's agreement and consent to the objective to avoid later misunderstandings. For large scale or complex negotiations on behalf of organizations, at least some form of written mission statement which has been blessed by appropriate personnel should be the starting point for planning. In negotiations, the side that knows what its core objectives are from the outset will enjoy an advantage and be able to move through the negotiation process far more smoothly than a party that is making up its mind as it goes along, often while under pressure and sometimes in the throes of panic. Good objective setting requires time and thought. This may be done far more easily and less subjectively when it is done early in the process. Hasty decisions made under pressure or in a state of panic are considerably more likely to be erroneous or dangerous and to carry major negative consequences.

STRATEGY (GOALS)

"[Strategy is] the art and science of developing and using political, economic, psychological, and military forces as necessary during peace and war, to afford the maximum support to policies, in order to increase the probabilities and favorable consequences of victory and to lessen the chances of defeat." [Department of Defense] The second phase of the initial planning process for the negotiation game is developing detailed objectives, setting priorities on the objectives, and devising a strategic plan. Keep in mind that strategy is the broad concept of managing and directing an enterprise or mission while tactics deal with short term day-to-day manipulations. A strategy for an attorney may be to bring a class action lawsuit. For a union's labor contract negotiator, trying to organize another of the employer's facilities to which the employer might shift work may be a strategic means of applying pressure. For a corporate purchasing agent on a large buy negotiation, a strategy might include floating the possibility the corporation will manufacture its own product if the potential supplier does not reach an accord. For a house seller, a strategy may be to convince an interested potential buyer that other potential buyers exist and are ready to step in.

You may well think that plans cannot be determined in advance because you must react to what the other side is doing. One of the greatest mistakes inexperienced negotiators make is being overly reactive to the other side's actions or feared actions, thereby letting the other side take the initiative and determine what is happening in bargaining. There are two excellent segments on this in Kenneth Burns' Civil War documentary series. In one, General Grant, early in the War Between the States, remarks on how as he went up a hill he was in fear of the enemy and then he realized that the enemy was as much in fear of him as he of them. Grant adds that it was a lesson he never forgot. The second clip quotes General William Tecumseh Sherman as saying that Grant is a better general than he is because he, Sherman, cares too much about what the enemy is doing out of his sight, while Grant doesn't give a damn about the enemy's plans and pursues his own. Students in my collective bargaining simulation classes at Cornell are exposed to these clips on the first day. The lesson is that you must plan your own strategy and tactics and while you may, and should, plan, or "war game," what the other side might do, you must not forget to devise and follow your own game plan. Professional football teams in the NFL have game plans and while they respect what the other team may do, they usually try with determination to impose their own game plan. That is a good lesson for transfer to negotiations.

TACTICS (EXECUTION)

"[Tactics is] the ordered arrangement and maneuver of units in relation to each other and/or to the [other side] in order to use their full potentialities." [Department of Defense] The final element in the initializing of a negotiation is a tactical plan. In the tactical phase such issues as how to organize negotiations, seating at the table, the words of opening speeches, agendas, the number of meetings desirable, and similar matters are considered. Since you can't cover everything that might happen, tactical plans at this level are still moderately general. On the spot and quick tactical decisions will have to be made in any negotiation when the other side surprises you or unexpected outside events cause problems.

No matter how well you plan, surprises will happen. But, as my negotiations consulting clients have often noted, when they were prepared with an advance plan, what would have been torturous decisions became much simpler. Baseball players on deck swing multiple bats so that when they get to the plate with just one, it seems lighter. A good strategic and tactical plan will add self confidence to any negotiator and negotiating team. Being prepared will make it harder for the other side to take you off your game plan.

Sometimes it is particularly difficult to negotiate with someone who doesn't quite know where they are going and flounders around, sending mixed signals. If both sides are well prepared they are more likely to have reasonable expectations and thus to be better able to reach timely agreements. You have to know where you want to go in order to have a good chance of getting there and not someplace else. Set a generalized mission statement first with the overall purpose and goal of the negotiations. Then think about strategy and tactics. The preparation task can take time and effort, but it is usually worth it. If you don't do it and the negotiations are complex or high value, expect to pay a price for not being prepared.

Finally, keep your negotiations in perspective. Unless you are negotiating on your own behalf, you should try to think of negotiations as a game. Personal negotiations carry the danger of your becoming overly involved in attaining goals and hence less objective. In commercial and labor negotiations, you play the negotiations game as an agent for someone else. Because your job success may ride on your achievements while bargaining, playing the negotiations game may sometimes be quite stressful. It is important to play the negotiations game to win, but it is also critical not to let the game become obsessive. Doing so will destroy your negotiating objectivity and reduce your chances of success, while possibly impacting your health. So play to win, but remember that in the last analysis most negotiations are only a game.

CHAPTER 2

PLANNING A STRATEGY

WHY PLAN?

"Few people have any next, they live from hand to mouth without a plan, and are always at the end of their line." [Ralph Waldo Emerson] Why plan? Planning makes life easier. There is a story, perhaps apocryphal, about a general who was awakened by a frantic aide who gave him the news, "The enemy has suddenly attacked our southern frontier," and asked, "Sir, what must we do?" The general yawned, and replied, "You will find that plan in drawer B," turned over, and went back to sleep. The time the general had spent planning paid off. Without a plan, there might have been panic. All major military forces maintain contingency plans. Attorneys plan trial strategies with contingencies in mind.

Why plan in advance of a negotiation? Time, power, and information are the three key elements in negotiating. With regard to time, it is far easier to make objective decisions on vital matters when the decisions are made with rational reflection and not under the pressure of a time deadline. For personal negotiators who have complete power over what they are authorized to do, having even informal plans may check their normal human tendencies to go further than they had intended or are really able to go. Individuals sometimes go too far because they have become too attached to attaining the house, antique, or new car they want. For them, negotiation is no longer a game. For those negotiating for others or organizations, the time for decision makers to collect data, come together, and decide a position is well in advance of negotiations. Without planning, there is a tendency to panic under pressure and time deadlines.

Portia Caesar is an amateur collector of ancient Roman coins. She finds a very interesting specimen at Joe's Antique Shop in a small town. She instantly decides that she must have that coin and estimates its value at $500. She decides she will not pay more than that for it. It has no price tag and the dealer says, "Beautiful, isn't it? I see you are interested. Make me an offer." Portia offers the dealer $300 for the coin, saying that it looks rather flawed. The dealer laughs and hands her the coin urging her to look at it more closely. Handling the coin, Portia finds it even more attractive. She responds, "OK, I'll go to $400." The dealer laughs again and invites her to touch the coin again. Portia, who now really wants the coin, begins to wonder if she has undervalued it. She goes to her "final price" of $500 and the dealer, who has noted the longing look in Portia's eyes as she handles the coin, grins and says, "Surely, you jest. That beautiful and rare coin would be a bargain at twice that price." Having reached her self set price limit, Portia begins to leave the store but she has absolutely fallen in love with that coin. When the dealer calls to her, "I'll let you have it for $800," almost without thinking, she snaps back, "$750, that's my final offer or I'm really leaving." The dealer responds, "sold." Portia, who as an individual negotiator has no binding negotiation instructions from a client or organization and is not risking her career by overspending as a professional negotiator would, has now paid one and a half times her improvised plan level for the coin because she became too attached to it. When she gets the coin appraised, its retail market value is set at $550.

Pollyanna Systems is in negotiations with Cassandra Industries to purchase a wide range of parts needed for its assembly operations. Its current supplier, Broke & Bankrupt, is going completely out of business next month. Pollyanna enters its negotiations with Cassandra with no thought that negotiations might break down, without opening simultaneous negotiations with other potential suppliers, and with no contingency plan. At first, negotiations appear to be going well and Pollyanna is confident that it will be able to reach an agreement with Cassandra Industries before supplies from Broke & Bankrupt dry up. However, at the last minute, Cassandra Industries insists that due to changing market condi-

tions it must have a huge price increase to close the contract, a price well beyond what the negotiating team is authorized to spend. A stunned group of Pollyanna executives hears a report to this effect from their negotiating team. Should they accept the higher price or try to find another supplier on short notice? Two vice presidents argue for the former course and two for the latter course. While they are arguing, the negotiating team is forced to stall negotiations until they are able to receive instructions on what to do. During the delay period, Pollyanna's assembly production managers are screaming they must have new parts soon or will be forced to shut down. Finally, Pollyanna's President and Chief Executive Officer has to break the deadlock and decide which way to go. That Pollyanna should have planned for the possibility of a breakdown in negotiations earlier is now evident. The message is never to leave yourself without planned alternatives.

A second reason for planning is that it allows time for debate and the resolution of any splits among the decision makers of your own side, be they business executives, an attorney's clients, or perhaps a spouse for a personal negotiation. On many complex issues, there may be more than one point of view on what should be done and what risks are acceptable. Negotiations involve a variety of stakeholders. In personal negotiations, stakeholders may include a spouse and children who will inhabit, for example, a new house and have different ideas about what it must include. Business entities may have rivalries between various profit centers. A commercial or labor negotiation may result in an outcome favorable to the business organization as a whole but which has a negative impact on one or more divisions or operations. These issues can be difficult and time consuming to thresh out. If they cannot be worked out in a business entity, they may require the decision of a common superior, such as the chief executive officer.

Bonaparte Corporation is planning for negotiations for a successor labor agreement between Local 100 of the Armaments Workers union and Bonaparte's missiles division. The negotiating committee has determined that there is a real risk of a labor dispute. Jon Money, Bonaparte's chief financial officer who originally opposed the acquisition of the missile division, argues that operating the division, which is only marginally profitable, requires that the wage settlement not exceed the area trend settlement of 3.0% per year and further that a strike should be taken if neces-

17

sary to protect that target. "If we are not making a profit in missiles, we should get out of that business," is his position. Alma Morter, Bonaparte's vice president for missile production, objects strenuously to risking a strike because she is "concerned that a strike will be too disruptive and imperil future contracts which will make the business very profitable in the long run." Morter knows it also means she will miss her bottom line objectives for the current year and drastically reduce her performance based executive bonus. Pat Ultimate, the corporate president and chief executive officer, understanding both Morter's business argument and her hidden personal agenda, finds the proposed wage limitation the better argument and decides to subsidize any losses in the missile division from profits earned in the small arms division. Of course, the vice president heading that division is upset and argues against the subsidy. The president has the last word, "I understand that each of you is primarily concerned with your area of responsibility. But, I have to be concerned with the good of the overall company and I'm willing to take the risk and shift profits around between divisions. And, in case you are wondering (she smiles), I'll protect those whose executive bonus performance is directly impacted by this decision from adverse action due to it." Such a discussion is far more likely to produce a thoughtful result if not done under crisis conditions.

A third reason for planning is to give the negotiators benchmarks against which to test proposals. Without pre-determined benchmarks there will be time-wasting squabbling between members of a negotiating committee or stakeholders in a real estate transaction or in a car deal. This is particularly true in democratic organizations, such as some unions, in which the negotiation leader must persuade and cannot override dissent. Planning will provide negotiators with the confidence level that stems from knowing where they are going and what they are doing. For organizations, planning also insures that its negotiators will be advancing the organization's goals and policies and not dispensing their own brands of business justice. Unions also need to plan.

The United Shoe Workers union is engaged in a negotiation with Footfall Tackle. Half of workers represented by the union are under the age of thirty and all the remaining workers are over age fifty. The composition of the union negotiating team mirrors this distribution. In the last hours of negotiation before the current contract expires, Footfall offers the union a choice of how to divide the eco-

nomic offer on the table between wage increases or pension increases. Footfall's spokesperson states, "We are giving the union the option to distribute the available monies between wages and pensions. We don't care which way you go as long as the total price to us is the same." The union has no plan of what to do to bridge the gap between the younger wage oriented workers and the older pension oriented workers. Under time pressure, the union negotiating team fractures.

Fourth, planning will help to avoid mistakes. Few of us do our best under pressure when we have to make last minute snap judgments. We make sounder decisions when we have both time to think and time for our decision to be examined by others for deficiencies or weaknesses. Mistakes are a great enemy in negotiations. They may prove to be very costly or difficult to retrieve. Minimizing the risk of mistakes is one reason why many negotiations are conducted through teams rather than through individuals.

With the time needed to make a decision rapidly disappearing, Rapid Data Processing quickly draws up a detailed plan for handling the payroll needs of BigShot Guns. BigShot, which is under pressure from failures in its aging payroll system, is simultaneously negotiating with other data processing companies. The company, which wishes to bring all these negotiations to a close, has set a deadline date for all potential suppliers and has firmly denied Rapid Data's request for extended negotiating time. Rapid Data's plan is put together by its chief spokesperson and its data processing manager, completed at two in the morning, and presented to BigShot at an early morning breakfast negotiation session. The plan is an elaborate one. BigShot is impressed, accepts the plan, and signs a contract. Two hours later, in the midst of a celebration of the new contract, Rapid Data's data processing manager suddenly realizes that a key element of the proposal cannot be carried out without the purchase of expensive new equipment. This discovery completely turns the expected profit on the deal into a sizeable loss. Had the data processing manager not been so tired on the last night of negotiations or had there been time to submit the new scheme to other managers, the defect might have been spotted.

⚐ TRAP

In business negotiations, try to get your plan formally adopted and signed off on by your organization's highest executive authority, with a proviso that its terms *cannot* be changed without that individual's express and personal approval. The purpose of this exercise is to be sure that if panic should set in at a level above the negotiating team but below the top, these intermediate level authorities cannot force an abrupt unplanned change of direction on their negotiators.

THE NEGOTIATION "WHITE PAPER"

"Have a plan for everything." [Bear Bryant] What is a "white paper" negotiation plan? This document, frequently referred to as a bargaining plan, is a blueprint for a negotiation. *As such, a white paper negotiation plan is the single most important piece of planning that may be done for any negotiation and is highly desirable in any complex or difficult negotiation. The paper is more than an exercise. It imposes discipline on the negotiation process. It forces you to examine and evaluate your bargaining power, to look at timing issues, and to consider all available information.*

While nothing like a formal white paper negotiation plan is needed for an individual negotiation for a house, a car, or to buy a Persian carpet, at least some of the planning elements involved may be applicable to these consumer transactions. Many of the factors examined in a white paper negotiation plan might at least warrant thought before beginning an individual consumer negotiation, at least for a big ticket item. Readers involved in personal negotiations such as buying a car or a house may want to just skim or to skip this section and move ahead to the next section.

⚐ TIP

Despite the work involved, try to be selected to draft the white paper negotiation plan. The person or people who actually write the white paper negotiating plan may exercise power within an organization far in excess of nominal rank or status. This is particularly true of the individual who writes the key objectives and strategies section of the plan. Many people do not like to write, but the way in which issues are framed and the language used in a negotiating plan gives the writer unusual influence. People tend to be lazy. A writer's proposed objectives and strategies may be modified, but many people prefer to modify someone else's work rather than to take on the work of rewriting the material.

A white paper negotiation plan should examine the current situation, how the situation is likely to evolve, and set forth a mission, a strategy, a general tactical plan, and a communications plan. The end purpose of a white paper negotiation plan is to be blessed by the highest levels of an organization, so that the bargaining team members will have a charter, a benchmark against which to work, and a bulwark against last minute panic laden changes that might tend to destroy the team's credibility.

Unwise Manufacturers is about to enter into a negotiation with SmartSeller for a one year supply of wemblies. Unwise's prior supplier has notified the company that it will be able to supply wemblies for only another ninety days. Unwise does not adopt or use any form of negotiating plan. SmartSeller does use such plans and by collecting information from network sources they are aware that Unwise's Vice President of Manufacturing, Waffler, has a reputation of caving under pressure. Maria Firmly, newly hired to be chief spokesperson for Unwise, is instructed by Vice President of Manufacturing Waffler that Unwise will absolutely not pay more than five dollars per wembly and that she has no authority to go any higher. As negotiations near the last critical date for locking in a supplier, SmartSeller insists on a price of five and a half dollars per wembly. Firmly, armed with her instructions not to go over five dollars per unit, crisply tells SmartSeller, "We simply will not pay that much. We won't do it. If you don't come down, we will be unable to reach an agreement." The next day, Vice President Waffler panics and orders Firmly, "Pay the five and a half." When an embarrassed Firmly returns to the table and eats her words about price, a deal is closed. However, Firmly is left looking ridiculous and with reduced future credibility throughout the industry. Two months later, Waffler gets Firmly fired for "botching up the SmartSeller negotiation."

While there is no magic formula for the contents of a white paper negotiation plan, one format for a white paper might be as follows:

- Introduction and summary;
- Negotiation policy and philosophy;
- Background (including last two negotiations between the parties, if any);
- Relationship with the other party;
- Influence of the other party's parent organization (if applicable);
- Profiles of committees or teams (the other side's and yours);
- Local and national business climate relevant to the negotiation;
- Wage rate rankings or price comparisons;
- Expected proposals from the other side;
- Your present situation and position;
- Your bargaining mission and strategic objectives;
- Strategic plan;
- Tactical plan;
- Emergency preparation (strike) plan or alternate route plan;
- Authorized authority; and,
- Communications plan.

The introduction and summary section of a white paper negotiation plan sets out how you have become involved in negotiations. For example, the need for negotiations may have been occasioned by the need to find a new supplier due to quality problems with the present one or may be caused by the expiration of a labor agreement.

The negotiations policy and philosophy segment of the white paper negotiation plan briefly outlines the organization's approach to bargaining. For example, an organization might have as part of its negotiating philosophy to hold its costs to a competitive level or to accept a work stoppage if a new agreement cannot be concluded on time, within budget. If your organization does not have a negotiations policy or philosophy, consider adopting one. It will make the task of preparing for negotiations considerably easier.

The background section of the plan reviews critical events surrounding the organization's needs as it approaches negotiations. For example, this section might detail that the organization has been going through a large scale expansion and expects this to continue. This section may also contain a review of the last one or two negotiations between the parties. While, as securities firms always warn, "Past performance is no guarantee of future results," in negotiations the behavior, methods, and goals of the other party in prior negotiations may be a very useful clue to what to expect in current negotiations (provided that nothing fundamental has changed for the other party).

The relationships review segment of the white paper negotiation plan looks at how the parties have gotten along in the past or at the factors that are bringing them together for the first time. This portion of the white paper negotiation plan also looks at critical institutional factors within the other party's organization. For example, is the other party now engaged in a major national sales effort to capture an increased share of the market as to the item on which negotiations are about to take place? In the labor-management context, the review might point out that a struggle is going on between various forces and groups within a union for control or that there is a power struggle between key executives within a corporation. The more you understand about the other party's internal workings, the better you will be able to judge the forces driving them to take or abandon positions.

Negotiations between organizations sometimes take place within a wider world. A seemingly "stand alone corporation" may, in fact, be largely controlled by a parent organization. It may sometimes be possible to influence negotiations (apply power) through its parent organization. To do this, you must know how the organization works. Relationships between local and international unions also take varying forms. In some relationships, the international union exercises strong control. In others, the local union leadership calls the shots. A portion of the white paper negotiation plan may be devoted to these issues, either to identify them or to conclude that they are not likely to be a factor in a given negotiation. If you don't have this information, the preparation of a white paper negotiation plan will tend to force you to obtain data (information).

✍ TIP

Other organizations with experience in dealing with the other side may be able and willing to give you background on how the other party negotiates and insights into the other party's internal structure. Today, many people network and have contacts in other organizations who might prove helpful. In ongoing relationships, information may be acquired from within the negotiating partner itself during routine intra-agreement period contacts. People will be freer with this information during agreement administration than during negotiations. Individuals like to talk about their work and to help others by answering questions. Properly approached, they may provide you with a wealth of data, but expect to have to provide some information in return.

The white paper negotiation plan segment concerned with committees is basically a personality profiling section. Why profile the other side's negotiators? Individuals on a negotiating team often have either personal agendas or personal weaknesses. It always helps to know your opposite numbers. Before he became the general commanding the Third Reich's Afrika Corps in World War II, Erwin Rommel wrote a book on armored tactics. In the movie "Patton," General Patton, leading the successful forces against Rommel roars, "Rommel, you magnificent bastard, I read your book." In negotiations, your opposite numbers will seldom be so kind to you as to give away their trade secrets (as the author is now doing in this book).

Once you know your opposite numbers, you can tailor your table behavior to play to their strengths and weaknesses. If you are going to do a presentation at negotiations based on numerical reasoning, it may best be aimed at the numbers driven financial manager on the opposing team, rather than being aimed its humanistic human resources manager. If you know that a key opposing negotiator has a family member with a severe cancer condition, that individual is less likely to reject a health care proposal or lawsuit settlement offer that includes monies for cancer treatment. A pension based proposal might best be aimed at older members of the other side. All of these factors require knowing as much as possible about the personalities and interests of opposing negotiators, provided such information can be obtained in an ethical fashion. The section on your own negotiating team may be briefer. You should already know your own side. You might wish to anticipate the other side's likely perceptions of the various members of your negotiating team.

🖋 TIP

Put some things in your offer, if possible, that provide personal rewards to members of the opposing team or which serve their personal agendas. They are not negotiating out of altruism. "Never appeal to a man's better nature. He may not have one. Invoking his self-interest gives you more leverage." [Robert A. Heinlein, *Time Enough for Love*, G.P. Putnam's Sons (1973)] A little bit of money or consideration which reaches the other guy's personal sweet spot can go a long way toward achieving a negotiated settlement.

Next, a white paper negotiation plan might examine the local and national business climate impacting bargaining. Are you negotiating to buy widgets? If so, you will want to know who has what market share, what the supply and demand picture is like, and who competes for the business in your particular geographic area. For labor-management negotiations, you will need to know area and national trends for labor contract settlements recently as well as the range of settlements. You should look at whether your own organization is likely to be expanding, holding its own, or contracting during the period for which you are negotiating.

Part of the necessary economic information may be how your prices (or the prices you are willing to pay) or your wages (or the wages you seek) compare with those of others similarly situated. Your position on this spectrum will either give you wide bargaining latitude or tend to restrict your options. For example, a company that determines that it is paying rock bottom low wages may have little choice but to provide large negotiated wage increases if it is to be able to retain or attract qualified employees with necessary skills, particularly in a tight labor market. Such an employer must recognize that it will be under enormous pressure to grant sizeable wage increases. Conversely, if the employer is already paying top of the line wages, there may be little room to further increase them without becoming uncompetitive.

Next, a white paper negotiation plan should try to anticipate what the other side may propose during negotiations, both in the form of economic (direct cost) proposals and detailed language (which often carries substantial indirect costs). Many parties will have enough knowledge of the other side to be able to predict at least the larger outlines of what will be proposed. Correctly anticipating what will be put on the table allows planning for preemptive proposals and thoughtful responses, positive or negative, to the other side's presentations.

When the above data has been compiled and analyzed, the authors of the white paper negotiation plan have a sound basis for planned objectives for their own organization. In the present situation and position portion of the white paper negotiation plan, its drafters, applying what they now know or theorize, may validly assess the general power position of the organization as it enters negotiations. Here, they may summarize the reasons supporting entering the negotiation.

The stage has now been set for a key portion of the white paper negotiation plan, the statement of the organization's mission and objectives in negotiations. A mission statement defines the overall goal of negotiations in general terms. Objectives define what it is the negotiators must specifically achieve, should strive to achieve, and what goals, while useful, may be traded away or used to make concessions. Without a set of objectives, negotiators will flounder and spend precious time trying to determine what they should be doing. The lack of defined goals will almost certainly lead to giving the other side "mixed signals" about your intentions, which will confuse them and complicate negotiations.

To achieve the mission and goals stated in the white paper negotiation plan, the plan must set forth a strategy. Strategy is a broad based look at how the negotiators will bring about success, not day-to-day tactical detail. For example, a strategic decision might be for a buyer to enter into two or three simultaneous commercial negotiations so as to put pressure on prospective sellers by heightening the aura of competition.

In the 101 seat lower house of the legislature of West Carolina, Republicans hold 50 seats and Democrats hold 50 seats. The remaining seat is held by an independent. Each party is desirous of controlling and organizing the house. Each opens negotiations with the independent. With only one vote, the independent representative has inordinate bargaining power. Rarely does an individual have so much clout.

In labor-management negotiations, shifting work away from the operation for which a negotiation is being conducted sets a strategic framework in which the pressures of possible job loss are brought to bear. In either case, a strategic decision might be to utilize the press and the media when large scale and complex negotiations are involved which contain issues that might interest the public.

Tactics represent day-to-day actions and responses to meet local conditions. While it is not possible to establish in advance a complete tactical or detailed day-to-day plan as to what a negotiating team will do, it is possible to address the subject of tactics for negotiation preliminaries (see Chapter 10) and for the opening phase of negotiations (see Chapter 11) in the white paper negotiation plan. Tactics look to the details of the bargaining process. Examples of tactical decisions include whether to seek to give the first opening speech at the table, who will speak for a side on various issues, and whether to keep meetings long or short. The white paper negotiating plan should address only initial tactics, reserving to the negotiators the right to determine day-to-day tactics based on developments.

Not all negotiations yield agreement. The emergency preparation or alternate route plans address the problem of what to do if negotiations are unsuccessful. Emergency preparation in the labor-management context means preparing for launching or withstanding a labor dispute (strike or lockout). This should be a detailed plan. An alternate route plan would be inserted in a commercial negotiation plan and would provide an outline of how the organization would manage if negotiations failed.

BlimpsRUs is the world's largest maker of helium filled lighter than air ships. Each blimp requires a large supply of helium. BlimpsRUs produces some of its helium requirements internally and buys helium on the open market to fulfill the rest of its needs. BlimpsRUs is in a negotiation with Gases Unlimited for helium. The strategic plan calls for simultaneous negotiation with HeliumOne. In the event that neither potential supplier meets the primary objective goals of BlimpsRUs, its alternate route plan lays out a timetable for increasing BlimpsRUs' internal helium capacity by expansion of its own helium production operations.

HeliumOne is also in negotiations with the Hot Air and Gases union. In the event that negotiations are not successful by expiration of the current collective bargaining agreement, HeliumOne has decided that if its employees do not strike, they will be locked out. The decision has been made for safety reasons, to avoid potential sabotage of equipment, and to deny the union control of the timing of a labor dispute, so that it cannot launch a strike, without warning, at the most critical time. HeliumOne has an extensive plan to maintain its helium sales. The plan specifies contracting out some helium production to competitors ("tolling"), shifting some helium production internally to facilities that are not unionized, and operating the struck facility using supervisors and salaried personnel from outside the bargaining unit. Knowing that it has this detailed plan will prevent HeliumOne's management from panicking if negotiations with the union are not successful and will allow HeliumOne to avoid last minute concessions on its vital objectives.

A critical part of the white paper negotiation plan is the grant of authority (economic authorization) to the negotiators. For example, in a labor-management context, management negotiators may be given specific authorization to spend up to a set amount for wage increases, pensions, and other items, and no authority to spend any more than that. If greater spending would be required for settlement, this operates as an advance organizational commitment that a strike will be taken or a lockout put in place. The statement of authority may also specify expressly what the negotiators are not empowered to do. In commercial negotiations, the grant of authority should set forth how far the negotiators may go and at what point they are to terminate negotiations.

✐ TIP

The hands of the negotiators should not be tied by an authorization that contains too many restricted "line items." The negotiators should generally have the freedom to move monies from item to item, at least within a general category such as employee benefits. They should also be left with authority to move monies between time periods of a lengthy agreement, keeping in mind that adjustments may have to be made for the time value of money (see Chapter 5). Restrictions should be framed around an organization's basic policies or economic constraints. For example, the organization may have a policy of not placing itself in the top third of wage payers in relation to competing companies, which would limit transfers from benefits to wages beyond that point. Because certain pensions must be funded over long periods of time, there might be restrictions on transfers from other items to pensions, beyond a specific pension increase limit.

Finally, the white paper negotiation plan might contain an analysis and plan for public and intra-organizational communications. In some complex and large scale negotiations, internal organizational support and public acceptance may be keys to being able to maintain positions. The important point is that the issue of communications at least be considered in advance and not ignored. Failure to consider communications may lead to losing the public relations battle and result in a negotiated settlement requiring major concessions that would not otherwise have to be made.

Apart from simple individual negotiations, a white paper negotiation plan should be part of the preparation for negotiations. Why do all that work? Again, the difference between highly successful negotiation and either marginally successful outcomes or failures, is planning and discipline. When significant sums of money are at stake, the cost of planning should easily be outweighed by marginal gains in negotiations.

WHAT DO YOU KNOW AND HOW CAN YOU USE IT?

"All men by nature desire knowledge." [Aristotle] This section applies primarily to people engaged in basic negotiations such as for a car or a single house who do not need or have the more elaborate white paper negotiation plans described in the previous section. For these basic negotiations, you might wish to sit down and draw up a list of the information you already have available about the prospective purchase or sale. Then, you might wish to target additional information that you will want to acquire.

When you are armed with good information about the car or real estate market, you may use this information to press the other side into a realistic settlement by making it plain that you know the facts. Another use for information is to determine when the other side is not giving you accurate information and cannot be trusted.

Knowledge (information) is power. Ed Durant is considering purchasing a new Messite luxury sport utility vehicle, which carries a sticker price of $38,000. Before entering the showroom, Durant draws up a list of things he already knows about the Messite sport utility vehicle and about Messite Center, the dealership. Durant learns that Messite's sports utility vehicle, despite its reputation for high quality, is not selling well. In fact, Durant has learned that the manufacturer, Messite Motors, has a large numbers of Messite sport utility vehicles in inventory. Secondly, Durant finds that the federal reserve has recently increased interest rates, which means that the dealer, Messite Center's, "floor plan" (the program under which banks finance a dealer's inventory) is likely to become more expensive for the dealer next month. By checking the yellow pages, Durant locates five Messite dealers within thirty miles of home.

Durant decides to research the question of who owns Messite Center. After finding that it is Hal Messite, Durant locates reports that Hal Messite is now involved in selling off a number of his deal-

erships due to a cash flow problem. Durant is also aware of a rapid upward trend in gasoline prices. While Durant can afford to pay a lot more for gasoline, as can many other Messite sport utility vehicle buyers, he considers that higher gasoline prices will not be likely to enhance sales of luxury sport utility vehicles. Durant checks a number of internet sites for information about dealer cost for new sport utility vehicles and for trade- in values for his old vehicle.

When Durant walks into the dealership, he is greeted by sales representative Pushem. Pushem tells Durant, "You need to buy today because the sport utility vehicle you want is in short supply and may be subject to a premium mark up next week." Durant laughs and counters with, "I'm in no hurry. I expect luxury sport utility prices to drop because they guzzle increasingly expensive fuel. Messite Motors needs to sell an overstock, the dealer's floor plan rates are going up, and your owner needs money. I'd dare say the real situation is that the owner needs to sell today because the owner has problems." Durant then offers a price modestly above true dealer cost. Eventually, the sales representative counters for slightly more, but offers Durant a "low ball" on his trade-in. Durant tells Pushem what the old car is worth and demands it. Pushem tries to make extra profit out of financing but Durant also refuses this bait. Because he has sufficient knowledge, Durant ultimately gets a good deal. Pushem hates dealing with this type of customer, because the customer has both the necessary information and the ability to spot and identify Pushem's normal sales ploys. A negotiating tactic that is supposed to be hidden is of little value once the other side becomes fully aware of what is being attempted.

✒ TIP

When you know a basic fact such as that there is an oversupply of a vehicle you may wish to buy, test the other side by asking a question about availability. If the other side tells you there is a shortage and you need to buy immediately, you will have determined that it would be most unwise to trust anything they tell you that you are unable to verify independently.

✒ TIP

Be very cautious about any claim that "you must buy today." You may be being pushed to hurry because the other party does not want you to think about aspects of the proposed deal or to have time to either get facts or research issues. You've probably seen how many great "holiday sales" are followed by "post holiday sales," followed by "pre-holiday sales" for the next holiday. Although exceptions do exist, most sales, particularly in relation to automobiles, are repeated in one form or another after the deadline date for a particular offer.

✒ TIP

Be particularly wary of all finance arrangements. Auto manufacturers today are not just selling cars, they are selling money, often at relatively high real rates of interest. Finance charges can amount to an appreciable percentage of the price of a vehicle. Be aware that "cash back" arrangements (which are offered instead of lowering the price on vehicles) exist to lure you into taking cash from the manufacturer for other purposes and then financing that amount with them. Special "low interest rates," such as 0.9%, usually require you to forego the "cash back" incentive. The real price of the interest then is the "low interest" to be paid, plus the money you would have received in the cash back incentive which you give up to get the special interest rate. Remember, the sales representative has far more information on how the combination of price, financing, and trade-in all work together, which gives the dealer a clear advantage. You may also want to review a proposed financing arrangement or a leasing agreement with your accountant or attorney. Although there is usually a fee for such a review, it may well save you far more than it costs.

GET THE FACTS AND VERIFY THEM

"There is no substitute for victory." [General Douglas MacArthur] In negotiations, there is no substitute for verified facts. Garbage in, garbage out. *If you make decisions based on bad data, you are very likely to make bad decisions.* For many negotiations, there will be a plethora of tools and places to go to research the other side. Some of these sources include: internet searches; directories at libraries; economic data (on line and in libraries); trade associations and groups; parent organizations; networking; and, reports filed with federal, state, or local government.

✒ TIP

Management negotiators, in the labor-management negotiation context, should order a copy of the local and international unions' LM-1 and LM-2 reports from the United States Department of Labor or the private Bureau of National Affairs. These reports, which must be filed by law, contain financial information about the union, including how it spends its income. In turn, union negotiators, dealing with publicly traded companies, can also obtain a great deal of information from reading the organization's annual report and other financial statements required to be filed by law.

Information from your own side should generally be obtainable, but sometimes obstacles may arise even in obtaining internal information.

Cy Jung Baseball Manufacturers is about to negotiate a grievance arbitration settlement or to arbitrate a matter with the Sports Workers Union on a contractual issue involving workers' compensation supplemental injury pay. In order to prepare for negotiations or arbitration, Bob Fellah, Cy Jung's Manager of Labor Relations needs to obtain as much information as possible about grievant Wilma Maize's claim for supplemental injury pay. Fellah requests Maize's medical file from company Medical Director, Dr. Alice McGraw. McGraw, a physician, refuses to release the file on the grounds of the confidentiality of medical records. Labor Relations Manager Fellah tells Dr. McGraw, "The Company could get a subpoena from the grievance arbitrator which would legally compel the release of Maize's medical records. We look damn foolish asking an arbitrator to subpoena one of our own records where we have a 'need to know' in order to defend the Company." Fellah carries this internal information dispute to Ken Landus, the Vice President of Human Resources, who oversees both the labor relations and medical departments. Landus directs Dr. McGraw to release Maize's record for negotiations to settle the grievance. Dr. McGraw seriously considers resigning. Attorneys, physicians, and other professionals with independent responsibility to conform to codes of professional ethics as part of their licensing requirements are most likely to have problems regarding the release of information for internal as well as external use. Internal information requests may also be resisted as a result of politics within an organization.

Even Santa checks his list twice to verify who has been naughty and who has been nice. All information, internal or external, should whenever possible be verified. One useful method of verifying data is to cross check it between two different and independent sources. Be particularly careful with survey and comparison data to verify whether what is being examined or compared has been validly chosen. Make sure that comparisons are made only against the same criteria. Don't compare apples and oranges.

Sasha Pope is negotiating with TempoTemps, a staffing agency offering certain types of temporary help. Pope, whose business has not used this type of help before, locates a recent survey showing an average cost to employers for the relevant workers of $1720 per month. When TempoTemps representative Jane Longstreet offers Pope qualified workers at $1499 per month, Pope looks no further and decides on the spot that he has been offered a great deal. Pope immediately signs a one year contract. Only subsequently does Pope learn that the survey figure he relied upon contained a transposition error. The figure of $1720 per month should have been $1270. Had Pope checked two or three different surveys, they would have shown consistency around $1270 per month and thereby flagged the survey error. Pope's mistake in failing to cross check has cost his company money.

☞ T I P

Suppose you find a survey done by a Tobacco Association. Will it show that smoking is good for your health? Always question who did a survey and what their goals and objectives might have been. A survey done by a true neutral is generally more reliable than one done by a partisan which will almost always show results in a form favorable to the direction the partisan advocates. When a survey reports data adverse to the interests of the party doing the survey, that part of the survey should be particularly creditable. Check a survey against others for consistency. A survey which is out of line with other surveys based on the same or similar criteria should be suspect.

DEMOGRAPHIC CONSIDERATIONS

"Before you start up a ladder, count the rungs." [Yiddish proverb] Count noses. In negotiations which require ratification (by the employees in labor-management bargaining), demographics are often a critical factor for both sides. Since resources are never unlimited, questions will always arise on how the available resources are to be spread. For the spending party, the question is one of putting money to work where it will achieve a satisfactory balance. For example, an employer may have to allocate resources between: a) achieving management objectives such as providing sufficient wage differentials for higher skills, to encourage and reward people for moving up the ladder; and, b) achieving sufficient employee satisfaction to cause employees to ratify any tentative contractual agreement. The other party, the union, will want to obtain a distribution of economic gains in a form that permits ratification but which is also in accord with union principles, such as equality differentiated primarily by seniority.

Betsy Ross Flags is in negotiations for a successor contract with the Flag Workers union. Approximately eighty-five percent of Betsy Ross' one hundred employee work force is made up of long service employees over the age of fifty. The parties ignore demographics and sign a tentative agreement, subject to employee ratification, with excellent increases in wages but with a zero increase in pensions. The agreement is rejected by the union body in a ratification meeting by a vote of 85-15. Each party should have taken stock of bargaining unit demographics and at least partially tailored the use of economic resources in such a way as to secure ratification. In short, each party must count noses. Here, failure to do so made the settlement devised unworkable.

THE "WE'VE NEVER DONE THAT" AND "WE'VE ALWAYS DONE THAT" INHIBITORS

"Mental inertia is death." [T. Thomas Fortune] Negotiations involve change. This change may be substantive (products), or it may be procedural (methods). As negotiation planners begin to work out their mission, objectives, and strategy, one of their greatest enemies is inertia. Inertia will not likely confine itself to the other side's negotiating team. Inertia lurks internally in the preparation phase. Two key phrases that should raise an alarm that the forces of inertia are at work are "but, we've never done it that way," and "but, we've always done that."

Thomas Edison said, "I have not failed. I've just found ten thousand ways that won't work." In searching for better ways to do things, negotiation planners should keep an open mind and be willing to go outside the box of conventional wisdom. Most provisions of ongoing pre-existing agreements were negotiated with some specific purpose in mind. However, as the years go by and contracts are routinely renegotiated, underlying purposes may be lost. No one may be left of the original framers and no one today may understand why a provision was originally adopted. Something that was right for the parties twenty years ago may have evolved into something that is wrong for today.

Each contract provision should be examined during the planning phase of each negotiation cycle to be sure that it still has a known purpose and warrants being continued. If you ask the question, "Why do we do this," and no one is able to respond with other than "we've always done it that way," consider whether your objectives should include change. If you ask the question, "Why don't we negotiate [whatever]," and the answer given is, "but we've never done that," don't let the idea drop until there is a real basis for doing so. Ideas should not be rejected merely because they've never been tried. Change may be substantive or mere housekeeping, but it is rarely easy to accomplish.

During the 1950s, Mama-Bear Ammunition first became a subcontractor to Papa-Bear Munitions. As part of their commercial contract, a clause was included that all Mama-Bear's ammunition supplied to Papa-Bear Munitions must be hand inspected three times. The two companies have renegotiated their contract every five years. This year, the negotiation planning team asked the question, "Why do we have to inspect three times? Doesn't this cost us a lot of money? What's wrong with the computers?" No

35

one knew why three inspections were required. Finally, a long retired employee, father of one of the planning team members, told his daughter, "Oh, that was a government thing left over from World War II, to comply with wartime regulations and to avoid any possible human errors." Today, all production is done under computer control and inspected electronically several times, only to be re-inspected by hand three more times. Armed with the reasons why the clause was adopted and how changes have made the inspection requirement irrelevant, Mama-Bear's negotiators added the elimination of the costly hand inspection process to their list of objectives. Although the triple hand inspection served no purpose, startled at the proposed elimination of this long extant clause, Papa-Bear's negotiating team at first resisted taking the provision out of the negotiated agreement (change), but subsequently agreed.

☞ TIP

Never accept the answers "but, we've never done that," and "but, we've always done that," without additional reasons, as valid responses to the question of whether something should be changed or abolished in negotiations. As for people who resort to these phrases regularly, consider removing them from participation in the negotiation planning process.

DEFINING OBJECTIVES BEFORE BEING UNDER PRESSURE

"The mistakes are all waiting to be made." [Chess master Savielly Griegorievitch Tartakower] Time, along with power and information, is a major factor in many (but not all) negotiations. Time pressure is the major cause of mistakes. The end phase of negotiations is the worst time to be fixing your objectives and deciding what it will take to reach an agreement.

Negotiating under time pressure is exhausting work. "Avoid making irrevocable decisions when tired or hungry. Circumstances can force your hand. So think ahead!" [Robert A. Heinlein, *Time Enough for Love,* G.P. Putnam's Sons (1973)] Keep in mind that last minute decisions are seldom well thought out, may result from panic, are often made by tired negotiators, and may create numerous problems for the future.

The best time to set objectives is during the negotiation planning process. Decisions at that stage allow adequate time for thorough discussions, so that decisions may be reached without excessive emotion. Negotiations are often an emotional roller coaster for the inexperienced. At one moment it may look as though an agreement is virtually at hand guaranteeing professional or personal success, while at the next moment the entire edifice may look as though it is about to topple on your head. Decisions made well in advance and firmly backed by those at the top of an organization provide bedrock support and benchmarks for a negotiating team. They are an anchor and enhance stability. They also allow team members to speak without fear that their positions will be undermined and their credibility destroyed. Yet, few negotiators are fortunate enough to enjoy these confidence builders.

Students in my negotiations simulation classes are frequently frustrated by negotiation instructions that do not give them free rein to reach settlement. What they sometimes do not understand is that these instructions provide them with the security to act from known objectives and therefore the sense of confidence of support that is vital to a high level of negotiating success. A negotiation team that is struggling to define goals under pressure will make lots of mistakes and have little confidence.

SETTING REALISTIC ATTAINABLE GOALS VERSUS AMBITIOUS GOALS

"Its kind of fun to do the impossible." [Walt Disney] One of the prime tasks of the negotiator, or the negotiating team, is setting goals for the negotiation, particularly those primary goals which, if not attained, will result in the failure of negotiations. If goals are set too low, they will easily be attainable, but will fall far short of what could have been accomplished in negotiations. If they are set too high, the negotiations may be doomed to failure and a fine opportunity lost. Determining the optimum goal level is one of the most important aspects of negotiation planning and warrants considerable time and attention. Unfortunately, there is no magic formula for just the right level of goals. Each case must stand on its own facts and in its individual context. It is in determining the optimum level for goals that the professional negotiator's skills are worth their weight in gold. Experience matters.

The optimum goal level may well be the one at which goals, while still attainable, must be sought with determination, knowledge, and skill. At the optimum level, the negotiating team will enter negotiations with no guarantee of success but with a bar that may be cleared by a team that goes about its business effectively. It will be very difficult for inexperienced negotiators to set or attain the optimum goal level. To the extent that an organization sanctions goals that are below the optimum, it is, in essence, bargaining against itself by conceding points that might have been won.

✐ TIP

For each of the relatively few primary objectives proposed, a review of the costs and benefits of foregoing the goal or achieving it should be evaluated, together with an assessment of the probability of attaining the goal. Goals should take into account the anticipated level of resistance of the other side, but the concentrated effort should be on how your own side can make the goal happen, no matter what the other side does. The party that is reactive, not proactive, is likely to lose the negotiation game.

✐ TRAP

Some parties spend little time in preparation and a lot of time in caucuses and actual negotiations. Failure to spend adequate time on negotiation planning is perhaps the largest of the mistakes waiting to happen that non-professional negotiators make. An hour of negotiation planning may save days of later struggle.

DURATION TARGET FOR AN AGREEMENT

"We didn't lose the game; we just ran out of time." [Vince Lombardi] All things must end. When you are negotiating an agreement that goes beyond a one time event such as buying a car, you need to think about how long the agreement should be binding. The duration of an agreement is itself a basic negotiable issue. Lawyers write duration clauses into agreements for reasons. People will seldom want to live with an unchanged contract for an indefinite period. They will want to know when their obligations and rights end. Even in one time personal negotiations for a car or a house, time limits for the completion of required activities (e.g. house inspection) and time limitations on offers remaining open (offer might be good for one week) are negotiable and should be addressed.

Edsel Olds is buying a new car. He and the dealer have reached agreement on the price and other terms and are about ready to sign a contract. The car is to be ordered from the factory. There is a possibility of a national auto strike. Edsel Olds wants to be able to cancel the order and buy a foreign car if he cannot take delivery on his order within thirty days. He must negotiate to include such a clause in the contract or he will have only such cancellation rights as are provided by law or the dealer may choose to give him in its form contract.

In commercial negotiations, which cover a wide range of activities, there are no set guidelines on contract duration. Each party should consider the upside of locking the other into an agreement for a set period, with stability being one of the key reasons for longer durations. On the other hand, it is rarely possible to predict the future accurately more than a few years out. Thomas Watson, then Chairman of IBM, said in 1943, "I think there is a world market for maybe five computers." Times and conditions may change and if conditions become unfavorable, a party may want to have a way out of an agreement or at least the chance to redefine its terms.

---

*Optimist Petroleum Products is entering into a long term contract to supply jet aviation fuel to Delamerited Airlines, the nation's largest air carrier. The contract is to be for a five year fixed term. Assume the price of jet aviation fuel is today at one dollar per gallon. Optimist agrees to supply all of Delamerited's jet aviation fuel needs for five years at market price, **but subject to a cap of one dollar per gallon.** Suppose that six months from now, the OPEC nations impose a major oil embargo on the United States. The price of jet aviation fuel soars to three dollars per gallon. Delamerited will want to force Optimist to adhere to its contract, although it might agree to modifications in price such that while Optimist will lose money, it will remain in business and able to deliver fuel. Optimist will then surely regret that the long term contract has no early cancellation clause covering market force changes. Suppose that the embargo collapses and the price of jet aviation fuel falls to fifty cents a gallon. As negotiated, on the*

price downside, the airline will reap the lower price, as the price is
not fixed at one dollar per gallon.

In the labor-management context, collective bargaining agreements are seldom for a duration of less than one year. Two and three year terms are frequently used. In recent years, more and more parties have found ways to reach agreements that cover four or five years. One of the difficulties of achieving long labor contracts is the National Labor Relations Board's "contract bar" rule (under which an extant labor agreement prevents a union from having to withstand possible challenges from other unions or efforts to decertify the incumbent union), which has a maximum time limit of three years. As a result, an insecure union will seldom agree to more than a three year contract.

In any long term negotiated agreement, changing economic or political conditions may make a good ongoing agreement today a bad one tomorrow. This is particularly true when trying to predict wage trends. If an employer keeps wages low for four or five years and there is high inflation, the employer's wages may be too low. However, if wages increases are programmed high and inflation is low, the employer will have a problem remaining competitive. If a union accepts what looks like good wage increases and inflation then erodes them, its members will be unhappy. However, if the union gains increases that the economy cannot support, it may bring on layoffs or even plant closure.

Geyser Chemicals is negotiating a successor labor contract with the Chemical Employees union. At the time of these negotiations, assume inflation is approaching eight percent per year. Geyser and the Chemical Employees enter into a three year labor agreement in which the union makes work rule concessions and the company responds by granting an above area and industry average wage increase package of ten percent in the first year, seven and a half percent in the second year, and eight percent in the third year. However, by the end of the second year, economic conditions have changed radically. Inflation is now down to one percent. Geyser has a "salary freeze" for all of its employees who are not union represented. Geyser is still legally obligated to increase wages by eight percent for bargaining unit employees. The company approaches the union about deferring or foregoing some of the increase. The union refuses. The stage is set at the expiration of the three year agreement for an almost inevitable labor dispute. The parties acted rationally in setting contractual wages but wrote no provision into the agreement that would "kick in" if economic conditions moved outside an expectable band.

✒ TIP

If a current agreement or one you expect to conclude is highly favorable to your side, lean toward a longer agreement. The goal here is to lock these favorable conditions in for a period approaching the limit for predictability. If the agreement looks unfavorable and the prospects for the next negotiation look better, try to obtain a short term agreement. The sooner an unfavorable agreement is reopened, the sooner you will have the opportunity to rectify its negative provisions.

✒ TIP

If you want and obtain a long term agreement or if both sides really want one, consider writing provisions into the agreement that trigger only when conditions become abnormal. For example, an increase or decrease in prices or wages may be conditioned on a cost of living adjustment which only comes into play if inflation is particularly high or low (as defined numerically in the agreement).

✒ TRAP

A labor-management agreement with an early "re-opener" provision for one or more of its terms is not to be considered an agreement for its stated duration. Having to re-open early, even on a single issue, opens the door to instability. If you are management and must agree to a re-opener, make sure that the agreement's "no strike pledge" covers the re-opened issue. If you are negotiating for a union, be sure you retain your freedom to strike over the re-opened issue.

41

CHANGE: HOW MUCH TO INTRODUCE AT ANY GIVEN TIME

"To change one's life even in small ways requires energy, participation, and enthusiasm." [Dr. David Campbell] People tend to resist change. Sometimes negotiations require the introduction of sweeping change. This will not usually be a problem in personal or commercial negotiations, but large scale change is increasingly necessary in certain labor-management negotiations as foreign and domestic competitive pressures require restructuring of industries and companies. A further complication to this process of change is that federal private sector labor law bars unilateral changes by management without prior discussion with the union and further limits unilateral change in the terms and conditions of employment except at impasse. For public sector employees, New York's Taylor Law, for example, prohibits virtually all unilateral changes in labor agreements, even at impasse between agreements, without mutual agreement. Unions are, in the sense of resisting change, "conservative" institutions. Many labor agreements even contain clauses requiring the employer to adhere to "past practices." The past practices doctrine tends to enshrine the methods of decades ago, whether or not they are currently relevant.

How then is an employer to negotiate change? Change may either be introduced in small steps, taken slowly over a long period of time (several negotiations, step by step), or if large scale changes are needed, they may be introduced all at once, in a single overriding reordering of the work world. In my experience, what will prove most difficult to negotiate are significant changes, frequently repeated. Accordingly, negotiators should try to avoid goals which involve major change again and again, unless there is a significant intervening period of stability.

Competitive Industries is a manufacturer in an industry undergoing rapid technological change. Its older manufacturing plants are labor intensive and require employees to complete many operations by hand. Its newer operations are largely computer controlled and highly automated, requiring fewer employees but necessitating high skill levels. Competitive Industries needs to convert its older Smokestack Works to the new technology. Employees at the Smokestack plant are represented by the Hand Workers union, which has been in place since 1935. The labor agreement contains many provisions that would be irrelevant to the new technology and which would impede the transition. Competitive

Industries decides to risk the bold strategy of seeking to renegotiate the entire labor agreement from scratch. It has determined that if the old plant is to be modernized, the entire work atmosphere must be changed. It seeks to introduce macrocosmic change all at once. Competitive has watched one of its competitors, which tried making a series of large changes each year for several years, undergo serious labor turmoil. Competitive intends to get all the turmoil accompanying the changes over at one time.

SlowGrow Associates is in a stable industry. It is negotiating a successor labor agreement with the General Workers union. SlowGrow has noted that its production employees do not seek to move up to higher level jobs and often choose to move from high level jobs to ones with less responsibility. The result is that the company's investment in training employees is often wasted. SlowGrow determines that the reason for this problem is that there is very little wage spread between the least skilled jobs and those which are the most demanding. SlowGrow therefore determines to "drive a wage spread" based on skills. However, it recognizes that it probably cannot negotiate a wage spread of sufficient breadth to achieve its aims in any one negotiation (which have been historically three year contracts). SlowGrow decides that it will seek to increase the wage spread gradually over the next three negotiation cycles (nine years), rather than introduce the change all at once and risk a labor dispute. Three cycles are chosen because at the level of change desired, change in just two larger increments is believed to be more than employees will be willing to accept.

The amount of change that may be successfully negotiated at any one time cannot be determined by any magic formula. Each case must be looked at in context. What is important is to remember that seeking large scale change in a single negotiation should not be discarded. Seeking such change may be a high risk, but high reward, strategy.

ANTICIPATING THE OTHER SIDE'S GOALS AND VITAL NEEDS

"For most people the pathway ahead is a little misty." [David Campbell] Successful negotiations often require that you be able to anticipate not only what the other side will say but more importantly, the other side's self-interest, real goals, and vital needs. Anticipating these factors allows you to determine how far you must go to accommodate their interests without undermining your own. It also allows you to create preemptive proposals (to provide material for trade offs and compromises designed to steer things back to the status quo), as a technique for avoiding concessions that your side really does not wish to make. The other side's goals and vital needs may be determined, as part of the key information gathering aspect of negotiations, through examining its history and determining its current economic and internal political situation.

Once you have either predictions of the other side's goals and needs, or have developed a sense of them from negotiations, you will have to decide just how vital their achievement is to the other side. Keep in mind that what you may be told at the table about the other side's level of interest in a proposal may not be accurate. **The other side's tolerance for risk is the critical factor and will be determined largely by their negotiating power and the time still available for negotiations.** Once it becomes clear that a side does not have much tolerance for risk, the other side gains a power advantage at the table. Once you determine that the other side cannot afford to walk away from negotiations (in commercial situations) or cannot take a labor dispute (in the labor-management context), its bargaining power will be seriously weakened.

The ability to take risk is relative. A side with superior resources can afford to take risks that the other side simply cannot endure. In personal negotiations, for most of us without great wealth, risking tens or hundreds of thousands of dollars even for high rewards if we are successful is an unacceptable gamble and one that we cannot afford to lose. For major corporations, ten thousand, a hundred thousand, or even a million dollars may be a minor amount which may be risked against a reasonable probability of success, which will bring rewards far greater than the amount risked. A risk assessment of the other side must take into account the risk limits and resources available to it, measured by the other organization's own risk taking abilities, not your own. This is one of the reasons it is so difficult for an individual to negotiate with a large organization.

The hypothetical state of West Carolina has a lottery program. There are approximately two million combinations of numbers available. Because there have been six drawings with no winner, the jackpot is now at six million dollars. Tickets cost one dollar each. You determine that if you buy all two million combinations and are the sole winner, you will be guaranteed six million dollars before taxes, less the over two million dollar cost of your buying program (tickets plus other costs). If there are two winners, you will make one million dollars, less taxes on your winnings and the costs of your buying program. However, if there are three or more winners, you will lose money (at a minimum, taxes and staffing). West Carolina law does not prohibit your scheme to buy every combination. You hire an army of people to make the purchases, trying to be certain you have all numbers covered. If so, you are a sure jackpot share winner. A good scheme? The odds are with you, and the scheme will probably work. But, can you afford the risk that there will be a maximum of only one other winner beside yourself? A person with many millions in assets who could stand the loss if there were many winners might find the odds attractive but for most of us it is simply beyond our risk limits.

✍ T I P

Look for any evidence that the other side has an alternate plan (in commercial negotiations) or a strike or emergency plan (in labor-management negotiations). If the other side is not prepared to break off negotiations or go to a test of strength, you will know that your relative bargaining power has increased.

PRIMARY, SECONDARY, AND "SMOKESCREEN" OBJECTIVES

"All animals are equal but some animals are more equal than others." [George Orwell] Certainly, not all your negotiation objectives will be of equal importance. One of the most critical parts of negotiation planning is to divide objectives into tiers of priority. A convenient method is to place objectives in three general categories, defined as follows:

- **Primary objectives,** the top tier, are those objectives which are of such importance that if they cannot be achieved in negotiations, the negotiations will be broken off (if personal or commercial) or a labor dispute (strike or lockout) will be endured (labor negotiations). Primary objectives, by their very

45

nature, should be held to just a few in number and strictly confined to issues which survive a vital interest test.

* **Secondary objectives,** the intermediate tier, are those objectives which are of sufficient value that they are worth striving to achieve in negotiations up until the last minute, which have solid value for your side, but which are not worth abandoning a negotiation or taking a labor dispute to achieve. Successful negotiators will usually achieve at least a number of their secondary objectives.

* **"Smokescreen" (or tertiary) objectives,** the lowest tier, are those objectives which if achieved would have some value to your side, but which are proposed mainly to have material with which to compromise, to trade away, or to preempt proposals from the other side which go the opposite way (so as to make the status quo seem a compromise). The most successful negotiators often achieve at least a few of their "smokescreen" objectives. These objectives should not be merely frivolous.

The purpose of categorizing objectives is to determine what may be conceded in negotiations and what must be the focus, or core, of what is sought and what must be obtained. Armed with this guidance, negotiators are less likely to send out false, or mixed, signals as to their intentions about proposals.

✒ TIP

Before determining that any objective is primary, ask yourself the question, "is it worth breaking off negotiations if this is not achieved (commercial) or worth taking or causing a labor dispute (labor-management)?" If the answer appears to be that it is worth such a risk, be sure that the highest levels of the organization (in commercial or labor negotiations) are in agreement with that assessment and, if possible, have them sign on to that decision, in writing. Make this decision early enough so that is done without pressure or panic. The *vital interest test* is done by looking at the item and asking, "if this was the *sole* issue left on the table that stood between the parties and a full settlement, would it, standing alone, if not achieved, be sufficient reason to break off negotiations or to cause a labor dispute?" Unless the answer to this question is "yes," the objective is not truly primary.

LONG RANGE PLANNING IN SERIAL NEGOTIATIONS— NIBBLING AWAY

"Luck is the residue of design." [Branch Rickey] Long range planning is a form of design. State of the art techniques for commercial and labor-management negotiations sometimes require looking beyond the current negotiation in hand. Long range planning is a form of institutionalized persistence. In negotiations, persistence usually pays. Some goals may not be possible to achieve in a single negotiation but capable of full achievement when stretched out as part of an open or hidden agenda in phases over two, three, or more negotiation cycles or renegotiations. In other cases, a proposal may be floated, not with the hope that it will achieve success in the current round of negotiations, but rather that it will set the stage for the next round.

Vega has been selling wemblies to Cygnus for the last fifteen years. Every three years, the parties negotiate to update their sales agreement. All of the previous contracts specified that only wemblies assembled at the West Carolina plant could be supplied to Cygnus. Vega now assembles wemblies at six different plants, with the West Carolina plant the smallest and most costly to operate. Vega wants to alter its contract with Cygnus so that wemblies assembled at any Vega plant may be sold to Cygnus, but Cygnus has a strong preference for wemblies produced within short shipping distance of its East Carolina facilities. Vega places a proposal on the negotiating table permitting it to be allowed to supply Cygnus with wemblies from any of its plants. This "any plant" proposal is a secondary objective. However, Vega has decided to make it a primary objective that it be permitted to assemble Cygnus' wemblies at a minimum of two plants. In the next negotiation, it will try to broaden this and in the cycle after that to obtain the right to assemble for Cygnus anywhere. Vega believes that once it gets its foot in the door on assembly at multiple sites, it will ultimately gain the freedom it wishes.

In the labor-management negotiations context, concrete proposals should not be placed on the table merely to foster discussion because

when a side proposes things and does not achieve them, in future interpretation disputes, ambiguities on that point will be held against the
party raising the issue who failed to get the proposal adopted.

✒ TIP

If you are putting a proposal on the table for discussion purposes only without any real hope of achieving anything formal, do not make detailed proposals. Instead, word your proposal as simply "discuss [the issue]." This is not the type of proposal that will give rise to any inference against you if no
changes on the subject are ultimately made.

TACTICAL PLAN AND "WAR GAMING"

"A pint of sweat saves a gallon of blood." [George S. Patton] As
with all planning, the processes of tactical planning and war gaming
require time, work, and "sweat." A tactical plan is concerned with day-
to-day issues at the bargaining table and the details of achieving strategic objectives. However, a tactical plan devised in the original negotiation planning stages will rarely be accurately projected much beyond
the opening stages of a negotiation. For example, an initial tactical
plan might specify that in the opening phase, you will strive to have
negotiations held at your site or at a neutral one. In an initial tactical
plan, it would usually be futile to speculate about how many economic offers your side might make to the other side, as this usually occurs
late in negotiations and much may change before then.

Since it is difficult to have a tactical plan that goes much beyond
the opening phase of negotiations, how do you prepare for tactical
issues that may later arise? One technique to stay ahead of the ongoing negotiation tactically is to "war game." War game theory starts
with projecting your own moves, the other side's reaction to your
moves, and the other side's probable moves. You then assign projected outcomes a probability and evaluate various methods of handling
at least the more probable cases. War gaming is analogous to what
goes on in the mind of a great chess player who thinks several moves
ahead, considering a wide range of variants. At its best, war gaming
may be combined with simulation training in which your planned ini-
tiatives and the other side's probable actions and responses are tried
out internally against mock opposition.

Arctic Enterprises has been negotiating a potential alliance with Equatorial Services. Arctic's negotiators are now considering putting a proposal on the table, not for a mere alliance, but for an outright acquisition of Equatorial. They are unsure how Equatorial will react to this shift in approach. Before putting the acquisition proposal on the table, Arctic considers what impact doing so might have on negotiations. They war game various scenarios including: A) Equatorial walking away from negotiations; B) friendly open discussion on the proposal; and, C) quick acceptance in principle by Equatorial, and decide that cases B and C are more probable. They then practice how they will handle the situation if those events occur, role playing them out, and putting less time into consideration of case A.

✐ TIP

War gaming is most effective if utilized only one or two moves ahead. As in chess, the more moves ahead you attempt to anticipate, the more complex the problem becomes and the more alternatives must be considered. Also, try to confine war game exercises to higher probability events. In the latter stages of a time limited negotiation, opportunities to war game decrease, then vanish.

✐ TRAP

It is possible to "over process" possibilities in war gaming. Your war gaming can be no more accurate than the information you have. Some of the exercise must be based on your best "guess-timates" of the other side's probable positions, actions, and reactions. Don't spend too much time on detail which is based on a pyramid of assumptions. The larger the pyramid, the less useful the exercise.

49

PREPARING TO "SELL" YOUR PLAN TO REQUIRED AUTHORITIES

"By indirections, find directions out." [Shakespeare] Internal approvals are just another form of negotiation, a "play within a play." In commercial and labor negotiations, whatever negotiation plan the negotiator or the negotiating team drafts, that plan is likely to require higher level approval. Top executive approval may also be required if the negotiation involves large sums or is complex or risky. Internal negotiations are often more difficult than negotiating with third parties, because insiders, who have far more information than third parties, tend to know the strengths and weaknesses of your case. Internal negotiations are subject to a set of internal limitations based on rank, tolerance for risk, and the likely personal and political agendas of those who must approve the plan. To a lesser degree than with outsiders, your plan should allow for the possibility that you will have to negotiate your goals and that they will be reduced by those who must approve them. **Many of the same techniques that apply to external negotiations also apply to internal ones.**

In some organizations which require the presentation of a bargaining plan to key executives or the chief executive officer, the presentation may be an ordeal. Mission, goals, objectives, strategy, and the requested money authorization may all be challenged. Absolute accuracy in the presentation of numbers may be demanded. **It is essential to be thoroughly prepared for a top management review of your negotiating plan.** A negotiator or negotiating team that leaves the impression in an executive review that it does not have complete command of its material is unlikely to enjoy the confidence of the approving authorities. These are the individuals who have the power to revoke or change negotiating instructions in mid-stream, actions that greatly complicate the life of anyone negotiating. Incomplete command of material also puts a negotiating team at risk for micro-management and over-supervision during a negotiation, greatly complicating its work by requiring it to spend even more time on internal relationships.

Altair Star, who joined Stone Mart when his former company was recently acquired, is regarded as a high potential person on a fast track for top management. Star has been appointed chief spokesperson of the negotiating team for Stone Mart as it seeks to purchase a very large campus office complex for its corporate headquarters in San Francisco. The negotiation team has pre-

pared a white paper negotiation plan and has been instructed to present it to the corporate president and several vice presidents. Notwithstanding warnings about the rigors of a Stone Mart executive review, instead of preparing for the plan review, Star, who had never been to corporate headquarters or to San Francisco before, spends the night before the executive review exploring the city's hot spots. At the review, the president asks a number of questions about the rationale and bases for a number of key objectives. Star is unable to answer completely. He is also unable to explain what appear to be some numerical inconsistencies in the negotiation team's proposed monetary authorization. The negotiating team is told to come back in two days for a further review, with answers to all questions. On his way out of the meeting, the vice president of human resources is heard to remark, "Had he done well today, Star could have been a vice president within a year. As it is, he'll be lucky to keep his current job."

TIP

Treat any review required for approval of a negotiating plan as an internal negotiation, one that may be more rigorous than an external negotiation. Be fully prepared to defend all major decisions and able to justify numbers, strategy, and proposed tactics. Before any meeting think about whether there may be any hidden agendas. Understand the organization's executive review style.

TRICK

Always make your presentation in the format generally used in your organization for internal reviews. Introducing a novel format will make it more difficult to obtain approval. If your organization likes "executive summaries," bulleted charts, and graphs, use them.

TRAP

Don't offer high authority choices and ask them what they prefer. They pay their negotiators and negotiating teams to present them with a carefully considered and defensible course of action. Generally, executives do not have negotiation expertise. Instead, they are relying on their negotiating team. A review is not a place to start the planning process over again, nor would you particularly want to have a new group of personnel, at the executive level and without full data, become involved in discussions of the negotiation points your team has already resolved. If you don't present your preferred course of action as the way to go, you may be trapped into modifications.

PLANNING A WAY TO "SELL" YOUR GOALS TO THE OTHER SIDE

"Business has only two basic functions – marketing and innovation." [Peter Drucker] In negotiations, you may achieve your goals in one of two ways. You may (rarely) have the sheer bargaining power to force the other side into agreement (win-lose model) or you may market the idea to them that there is mutual benefit in reaching accord with you (win-win model). Bargaining power is not usually distributed heavily in favor of one side. A negotiated agreement that both sides at least perceive as providing gains tends to bring willing adherence to the bargain, and as a result is far more likely to prove workable. But, how do you "sell" your goals to the other side?

There are several things that will facilitate selling your ideas:

- Avoiding personal attacks;
- Breaking large issues down into smaller manageable parts;
- Stressing the facts (these may need to be repeated a number of times);
- Starting with the easiest and least emotional subjects (get some success experiences);
- Using informality and humor;
- Being flexible (it is the goal that's important, not the method);
- Citing real world constraints;
- Personalizing your arguments; and,
- Finding ways to continue talking face to face.

One of the most important ways to sell ideas is to have a sense of empathy with the other side. Make an effort to understand their goals and how difficult it may be for them to give up on certain items they seek. If you are discussing some broad general concept, try to use illustrations or examples that show how your concept would work in specific cases. Caveat: If your illustrations show the negotiators on the other side that they would personally be hurt by your proposal, don't use them at the table or try to find the positive aspects of your proposals as they would apply to the specific cases. If you cannot do this, understand that your proposal is likely to bring a negative reaction. Have a rationale to show why your proposal is still necessary.

ACTIONS MAY HAVE UNINTENDED CONSEQUENCES— HAVE CONTINGENCY PLANS

"[A scout] is never taken by surprise; he knows exactly what to do when anything unexpected happens." [Robert Baden-Powell] For most of us, unexpected things do happen. In mathematical chaos theory, a butterfly flapping its wings in South America might impact the weather in New York weeks later. Certainly, the butterfly had no such intent. Almost all of us have had experiences in which our intentions were good but there was an unpredictable and unfortunate outcome. It is particularly frustrating for negotiators to make concessions or to try to accommodate the needs of the other side and then to receive not mere criticism of the concessions as "too little, too late" (which is to be expected), but to be met with abuse. **You will not always be able to predict the reactions to your words or acts and once a chain of events has started, it may be hard to stop or limit. When a negotiation is really important, any speech or acts may give rise to unexpected events.**

A week ago, hurricane Zelda swept through the Carolinas where BoilNBubble Chemicals has a manufacturing site. In the West Carolina town of Cawdor, home of BoilNBubble's Special Mixtures Plant, the floods caused by Zelda severely damaged the homes of sixteen employees. Company president Beth Mack, after a routine visit to the plant site, toured the devastated homes. Two days later, Mack announced that the company would supply, without charge, materials needed for repairs of employees' flood damaged homes in Cawdor from the company's surplus stocks and that the company would provide skilled workers to do the repairs on company time. In announcing the employee flood relief program, Mack said the company was glad to help out because the Cawdor plant "has been the crown jewel of our specialty mixtures business."

BoilNBubble has another specialties mixture plant at Glamis, Pennsylvania. The Glamis site is unionized and employees there are represented by the Chemical Employees Union (CEU), which is in the midst of a labor contract negotiation with BoilNBubble. CEU's negotiators, frustrated by the company's refusal to meet their wage demands, put out a press release stating, "BoilNBubble, the huge multi-national chemical company, while denying our just wage demands, seems to have plenty of money to spend on non-union employees in Cawdor, West Carolina, where BoilNBubble volunteered to remodel employee homes with company money." When president Mack saw this article, she was outraged. "You try to be a good corporate citizen and you get criticized," Mack was quoted as saying. "I never thought that our corporate good deed would be taken this way." At a negotiating session the same day, CEU said that employees at Glamis felt insulted by Mack's "crown jewel" remark and that this comment would make negotiations more difficult. Privately, CEU was actually pleased with Mack's remark because it helped solidify rank and file support behind the union.

Unpredictable consequences may sometimes be spawned by real world events that are not foreseeable. Further, once a sequence of unexpected events begins, the sequence may take on a life of its own and spin out of the control of the parties. There is little that can be done about this apart from "spin control."

Suppose the facts are as in the example above and that the union is also trying to organize the employees of the Cawdor plant. Employees at Cawdor learn of the critical comments made by the union at Glamis concerning the company's flood relief program when their nationally famous religious leader preaches a sermon on radio that Sunday, taking as his theme the sin of spurning good deeds, using CEU's reaction to BoilNBubble's voluntary flood relief effort as his key example of sin. The union's organizing drive at Cawdor, which was making good progress, now loses substantial ground. Certainly, when the union commented about the company's flood relief program it did not expect the comment to chill organizing at Cawdor or to attract national attention. BoilNBubble never anticipated Mack's "crown jewel" remark as having a serious impact on negotiations at Glamis. Both sides have seen things spiral out of their control.

Understand that uncontrollable events do happen. There is little that negotiators can do in advance to prevent them, other than to try to coordinate the activities of other elements of their organizations. This will be difficult at best and impossible if the negotiations are not over issues of truly substantial concern to the organization. What negotiators can do is to attempt to limit negative consequences with "damage control."

PRODUCTIVITY REPORTS AND EMERGENCY PREPARATION PLANS

"Not everything that can be counted counts, and not everything that counts can be counted." [Einstein] Productivity is about numbers. In the context of this book, a productivity report is the result of a study by a team or task force identifying areas for productivity improvement which require negotiations. A productivity study looks at the way an organization currently does business and tries to identify any cost inefficiencies that might be remedied through negotiations. An emergency preparation plan is the blueprint for how an organization will cope with a labor dispute (strike or lockout). In commercial negotiations, a productivity report may be also be useful. There the analog to an emergency preparation plan is an alternative route plan, which spells out what the organization will do if the commercial negotiation fails. Personal negotiations and some commercial and labor-management negotiations will not require a productivity study, but the latter do frequently warrant this type of study.

A pre-negotiation productivity study would look at existing agreements, if any, and the impact they have on the bottom line. If there is no extant agreement, the productivity study would concentrate on how the organization would be impacted by entering into a first agreement. A productivity study should be an exercise in creativity. The productivity team should not be concerned with what may actually be achieved in negotiations. Their primary purpose is to identify costs associated with an existing or proposed agreement and to suggest ways in which future costs could be avoided and current costs reduced or eliminated. Their analysis would then be passed on to the negotiators for their review which, of course, at this level, must be conducted in light of what is deemed achievable. The negotiators translate the productivity recommendations into goals and objectives as part of negotiation planning. Accordingly, the productivity study should be completed prior to the beginning of the negotiation team's planning.

✒ TIP

People selected for a productivity study team must be creative. Individuals who frequently base decisions on "but, we've always done it that way" or "but, we've never done it that way," are not good candidates to conduct a productivity study. The productivity report should identify, quantify, and place in priority order possible cost avoidances and savings.

An extant contract under which SmallOne supplies BigGuy with wemblies is being renegotiated. SmallOne establishes a productivity committee. In examining the arrangements for shipping wemblies, the productivity committee finds that presently SmallOne pays shipping costs. They recommend that SmallOne negotiate to shift shipping costs to BigGuy, even if the price SmallOne charges has to be reduced by the amount of the shipping costs to be paid by BigGuy. The committee notes that BigGuy's size means that it produces sufficient shipping volume to obtain far lower rates than SmallOne's lesser purchasing power makes possible. The negotiators decide to push for the shift with a mutual gains proposal that the resulting savings in shipping be shared between the parties, noting that the present arrangement, under which SmallOne pays shipping and passes its higher shipping costs through to BigGuy, benefits neither party.

An emergency preparation plan is an organization's blueprint for dealing with a breakdown in negotiations. The best emergency preparation plan or alternate route plan is one that will never have to be used. Paradoxically, the better the plan, the more likely it is that it will never be needed. The probability of a labor-management negotiation ending in a labor dispute is reduced if each side is aware that the other is fully prepared. The probability of reaching a commercial negotiation agreement is also enhanced if the other side knows your side is prepared with alternatives if negotiations do not meet your needs. Under these circumstances, the desire for settlement is likely to increase and you are likely to achieve a more satisfactory outcome.

USE OF EXPERTS

"An expert is someone who knows some of the worst mistakes that can be made in his subject and how to avoid them." [Werner Karl Heisenberg] Many negotiations are complex and difficult. Remember that information is a key factor in negotiations, along with power and time. Planning for bargaining often involves a range of information skills no single negotiator, or even a reasonably sized negotiating team, can fully hope to master. One advantage that organizational negotiators have over individuals who are buying a house or a car is that they generally have access to staff support or the means to bring in outside experts. **Always use internal or outside experts when the subject matter is complex, the monies involved large, the consequences of error are significant, and when experts are available at a reasonable cost.** The use of experts should be considered on a cost to benefit ratio basis. The use of an outside expert who charges a few hundred dollars an hour for a few hours may pale in relation to the cost of an error that could cost tens to hundreds of thousand of dollars or more.

OldTech is concerned about the growing cost of health care benefits for its employees. Demographic studies at the company show that the work force is very stable and that it is aging, indicating that health insurance premiums may continue to rise rapidly. Accordingly, OldTech has decided to negotiate a new health care insurance plan. It has contacted a number of health care carriers and started negotiating with them. The carriers have asked about how the company wants the plan designed, offering to help. OldTech decides that it wants a plan design from a neutral party, not one who is selling them something. OldTech's personnel staff is small and contains no experts on the subject and there are none on its negotiating team. Because the costs of health care are substantial, OldTech engages the firm of Mudd & McLellan to help the negotiating team with plan design and cost evaluation. The firm suggests a number of items which save OldTech several times Mudd & McLellan's fee and which OldTech's negotiators, acting on their own, would not have identified.

Tom and Mary Dairy have a corporate identity as T&M Dairy, Inc. still in place from a prior venture. They are simultaneously negotiating with the sellers of a "The Country's Best Taste" (TCBT) franchised yogurt store to acquire the franchise and the store and with the current store owner's mall landlord to assume the store's lease. The couple is reluctant to pay the cost of retaining a lawyer, so they negotiate on their own. After the deal is closed, when the business is still marginal and problems arise with the landlord, they have the lease examined by counsel. The attorney finds that while they bought the franchise and store in the T&M corporate name, they signed the lease with the mall landlord as Tom and Mary Dairy (in their personal, not corporate, capacity), something the attorney would strongly have advised them not to do. By negotiating without the expert assistance of counsel, the couple has ended up risking their home and personal assets if the business should fail.

⚡ TIP

A lower per hour rate for professionals who consult is not always an indicator of ultimate lower cost to the client. An experienced attorney or accountant may charge more per hour but because of extensive experience may end up spending fewer hours on a given project. While experience and high price do not in themselves guarantee quality or efficiency, it is most often the case with experts, as in other things, that you receive what you pay for.

If the planning process for negotiations seems elaborate, keep in mind that not all negotiations, and few personal ones, require all of the steps outlined. You would not go through an elaborate planning process to buy a car or an oriental rug, but you should do what is necessary to be prepared to negotiate a price. Every situation is different and you will need to pick and choose which topics pertain to your negotiation. In the next chapter, we will look at some of the legal, economic, and public relations factors which may bear on a negotiation.

CHAPTER 3

LEGAL, NEGOTIATIONS MANAGEMENT ISSUES, AND ETHICS

AVOIDING LEGAL PITFALLS

"The more laws, the less justice." [Marcus Tullius Cicero] Negotiations are so intertwined with law that professional negotiators are often lawyers. Many lawyers spend more time in negotiating settlements than they do in litigating cases. Although this chapter is designed to give you some insights into the legal factors surrounding negotiations, the intent is neither to make you a lawyer nor to serve as a substitute for competent legal counsel. To spare the non-lawyers, this chapter contains only general comments on the law, presented without statutory or case law citations. Although it may be a relatively dry subject, knowing the law may be critical when you are negotiating. For attorneys negotiating settlements, it is assumed that you know the law regarding settlements, representation of clients, and the canons of professional ethics.

In those portions of this chapter that are concerned with labor-management negotiations, my comments are essentially limited to the federally regulated private sector, covered by the National Labor Relations Act (NLRA). While NLRA generally leaves the parties great freedom in arriving at the terms of a negotiated agreement, it provides a more restrictive framework for the negotiating process than is applicable to personal or commercial negotiations. NLRA includes private health care facilities, the Postal Service, and private colleges and universities, but it excludes most railroad and airline employees (who are covered by the separate Railway Labor Act). The labor relations of all but certain small private sector employers is also covered by NLRA. The remaining employers are left to a patchwork quilt of state laws which may or may not differ from NLRA. Public employees are covered by federal statutes for employees of the United States government and by varying state laws for state and local employees.

Commercial negotiations are less regulated than labor-management ones. Here, parties have great freedom to make their own rules, both as to the process of negotiating and the terms of any resulting contractual agreement. However, even in commercial negotiations, you need to be sure that no laws are violated. Great care must be taken to put the negotiated agreement in proper legal form. There are many technical legal nuances to a negotiated agreement including such factors as a choice of laws provision (which designates which state's law is to govern the agreement) and the need to preserve the rest of the agreement if any part of it is, or becomes, unlawful.

For individuals negotiating for homes or cars, the legal context is relatively simple, but it is unlikely that the average individual will know the details of what is impermissible or the parameters of consumer rights. Consumers generally are presented with a form contract which they may have little ability to alter. In real estate transactions, licensed real estate brokers will be able to guide most individuals as to seller disclosure forms, environmental requirements, the process of offer and acceptance, and purchase agreements. When complications arise, when the transaction is complex, or at closing, an attorney is usually needed. In auto purchase transactions, states may have "lemon laws" which provide a remedy when a vehicle is severely defective, may legally mandate a revocation right for a few days after an order contract is signed, or spell out what happens if a dealer is unable to deliver what was promised.

One of the fastest growing and rapidly changing legal areas is alternative dispute resolution, or ADR (which is discussed later in this chapter). For many decades, ADR clauses related to contract administration have been negotiated as part of virtually every labor-management contract. The significance of ADR to consumer and to many commercial negotiations is that today companies are often placing in their standard contract forms, on a take it or leave it basis, a clause that requires the other side to agree in advance to submit any future disputes with the seller to binding arbitration. The buyer loses the right to a day in court. Arbitration is the use of a neutral third party to issue final and binding decisions on an issue. Appeal or court review of arbitration awards is extremely limited. Consumers should keep in mind that for all practical purposes they have little or no bargaining power to force removal of these binding arbitration clauses.

Tawana Tide is purchasing a washer and dryer from Sirs, a national chain of department stores. The purchase agreement she is given to sign contains a clause which reads, "any disputes between the parties arising out of the purchase of the appliances described herein shall be submitted to final and binding arbitration, under the rules of the American Arbitration Association." Tide, an unusual person who actually reads form contracts, wants to strike out the clause, but the sales representative says, "I can't change the contract and I can't sell you the appliances without that clause."

Suppose you fail to conform to the law when negotiating. Among other consequences, the resulting agreement, or parts of it, may be unenforceable. Your actions may be violations of federal or state law which, while not criminal, may carry sanctions such as cease and desist orders, back pay, or other financial penalties. It will do you little good to have a successful negotiation with a favorable agreement, only to see it eroded or set aside because of legal defects. For this reason, once a negotiation gets beyond routine matters, you may find that legal counsel is an excellent investment.

Much of the law surrounding negotiations turns on the specific facts of a given case. Because those facts are not known and because the information here is of a general nature, Also note that some portions of the law impacting negotiations (such as those related to discrimination and sexual harassment in the work place) change and develop rapidly. For this reason, older legal information or texts, not updated to the moment, may actually be more dangerous for you than having no legal information at all.

✒ TIP

Not all attorneys are sufficiently specialized to provide high quality advice on labor relations and commercial negotiations.

When selecting an attorney, try to find one with particular expertise or specialization in these areas of the law. Be prepared to pay a bit more for specialized counsel. If the attorney is to be used in negotiations, select someone who has considerable table experience, preferably in your type of situation.

✐ TIP

There are desk reference tools that may be prove useful in educating yourself in the relevant law. For labor-management negotiations, obtain a copy of *The Developing Labor Law,* published by the Bureau of National Affairs (BNA). For sex discrimination and sexual harassment law, including collectively bargained agreements, and alternative dispute resolution, see my books, *Sex Discrimination and Sexual Harassment in the Work Place, and Alternative Dispute Resolution in the Work Place,* both published by American Law Media's Law Journal Press. There are also commercial services which for a fee (sometimes substantial) permit you to research the law from your computer via the internet (LEXIS and Westlaw). These tools, while no substitute for counsel, can lower your professional fee expense by helping you to frame the problem for your counsel and assist you in asking counsel the right questions.

INFORMATION REQUESTS IN LABOR AND OTHER NEGOTIATIONS

"Knowledge is power." [Francis Bacon] Information, along with bargaining power and time, are the three key factors in any negotiation. The more information you have, the better you will be able to apply your bargaining power. Arthur C. Clarke noted that it is the application of power, not its amount, that matters. In most personal and commercial negotiations there is no general legal right of access to information held by the other side. There are exceptions. For example, in mergers and acquisitions, real estate transactions, and auto sales (mileage, prior damage) there may be some duty to disclose. Because governing state laws vary and are numerous, they are not addressed here. Be sure to consult with counsel.

In labor-management negotiations conducted under the National Labor Relations Act (NLRA), both management and the union have a duty to disclose to each other, on request, material which is relevant and necessary for collective bargaining. Failure to do so is an "unfair labor practice." For management, particularly, failure to disclose may turn what would otherwise be a simple economic strike into an unfair labor practice strike, with the potential consequence that the employer might be ordered to pay back pay to those on strike. Consult counsel before declining any information request.

There are limits on the type and nature of what may be requested under NLRA. An employer is not required to create data it does not already have, nor does it have to deliver information in a specified form that does not already exist. It must respond within a reasonable time, not necessarily immediately. Data requests should relate to "hard data," which means that requests for management's internal opinions, projections, and estimates are not appropriate. Obviously, an employer is not required to supply either its negotiation plans or documents relating to its negotiation efforts, nor is it required to disclose the legal advice of its counsel. Data held by true third parties, such as medical records, and not within the control of the employer may be unavailable, but generally confidentiality is not a defense against supplying requested information.

Information requests from employers to unions are relatively rare. But, unions may be required to provide data they hold to which the employer has no independent access. The same rules on form and nature apply to requests from management to a union as when the request is made by a union to management.

The Whistle Workers union is in negotiations for a successor labor agreement (any agreement subsequent to the initial one) with Music Enterprises. The employer has proposed certain changes to reduce health care costs, while the union has proposed expansions in health care coverage. The union hands the employer a written information request for the current cost to the company for single employee coverage, employee and spouse coverage, and family coverage. The employer must provide the data, but as it currently offers only single and family coverage and has no data on the cost of employee and spouse only coverage, it need not compile nor provide that information.

✒ TIP

While the law does not mandate any particular wording for an information request under NLRA, start the information request with the specific words, "Under the National Relations Act, we are hereby requesting that [name] provide the following data which is required for bargaining: [specified data]." In the event that your request is refused and legal action is later taken, this will eliminate any ambiguity as to whether you actually made an NLRA request and will put the other side on notice that your request is subject to a legal requirement of disclosure.

IMPASSE IN LABOR NEGOTIATIONS

"Never mistake motion for action." [Ernest Hemingway] Nor should you confuse apparent action with real motion. Impasse means a lack of motion on both sides. This section applies only to private sector labor negotiations. Under the National Labor Relations Act (NLRA), an employer may not make unilateral changes in the terms and conditions of employment, that is changes without negotiating. However, when the employer and the union have bargained to "impasse" over a new agreement, the employer may unilaterally implement such changes as it has on the table (once the prior labor agreement has duly expired). Keep in mind that an employer's duty to bargain does not end merely because the prior contract expires. "Impasse" is very much a legal term. It means that each party has simultaneously reached a position where it has no movement it is willing to make. Impasse need exist only at the moment when the unilateral change is announced. The problem is that so long as either party indicates it is ready to make any movement at all, whether or not meaningful, impasse does not exist.

✒ TIP

A union wishing to avoid unilateral implementation of terms by management should always express some willingness to move. Further delays can still be had by way of caucus time. The movement may be small scale and insignificant.

The Whistle Workers Union and Music Enterprises are continuing to negotiate after the expiration of their prior agreement. The con-

tract has not been extended. The employees are working without a contract. Music Enterprises wishes to implement its last offer on the table and change the terms and conditions of employment. To that end, the spokesperson for Music Enterprises indicates that the company has no movement at this time on either its own proposals or the union's demands, then asks if the union has any movement. The union spokesperson, wishing to avoid impasse, replies, "We do have some movement for you. We will caucus and get back to you with it shortly." Four hours later, the union returns to the table and alters its position insignificantly on a very minor issue. The company spokesperson repeats the earlier question about movement. The union responds, "we do have some more movement but it is late and we need to adjourn for the day. We'll see you at the next scheduled session." In a technical sense, the company would be at legal risk if it were to declare that an "impasse" exists.

Because the law surrounding impasse is highly technical, an employer seeking to unilaterally implement its negotiation proposals should first consult with counsel. The law of "impasse" is just one example illustrating why labor attorneys are sometimes utilized as chief spokespersons.

"TAKE IT OR LEAVE IT" OFFERS

"Choice has always been a privilege of those who could afford to pay for it." [Ellen Frankfort] However unwise it may be to do so, in commercial and individual negotiations you are generally legally free to make a "take it or leave it" offer if you are able to afford doing so. Although lawful, one reason that early "take it or leave it" offers are not good negotiating tactics in personal or commercial negotiations is that the other side has, as yet, no investment of time and energy in the negotiation. The other side will be less inclined to accept an upfront ultimatum than it will be to accept a firm last offer (on the same terms the early ultimatum would have contained), tendered only after it has invested considerable time getting you to make that offer.

Robin Byrd is considering buying a new Jupiter Oriole four door sedan. She visits Hummingbird Motors and talks with Ken Grebe, a sales representative. She spends almost two hours with Grebe, then leaves, saying, "I might be interested. I'll come back with my husband in a few days. A week later, Byrd and her husband, Cal Cardinal, return to the dealership and spend another hour with Grebe. They leave to talk over the prospective purchase. A third visit to discuss price stretches to an hour and a half. By the fourth visit, they are ready to make an offer. By now, Grebe has already invested four and a half hours on negotiating a sale. When Byrd makes a low but reasonable "take it or leave it" offer, Grebe takes it. Had he not invested so much time in the process, Grebe might have tried to bargain further. Had Byrd made the same "take it or leave it" offer on her first visit, the offer would probably not have been accepted. So, even in personal negotiations, investment of time and energy in the negotiation process is important.

Compare the wide open legal view of the negotiation process in commercial and individual negotiations with that in labor-management negotiations, where the process of negotiating is regulated by law, although not the terms of the final bargain. The National Labor Relations Act (NLRA) contains two interesting and seemingly contradictory provisions. One provides that an employer is required to meet at reasonable times and places to bargain in good faith with the union representing its employees, while the other says that the employer is not required to make concessions. In practice, an employer who makes no concessions on any issue is very likely to be found to have negotiated in bad faith. If you are negotiating for an employer or a union, you need not make any concessions whatsoever on *some* of the issues, or may eventually stop making concessions on any, or all, of the other side's proposals, for the requirement to negotiate in good faith is judged on the whole record, not issue by issue.

Suppose you, as an employer negotiator, decide to avoid spending a lot of time and effort in the labor-management negotiating process and to simply short circuit the process at the outset of negotiations by immediately putting on the table your "final offer," saying that the offer represents the furthest your company would eventually go after extensive bargaining and the union may "take it or leave it." By doing this, you will make your opposite number, the union negotiator, look irrelevant and make union representation appear futile.

In 1960, General Electric conducted its own research on anticipated union demands. It then put together an offer to the union that reflected the company's ultimate position on the issues. The company made only four changes in its initial offer and also presented an insurance proposal on a take it or leave it basis. The offer was published in the media. GE was found to have violated the NLRA by failing to negotiate in good faith. The courts eventually held that the statutory negotiation process under NLRA requires bilateral negotiations and that a joint attempt to reach terms must be undertaken. The law is grounded in the concept that labor-management negotiations require a process, not just simple offer and acceptance. The process itself is valued in labor relations and a "take it or leave it" early negotiation offer is not lawful as a labor-management negotiation technique, because it bypasses the role assigned the union by law in collective bargaining. As a result, if you are negotiating a labor agreement, keep in mind that you must go through the "ritual dance" of phased movement, while no such requirement exists in commercial negotiations. After a long conventional negotiation, you may make a final offer which is in essence a "take it or leave it" proposal.

✒ TIP

Never place your ultimate position on the table as your first position. Always leave yourself room for movement. This requires that initial proposals be "over stated," so as to leave the needed room to compromise. After you have made several moves on a specific proposal, it will then be safe to freeze your position, if you wish, and to make no further concessions on that proposal. Avoiding an early "take it or leave it" position does not prevent you, at some later point, from ceasing to make further movement.

ECONOMIC AND UNFAIR LABOR PRACTICE STRIKES

"All is fair in love and war." [proverb] Perhaps so, but not in labor-management negotiations (the exclusive concern of this topic). Under the rules of baseball, a fair ball hit with the bases loaded which clears the foul pole by inches is a grand slam homerun. A few inches the other way and it is merely a long foul ball. Under the rules of the National Labor Relations Act (NLRA), the failure of negotiations may result in either of two kinds of strikes, those for economic reasons (fair) and those done in response to employer unfair labor practices (foul).

The consequence of an unfair labor practice work strike (foul) in labor relations is far more serious than a foul in baseball. The offending company may be ordered to pay costly back wages to the striking employees for the entire duration of an unfair labor practice strike. Those strikes which have both economic objectives and are also at least partially in response to an employer unfair labor practice or practices are also considered to be unfair labor practices strikes. If you are negotiating for management, you must know the applicable law in order to avoid committing unfair labor practices at the bargaining table that could lead to full back pay for striking employees.

Under NLRA, unfair labor practices include: refusing to bargain with a union certified or recognized to represent a majority of the employees in the bargaining unit; discriminating against employees for engaging in union activity; failing to provide legally required information; establishing a company union or dominating a union; and, retaliation against an employee for using the protections provided by the Act. Unions can also commit unfair labor practices when they discriminate against employees for refusing to engage in union activity and when they refuse to bargain in good faith with the employer. This text cannot begin to cover the range and the many technical ways in which an employer or union may commit unfair labor practices. Negotiators should consult competent labor counsel. Inexperienced bargainers need to be extremely cautious.

⚜ TIP

Union negotiators will find it useful to try to draw management negotiators into committing at least one unfair labor practice at the bargaining table. Once management has done so, provided it doesn't subsequently purge its violation, the union will be in a far better position if it strikes and be able to offer employees the hope of securing them back pay. Success in the effort to induce an unfair labor practice will be considerably more likely with labor law advice. Although counsel costs money, this may be a very wise investment.

CONFIDENTIALITY—NOTHING IS REALLY "OFF THE RECORD"

"Loose lips sink ships." [World War II slogan] In negotiations, informal "off the record" meetings with calculatedly loose lips may serve several useful purposes:

- Information can be more readily exchanged when conditions are informal and no one is taking notes;
- Participation is possible by individuals who caution would indicate should be silent at the negotiating table; and,
- Doors remain open when official positions have hardened and the parties are deadlocked.

From a legal perspective, "off the record" negotiations do pose a confidentiality problem. Just how confidential are these informal meetings, even if the parties have agreed to make them "off the record?" Can what you say at an "off the record" meeting ever be made subject to public disclosure?

In commercial, real property, and automotive negotiations, the parties may draw up binding agreements that conversations, or documents, exchanged between them will not be admissible in future civil legal actions. Sometimes, these agreements are effective. However, in labor-management negotiations, should one party bring an unfair labor practice charge against the other, testimony may later be required concerning the content of "off the record" discussions. Unfortunately, the knowledge that what is said in an "off the record discussion" may ultimately have to be publicly disclosed may well serve to chill the effectiveness and very purpose of these meetings.

Football Players Trust Company and the Bank Employees Union are engaged in negotiations for a successor labor agreement. The parties are near impasse. The company and union chief spokespersons agree to meet after hours at a local bar to see if something cannot be worked out "off the record." During that discussion, the company spokesperson admits, "not for the record," that one of the members of her bargaining team committed an unfair labor practice for the company at the table. Negotiations do not result in a contract on time, the union strikes, and files unfair labor practice charges. The union's counsel questions the company spokesperson under oath about the admission made during the "off the record" conversation. Although the company objects to this line of questions, the company spokesperson is required to answer. Because unfair labor practices are not crimes, there is no Fifth Amendment protection against making incriminating statements.

✒ **TIP**

Always be careful about what you say in an "off the record" discussion. Assume that it may become public at some future time. The parties could sign an agreement to hold the content of an "off the record" discussion confidential in legal proceedings, but there is no assurance that such an agreement would be honored, particularly by the National Labor Relations Board, if the agreement related to labor-management negotiations. Apart from legal considerations, negotiation ethics would dictate that a party should avoid seeking to disclose even favorable "off the record" comments, unless compelled by law. Self interest would also apply. If you break such confidences, don't expect to receive them again.

NEGOTIATOR AUTHORITY

"Once the game is over, the king and the pawn go back in the same box." [Italian Proverb] Legally, must a negotiator be a powerless pawn or must the negotiator be vested with the authority of a king? In commercial negotiations the parties are free to determine how much power to confer on their negotiators. Keep in mind that when individuals act for corporations, they may need legally satisfactory authorizations from their corporate authorities, and sometimes enabling corporate resolutions, to have the power to sign legally binding agreements. Giving your negotiators insufficient authority to bind the organization (making them pawns) may leave the other side believing that dealing with them is futile. Giving those same negotiators too much authority (making them kings) will deprive them of the sometimes useful device of having to refer matters upwards to others and may lead to hasty mistakes that cannot be cancelled.

The Italic City School District is negotiating with the Italic Teachers Union for a successor labor agreement. Because this is a public sector negotiation, the union is dealing with the Board of Education in its corporate capacity. That is, the Board can only act when it is sitting together in a legal meeting. You are appointed as the Board's chief spokesperson, but given no authority to make any commitments without referring them back to the Board for approval. In meeting after meeting, you can only say, "I'll get back to you on that." After a short time, the union and its members come to believe, perhaps correctly, that you are merely a messenger.

MacWorld and MacCenters are negotiating for MacWorld to sell a number of its retail computer outlets to MacCenters. As negotiations progress, MacCenters asks the MacWorld chief spokesperson to make certain commitments about what is to be included in, and excluded from, the sale of the stores. The spokesperson replies, "I have no authority to decide that. I'll refer it upward." As the days pass, a whole series of additional questions arise, many of them minor, and the MacWorld spokesperson keeps responding with a denial of authority. After several repetitions, the MacCenters spokesperson says, "You people can't decide anything. We're wasting time here. Either put someone on your team who can speak for your company or there is no point in negotiating with you. We need to speak with people who have authority and who can act."

✒ TIP

At the outset of commercial negotiations, inquire into whether the other side's representatives have the authority to enter into binding agreements or to sign documents on behalf of their organization. Before signing final agreements, secure written evidence of necessary authority. To determine what is required, consult counsel.

In private sector labor-management negotiations, it is expected that management negotiators will be given sufficient authority to bind their organizations without any need for ratification by executives. In the public sector, sometimes both sides' negotiators have to submit their agreements to their principals for ratification. Coming to the table with negotiators who have no power to make any commitments may be an unfair labor practice. In labor relations, resolutions of an employer's corporate board of directors are not necessary to make management negotiators authorized agents of the corporate body. On the other hand, the law does not require parity of union negotiators. They need not have the power to enter into finally binding agreements with management, but may reserve final approval for ratification by the union body. Perhaps the basis for the distinction is that management structures are usually hierarchical while union structures are, at least theoretically, democratic.

☞ TIP

When ground rules are being discussed at the outset of negotiations, establish what level of authority has been assigned to the other side's negotiators. For example, ask whether union agreement to a labor contract will require ratification. Not all unions put collective bargaining agreements to a vote and others use varying practices. At least one major international union sometimes allows ratification by a one-third vote of the union body, when a contract settlement is recommended by the negotiating committee and endorsed by the business agent.

YOUR RIGHTS (OR LACK THEREOF) TO INFLUENCE WHO NEGOTIATES FOR THE OTHER SIDE

"Off the field I pick my own friends." [Snoopy] On the field, you play with, and against, those who have made the teams, or not at all. In commercial negotiations, including those to buy or sell a house or a car, you do have the right to pick your own friends and even to influence who will be your opponents. You may demand someone you can work with or, failing that, if it is within your authorization, you may walk out of negotiations. In these negotiations, there is no violation of law in requesting, or even demanding, a specific negotiator to represent the other side, although you will rarely have the power to force such a decision.

Shelley Transferee is being promoted and transferred from a field location to a distant corporate headquarters location. She is looking for a home close to her new office. The company recommends a real estate agent, Claudia Homes. Transferee tells Homes about her needs and location requirements for the new house. Homes takes transferee to see several properties, none of which are in Transferee's preferred location and none of which meet her preferences. "This is where your corporate people want to live and these are the kind of houses they like," Homes informs Transferee. Transferee demands that Homes show her properties that have the location and features she prefers. Homes ignores these instructions and takes Transferee to several additional sites that don't meet her criteria. Transferee breaks off her dealings with Homes and finds another realtor. Transferee's interchanges with the realtor are a form of negotiation in which realtor Homes failed to listen, losing a client and a commission.

Of course, it is unusual for one party to make demands on the other as to who will represent the other side. It may be considered discourteous and may be an inherent "deal breaker." However, if you are negotiating with a government representative such as an IRS agent, you may have no choice whatever as to with whom you will negotiate.

⚡ T R A P

It is usually a bad idea to permit the other side to have any say over who will represent your side in commercial negotiations. Sometimes the other side wants a change in your negotiator solely to get a weaker bargainer. To this general rule, there are exceptions. An individual, or a company, may be uncomfortable dealing with a particular personality, or may have had a prior bad experience with a specific negotiator. Under those rare circumstances, and provided you have someone else who is equally able to represent you, at least consider making the change.

Now, if you are involved in private sector labor-management negotiations under the National Labor Relations Act, the rules are different from those applicable to commercial negotiations. In labor negotiations, each side is legally vested with the sole right to choose its own representatives. Neither management nor union may interfere with, or insist on, changes in the other side's negotiators. To do so is an unfair labor practice. The underlying principle of this rule is that each side is sovereign in its own house and is to be prevented from using its negotiating power to force the other side to negotiate through potentially weaker representatives.

> ## ✒ TIP
>
> In labor-management negotiations, no matter how much the other side objects to a member of your bargaining team and demands change, stand firm and refuse to allow the other side to alter your team assignments. Failure to do so is a very clear signal of weakness and will likely result in other demands. Remind the other side of the principle that each side has a protected legal right to pick its own representatives.

END RUNS AROUND THE PEOPLE AT THE TABLE

"I do refuse you for my judge; and here, before you all, appeal unto the pope." [Catherine, Queen of England] There is nothing new about trying an end run around a particular decision maker. After World War I, President Wilson appealed directly to the public for his League of Nations as a means of trying to overcome Senate opposition. So too, in negotiations. On occasion, one side at the negotiating table may become highly frustrated with the other side's bargaining style and positions. Pleas to change the people at the table may have been denied. One tactic that negotiators sometimes use under these circumstances is to try direct contact with a high level decision maker, seeking to show that the other side's people at the table are irrelevant and may be bypassed. This tactic does carry substantial risk. The people against whom the end run is being attempted may be personally antagonized and in a position to punish those who sought to bypass them.

Bypassing, or attempting to bypass, the other side's authorized negotiators is not a violation of law in individual and commercial negotiations. However, in private sector labor-management negotiations, it may constitute the unfair labor practice of refusal to bargain in good faith. And, in settlement negotiations between attorneys, it is unethical to bypass a party's attorney and to try to deal directly with the opposing party.

> ## ✒ TIP
>
> Prepare for the possibility of an "end run" around your position as a negotiator or chief spokesperson. Discuss the possibility of an "end run" with the people who supervise your work as a negotiator and who might be contacted by the other side. Be sure that they fully understand that they must

supress any temptation to being amenable to any effort to get them directly involved in negotiations or to have them supplant the negotiation spokesperson or team. The best way to combat attempts to bypass you as a negotiator is to have those whom the other side contacts simply refer them back to you with an injunction to deal directly with you.

The Fussbudget Workers Union is in negotiations for a successor contract with Lucy's Fussing Emporium. Negotiations are stalled. Although the Emporium's negotiating team has full necessary authority, the union is unhappy with Emporium's blunt style and with their own inability to win major concessions. The union's chief spokesperson decides to try bypassing the company team and places a direct call to Lucy, the president and chief executive officer of the Emporium. Lucy takes the call. The union spokesperson says, "I think we might be able to settle if you came to the table yourself and take over or at least if you were to personally review the positions your negotiator has asserted." Lucy decides to go to the table. In doing so, she has destroyed the credibility of her negotiators and her negotiating team. Instead, she might have replied, "I have complete confidence in my team. You will have to deal with them. Please don't call me directly again." She should then notify her team of the contact and its result.

RETROGRESSIVE BARGAINING

"One step forward, two steps back." [Lenin] When you retrogressively bargain, you move backwards from a current compromise or position to a harsher position, perhaps one which was taken earlier and then abandoned. For negotiations to work, the parties should be progressively narrowing, not expanding, their differences, as the negotiation process moves from its opening phase to its end game. When a party retrogresses, it is widening the differences between the parties and moving away from any mutually satisfactory resolution. Doing this can absolutely torpedo a negotiation.

In individual or commercial negotiations, there is no legal impediment to backwards movement, but doing so is generally unwise and destructive of credibility.

Obsolete Press and Quentin Quill, an author, are negotiating a publishing contract for Quill's new work, "The Coming Golden Age of the Large Floppy Disk." Quill is concerned that the publisher will not adequately market his new book and wants a clause in the contract that should Obsolete Press fail to sell at least five thousand copies per year, the book will be declared out of print, with the copyright reverting to Quill, so he can find another publisher. Obsolete Press counters by agreeing to include the clause, provided the out of print trigger is set at three hundred copies per year. Obsolete Press and Quill are unable to agree on a number of other issues and temporarily break off their negotiations. When negotiations resume, Obsolete Press now refuses to include any out of print clause, although they had previously agreed to one with the three hundred copy per year trigger. This is retrogressive bargaining. Although Quill is unhappy with the Press for its retrogression, there has been no violation of law and the parties ultimately reach a full agreement, because both parties resolve other more important issues. In many negotiations though, this type of retrogression may undermine confidence sufficiently to prevent any settlement.

In a negotiation between neighboring Olympic Electronics and Everest Office Supplies, one of the issues is how reserved parking spaces will be allocated in a shared parking lot. As the lot is marginally sized to serve both firms and parking spaces are at a premium, the issue has been divisive. Last week, Olympic reduced its demand for spaces from 60% of those available to 55%. The parties have made no progress since on that issue or any other. Annoyed, Olympic's negotiator, in reviewing his side's position, announces that, "As you've done nothing, we are now demanding 65% of the parking spaces in our shared lot." Olympic has clearly retrogressed. Everest's team walks out of the negotiation session. Relations between the two sides are permanently poisoned.

Retrogressive bargaining is a *legal* problem only in labor-management negotiations. In this context, retrogression is an indicator of bad faith bargaining which constitutes an unfair labor practice under the National Labor Relations Act. Retrogression may turn an economic labor dispute into an unfair labor practice one, with significant financial consequences for an employer.

Charlie's Chocolate Works had been in negotiations for a succes-sor labor agreement with the Umpa-Lumpa Candy and Confectionary Workers Union. On December 21, the Chocolate Works placed an offer on the table of a 3.5% increase in wages for a one year contract. On December 22, when the parties resumed negotiations, the Chocolate Works announced that because of lack of progress with negotiations, it was reducing its wage offer to 2.5%, and said it would reduce the offer further if the union did not accept the offer by December 24th (at which point the extant contract expired). Wages had been and remained the only issue between the parties. On December 24th, the union had not accepted the offer and the employer cut it further to 2.0%. The union went on strike and filed a refusal to bargain in good faith charge with the National Labor Relations Board. After a four month strike, the National Labor Relations Board found that the employer had committed an unfair labor practice, that the dispute was an unfair labor practice strike, and the Board ordered the employer to pay the striking employees full back pay.

✒ TIP

If you have made a mistake and conceded too much or need to retrieve a position, do not retrogress on the point as such. If you offer a positive concession in another area but tie it to a negative change (otherwise retrogressive in nature) on the issue as to which you gave too much away, you will not have retrogressed, provided the overall package of the two things is not, in itself, retrogressive. Under these circumstances, a new concession is merely being tied to a relinquishment of some-thing already won by the other side.

CONTRACT INTERPRETATION RULES; AMBIGUITY AND THE DRAFTER; SPECIFIC AND GENERAL

". . . [N]o law in the world can punish a man for his silence. Tis God only that is the judge of the secrets of our hearts." [Sir Thomas More] When you negotiate a settlement, there is no way you can ever incor-porate every possible nuance of your agreement into a written document. There will always be some silences, some ambiguities, and some application questions you did not consider. To fill these gaps, certain general legal rules have been developed. When you negotiate, knowing these general rules may help to avoid subsequent problems when the time comes to interpret the negotiated contract. While the parties can opt out of the general rules by mutual written agreement, language to do so should be drafted by, or at least reviewed in advance by, counsel.

Sometimes, when you cannot prevail on a given point in negotiations or both sides want to get through a difficult issue, you may be forced to deliberately write or accept ambiguous language, or you may do so by accident. While ambiguity is a useful device for resolving the immediate problem of reaching an overall agreement, you should be aware that it contains within itself the seeds of future conflict. The general legal rule is that ambiguities are to be construed against the party that drafted the language.

In a negotiation between neighboring Titanic Maritime Services and Mohegan Overseas Shipping Lines, one of the issues is how many customer service agent positions will be allocated to each of them at a shared dockside office. The parties are totally unable to agree. Titanic suggests that the parties agree to disagree and proposes the following language: "The allocation of customer service agent positions at the common dockside offices shall be as appropriate in light of number of employees and customer volume." Mohegan accepts. The final negotiated agreement between the parties contains the language suggested by Titanic and also a broad based dispute arbitration clause. Two months later, the parties are at odds over marking the positions for their respective organizations. Titanic, which has fewer customers but higher priced unit sales per customer than Mohegan, maintains customer volume means the dollar volume of sales. Mohegan, which services large numbers of people at relatively low prices per unit sold, claims customer volume means literally customer population, regardless of dollar volume. The parties are unable to agree and Titanic invokes the arbitration clause. With no overridingly clear evidence presented, the arbitrator finds against Titanic on the basis that it was Titanic that wrote the language containing the ambiguity, so the clause must be construed against them. She notes that had Titanic wished to use dollars of sales volume it should have used those words.

☞ TIP

When accepting ambiguous language, try to get the other side to be the party to draft the language. When proposing ambiguous language, always realize that your side is taking the risk that the lack of clarity will be held against you.

Another general legal principle of contract interpretation applicable to a negotiated agreement is that a specific provision will override a general one. Suppose your negotiation produces an agreement containing both the phrases, "clerks are to be assigned to the day shift," and, "those clerks in the plant who work on the midnight shift will receive a fifty cent per hour shift differential." The question may arise of whether clerks may ever be assigned to the midnight shift. The first clause implies a negative answer, the latter clause a positive one. The second clause about plant clerks working on midnight shift, being specific, will be read to override the more general clause about clerical employees being assigned to daytime work.

ASSIGNING A CONTROLLING LEGAL JURISDICTION; CHOICE OF LAW PROVISIONS

"Location, location, location." [Adage] These are the three most important words in real estate. Location is also important in legal disputes. Suppose that you subsequently have a dispute over what you negotiated that results in litigation. But, in which court, federal or a particular state, do you litigate? And which jurisdiction's law does that court apply? The rules of law may differ in varying degrees between jurisdictions, so the outcome of your case may very well turn on whose law is used. Further, the location of a litigation, conveniently or inconveniently, may increase or diminish legal and other costs connected with the logistics of a lawsuit. Understand that a court in, for example, Illinois, in certain disputes may be required to apply the substantive law of the jurisdiction specified in the negotiated agreement, for example, New York. So, you may want to negotiate choice of law language that specifies which law governs and where cases will be heard. Having such language may give your side an advantage in later disputes. Use counsel to guide you through this legal thicket.

East Asia Trading Corporation is negotiating a commercial sales agreement with Eurasian Imports and Exports. East Asia is head-

> quartered in California and Eurasian has its main offices in New York. Neither does business in Illinois. The two sides send their negotiators to Chicago, Illinois, for bargaining sessions. The resulting agreement involves transactions in sixteen states, but none in California, New York, or Illinois. The parties do not specify a governing law in their agreement. Assume that a serious dispute later arises between them. The side claiming to be aggrieved may want to bring an action in a state that allows for jury trial and both compensatory and punitive damages. The other side may prefer a state in which judges, rather than juries, decide the facts and where punitive damages are not available. Millions of dollars may hinge on which state courts have jurisdiction and which law is to be applied. Failure to insert a choice of law provision in the agreement will make these threshold issues into matters of great importance.

In commercial negotiations, the parties usually start out with the assumption that the more familiar law of their home location, particularly if they share that location, will govern whatever agreements they may negotiate. That does not have to be the case. If the parties can agree on a controlling law, or if one side has the power to force this decision on the other, the agreement may contain specific provisions to alter the governing law. In consumer negotiations, the purchaser of a car, computer, or appliance is usually presented with a form contract and its terms are, for all practical purposes, not open to negotiation. One of these terms may well be that the controlling law under which the terms of the agreement will be applied and interpreted is that of a named state, which is the preferred state law of the seller. That state may give the seller far more protection than the purchaser's home state.

Why is the question of controlling law so important? For example, if you are buying a consumer product such as a car and it subsequently bursts into flames severely injuring you, you may be unpleasantly surprised to find that the state law made controlling by the contract you "negotiated" with the dealer bars you from recovering certain substantial damages which your home state might permit. The contract may also specify that disputes be settled by arbitration instead of in court and that hearings will be held in a state far distant from your home. Parties who are legally well advised try to make the controlling law the one most favorable to them.

Hal who is planning to build a house near Seattle, Washington is negotiating to purchase the desired pre-cut home package from an upscale housing company in Massachusetts. The contract form used by the seller contains a clause that all disputes arising out of the sale or the application and interpretation of the agreement shall be governed by Massachusetts law and resolved by an arbitration which is to be held in Boston, Massachusetts. The seller refuses to alter any part of the clause. Hal, already committed to building and needing to move ahead, enters into the contract and finds himself in a three thousand dollar dispute with the manufacturer over the proper application of sales tax to the purchase. The seller refuses to budge. Under the terms of the "negotiated agreement," Hal's only alternative is to go to arbitration. To do so, he will have to pay half the arbitrator's fees, his own attorney, and travel to, and stay in, Boston for one or more days. His calculations show that even if he prevails in arbitration, he will likely incur three thousand dollars or more in costs. For all practical purposes, the choice of law provision and the location requirement for the arbitration have left Hal with no remedy and the seller with immunity from smaller claims.

In commercial negotiations, the law allows the parties great freedom in assigning a controlling law. In some cases, it may even be possible to specify whether state or federal law will govern. When the parties to a negotiation are relatively equally matched, the question of a controlling law will be a negotiable item, like many others. Before selecting a controlling state law, always be sure and consult with counsel.

In labor-management negotiations, the controlling law as to the labor relations aspects for most private sector employers, will be the federal National Labor Relations Act. The parties may not legally opt out of this Act by mutual agreement. However, if the parties agree, other aspects of the negotiated contract may be made subject to a choice of law provision. Because choice of law is always a complex legal subject, the advice of counsel should be sought before taking a position on a controlling law.

EXPIRATION AND "SUNSET" CLAUSES

"I don't know what you could say about a day in which you have seen four beautiful sunsets." [John Glenn] If you are negotiating an ongoing relationship, one of the most essential elements is a "beautiful sunset," a termination date and time for an entire agreement. One of the more frequent mistakes non-attorneys make in negotiating agreements without legal advice, particularly in commercial contracts, is the omission of a specific expiration clause. Most negotiated agreements require a defined ending date and legally sufficient language to insure that any obligations you intend to survive the expiration of the contract are clearly spelled out.

The labor agreement between MegaProducts and SoleSource contains the following language: "This agreement and the pension agreement, pension plan, and insurance agreement negotiated simultaneously, shall expire and be of no further force and effect as of 11:59 P.M., December 21, 2002."

The negotiated agreement between Mini-Soft software and Computer-Users provides that Computer-Users will pay a royalty fee for the use of licensed software. The contract expires at a specific time and date. It also contains a clause that, "The provision of this agreement requiring the payment of a royalty on the software provided hereunder shall survive the expiration of this agreement and Computer-Users shall continue to pay royalties as specified herein until all copies of the provided software have been surrendered to Mini-Soft."

Jon Konsultant and All Eternity-Services have negotiated an agreement under which Konsultant will make himself available to All Eternity-Services for consulting for two weeks each year. The contract, negotiated without attorneys, contains no expiration date. Two years after its effective date, Konsultant wishes to reopen the arrangement. All Eternity-Services claims the contract is ongoing and they have no need to reopen at this time. Konsultant should have written an expiration clause into the agreement.

While an expiration clause ends an entire agreement, a specific "sunset clause" is a provision that automatically wipes away a specified portion of a negotiated agreement as of a certain date, unless the parties agree to extend the language in question. Sunset clauses are useful ways of eliminating obsolete language from an agreement, without the need for the parties to take any further affirmative action. The elimination of a clause at a date certain, unless extended, may be useful either substantively (for an experimental program) or procedurally (for housekeeping).

The labor agreement between Auto Parts and the Unified Auto Assemblers provides that: "Effective January 1, 2000, accident and sickness pay shall be at the rate of $300 per week, per eligible employee. This provision shall be automatically deleted from this agreement as of 11:59 P.M. on December 31, 2000. Effective January 1, 2001, accident and sickness pay shall be at the rate of $310 per week, per eligible employee. This provision shall be automatically deleted from this agreement as of 11:59 P.M. on December 31, 2001. Effective January 1, 2002, accident and sickness pay shall be at the rate of $320 per week, per eligible employee." There is no sunset clause for the last provision because the entire contract expires on December 31, 2002, and any change beyond that date will need to be negotiated. The effect of these sunset provisions is to keep the agreement's language automatically up to date.

Suppose the agreement also provides for Auto Parts to offer an experimental, partially subsidized, child care program for a period of one year. Because the program is experimental, Auto Parts does not wish to have to negotiate if it should decide to discontinue the program after the one year trial period. The Unified Auto Assemblers believes that it does not have the bargaining power to force a permanent program now and that once Auto Parts puts the benefit in place, inertia and fear of a negative morale impact will tend to force the company to make the benefit permanent. The union therefore accepts the experimental concept. The parties agree to the following language: "The child care program hereunder is experimental. One year after the effective date of this agreement, all contract language relating to the experimental child care program is automatically deleted from this agreement and shall cease to be of any further force and effect, unless the employer, in its sole judgment, agrees to extend the program."

⚡ TIP

Expiration provisions should be included in every contract. If you wish to have a flexible expiration date, write a clause that makes the contract indefinite in duration, but subject to cancellation after a specified date, on written notice of termination, delivered to the other party, at least a certain number of days in advance of cancellation. Use sunset clauses to eliminate time dependent provisions and for housekeeping purposes. Without a sunset clause, temporary provisions have a way of becoming permanent. Consider that a "temporary telephone tax," adopted to finance the Spanish-American War of 1898 was only repealed in the year 2000.

INTEREST ARBITRATION

"There is no substitute for talent. Industry and all the virtues are of no avail." [Aldous Huxley] But, there is an available substitute for negotiations, "interest arbitration." In interest arbitration, the parties confer on a neutral third party the authority to make a binding contract for them, perhaps hedged only with certain rules and restrictions. In pursuing this route, you give up your freedom to reach your own agreement and risk obtaining binding terms that you would never have accepted on your own. Because of the risks it carries, interest arbitration is relatively rare, although Congress has several times imposed it by law in the air and rail transportation industries. Arbitration is more frequently used to resolve questions of interpretation and application of an extant agreement.

Tough Beef Company and the Emperor Old Cattle Ranch are in negotiations to renew a longstanding contract. Unable to reach mutually acceptable terms, the parties agree to submit the making of their new pact to an interest arbitrator. The arbitrator, who does not understand the way work is structured for either party, creates a distribution and processing system that is extraordinarily costly and cumbersome for both parties. To alter this system, they are forced to resume direct negotiations to obtain changes in the contract imposed on them by the interest arbitrator.

✐ TRAP

Interest arbitration may not be widely used because of the risk it carries. Since an interest arbitration award is legally binding, the danger always exists that an interest arbitrator will issue a decision that you, the other party, or both of you, find absolutely unacceptable and impractical. The legal right to appeal arbitration decisions is extraordinarily narrow, so it may prove impossible to avoid having to comply with an interest arbitration award that contains unacceptable terms. For a full discussion on the limits on appeals of arbitration awards under the law, see my book, *Alternative Dispute Resolution in the Work Place*, published by American Law Media's Law Journal Press.

ALTERNATE DISPUTE RESOLUTION

"People take different roads seeking fulfillment and happiness. Just because they're not on your road doesn't mean they've gotten lost." [H. Jackson Browne] There are many different routes to the same end— a successful negotiation. Sometimes, you may have trouble getting both sides to be on the same road. In these cases, consider professional mediation or arbitration. Alternative dispute resolution, as related to the negotiation of agreements (as opposed to interpretation and application of extant agreements), may be divided into two basic forms, mediation and arbitration.

Mediation is a process in which an individual serving as a neutral third party, who is permitted no authoritative decision making power, is brought into a negotiation to assist both sides to achieve their own, mutually acceptable, resolution. A mediator's functions are not defined by law, but may include:

- Defining issues;
- Clarifying the parties' interests;
- Providing a channel for communications;
- Focusing the negotiations on productive areas of discussion;
- Proposing options for the settlement of issues being negotiated;
- Assisting the parties in documenting any agreements; and,
- Coordinating and educating the parties.

Mediation may be either facilitative or evaluative. In facilitative mediation, the mediator attempts to bring the parties together without giving advice or predicting an outcome. In evaluative mediation, the mediator analyzes and weighs the parties' positions and offers opinions to both sides on how the issues might be settled. Which style of mediation is chosen, if any, is up to the parties, but, to avoid misunderstandings, the potential mediator should be clearly informed of each side's preferences.

In commercial negotiations, mediation is a purely voluntary program and will only work if both sides wish to bring in a mediator. In labor-management negotiations, there is a critical legal requirement that the federal and state (if any) mediation services be notified of an upcoming contract negotiation. Failure to give this notice within the time limits specified in the National Labor Relations Act (for most private sector employers) deprives you of the right to use your economic weapons (strike or lockout), until you provide proper notice to the mediation services for the necessary period. However, the giving of notice does not require you to accept the active services of a mediator. If one party wants to bring in a mediator and the other party chooses not to cooperate with the mediator, the mediator will accomplish little or nothing.

Cooperative Cooperatives is in negotiations with the Union of Aggressive Employees for a successor labor agreement. The parties use completely different negotiating styles and are at a virtual standstill. To try to break the impending impasse, Cooperative Cooperatives calls the mediator assigned to their case by the Federal Mediation Service when it received the required legal notice of an impending labor contract negotiation. The union has a particular distaste for this mediator. When he shows up at a negotiating session, the union refuses to sit at the table. When the mediator tries to meet with the union privately, they receive him politely, offer him coffee, and then suggest he drink it in the lobby. The mediator will accomplish nothing.

The second form of alternate dispute resolution in negotiations is interest arbitration, as defined in the previous section. Once agreed to by the parties, interest arbitration is generally governed by the Federal Arbitration Act. This Act makes written agreements to arbitrate "valid, irrevocable, and enforceable," except on grounds that would be sufficient to set aside other contracts. The important thing for most private sector negotiators to remember is that interest arbitration is not mandated by generally applicable federal or state laws, either in commercial or labor-management negotiations. The parties have the right to negotiate their own bargain without being compelled to turn their negotiations over to a third party for binding resolution.

SOLE SOURCE; DISPARATE POWER; UNCONSCIONABLE AGREEMENTS; AND OVERREACHING

"Power tends to corrupt, and absolute power corrupts absolutely." [Lord Acton] This section is about the negative consequences of excessive power. Sole source means that the other party in a negotiation will be the only supplier of a particular type of goods or services to the buyer. Sole source negotiations may lead to excellent pricing for the buyer and an assured market for the seller, but negotiators need to exercise extreme caution when negotiating a sole source agreement. The critical factor is whether the sole source may be counted upon to deliver the promised goods at the specified times, regardless of such events as fire at a factory, a labor dispute, or other impediment to production. The legal risk is that the other side will use its control over your sourcing to extract from you changes in the negotiated agreement, during its term.

Disparate power impedes real negotiating. As used here, disparate power is not limited to anti-trust violations, but means any wide variation in bargaining power creating the ability of one party, often a supplier, to impose terms and conditions on the other party, often a buyer, on a take it or leave it basis. Under this definition, we all encounter disparate power when we rent an automobile, ship a package, or purchase computer software. These transactions are generally conducted on forms provided by the large player and you, as the less powerful party, are given no option to modify or negotiate the basic contractual agreement. Your only power is to go elsewhere, assuming there is somewhere else to go. In some fields, there may be only a few suppliers and all of them may require essentially the same "boiler plate" contractual language, not subject to modification. One such contractual clause may be an agreement to submit disputes under the agreement to arbitration. When buying stocks, for example, brokerages almost universally require a customer to sign an agreement which includes mandatory arbitration of future disputes.

The courts will not enforce unconscionable agreements. These are agreements in which one side has used bargaining power to impose on the other provisions which violate the law or are so overreaching in their impact as to "shock the court's conscience." Do not expect a court to be easily shocked. Few negotiated agreements are ever held to be unconscionable.

CONTROLLING AND COPING WITH THE FLOW OF INFORMATION

"All of the books in the world contain no more information than is broadcast as video in a single large American city in a single year. Not all bits have equal value." [Carl Sagan] We are often overloaded with documents and information and faced with the problem of identifying and keeping track of the information that really matters. All but the simplest negotiations are likely to produce a torrent of documents, including proposals, tentative agreements, and written examples and explanations. In complex negotiations, when the number of proposals exchanged may be measured in the dozens, each having several subsequent modifications, you may find yourself drowning in the flow of paperwork. In addition, you will need to keep other documents such as your negotiating plan, survey, and research in some form of order. The keeping of orderly records of proposal and counterproposals is essential should legal disputes arise post-negotiations on the application or meaning of the final negotiation contract or deal. You may need to know when and what was put on the table.

✐ TIP

Put the date and time on your master copy of each piece of paper handed over to the other side at the time it is distributed. Then keep a special loose leaf binder in which all materials turned over to the other side and received from them are maintained in chronological order. When several drafts of a proposal are utilized, it may help to put a revision number in the upper right hand corner of each subsequent draft, so that different revisions do not get mixed up. Consider using color coded paper to make sure that the wrong version of a proposal or document is not accidentally turned over to the other side.

✐ TIP

Do not bring to a negotiating meeting proposals you are not prepared to distribute at that time. If you anticipate the remote possibility of reaching these proposals, consider putting them in a separate case to be opened only if needed.

☞ TIP

Take the time to organize your materials after each session or during caucus breaks. Being disorganized opens the door to making a potentially costly error at the negotiating table. Some negotiating teams assign an individual, perhaps the note taker, the task of maintaining the master records book. After the conclusion of the negotiations, be sure that the master book is retained, preferably for seven years after the conclusion of the agreement in commercial negotiations, and indefinitely, so long as there are successor contracts, in the labor-management context.

NUMERACY, THE VITAL INGREDIENT

"Gigo." [Acronym meaning "garbage in, garbage out."] If your numerical data is wrong (garbage in), the conclusions based on that data are likely to be flawed (garbage out). Few things will be as embarrassing to you or as detrimental to your credibility as being found to have committed a numerical error in a proposal or offer. The other side will wonder whether you really made a mistake (showing incompetence) or tried to trick them (being unsavory). Either way, you will lose. Numerical errors in your internal planning documents may lead to erosion in the confidence level of those who need to approve your plan and whose support you need to back your judgment calls in negotiations.

Passionette Advocate is negotiating a possible settlement to a lawsuit with the other side's attorney, Justine Justice. Advocate offers Justice a calculation sheet, setting damages in light of a cut-and-dried formula that Advocate and Justice agreed on at their last meeting. Justice asks an associate to check the figures. Ten minutes later, he calls Justice aside and says, "Of these twelve figures, four are wrong, all in favor of Advocate's client." Justice is left wondering if Advocate is just careless or whether the errors were intentionally made in the hope she would not check the figures. In any event, she decides she will never trust any future numbers provided to her by Advocate.

If you are unfortunate enough to make a numerical error that is in the other side's favor, they may never point it out. If your error is in your own side's favor, as noted, it may be perceived as possibly deliberate, damaging your credibility. The absence of a calculation error is no guarantee that there has not been a logic error in either computerized or manually derived formulas. In negotiations with large monetary stakes, logical and computational errors, may be extremely costly. When a negotiated agreement contains both a formula and the results and they are incompatible due to error, the basis for a future legal dispute is created.

✐ TIP

When a proposal involves numerical data derived from a formula which has been generated on a computer using, for example, a spread sheet program, test the computer output by running a number of calculations by hand for each variant of the formula. This should be both an arithmetic check and a logic check. Complex formulas may seem to produce accurate results, but a slight error in input in the formulas may have a significant impact on the output.

Labrador Puppy Biscuit Company and the Canine Bakers union are negotiating a successor labor agreement. Labrador has proposed a "one time bonus" under which the amount each employee will receive is conditioned on a complex formula based on a set dollar figure times years of service, plus a different set dollar amount multiplied by an employee's skills level designator, but subject to a "cap" of the lesser of the computed amount or a specified maximum dollar limit. The computational problem is handled by using a computer spread sheet and a computer generated printed output. Labrador does not hand check the logic or arithmetic of the output. Only after the new contract is signed and ratified does anyone from management notice that the computer formula was flawed, in that the maximum figure was not applied to a particular skills group. The error is found to have been in the entry of the spread sheet formula for calculating the final bonus figures. During negotiations one of the union's bargaining team members, whose bonus should have been capped, noticed the error because it impacted her personally. She decided to say noth-

ing and the employer is ultimately bound by contract to make the larger payments.

✒ TIP

Check all arithmetical computations three times, preferably with different people running the calculations. Verify all formulas in any cases in which the three calculations do not give the same result, although it is highly probable that if two out of the three calculations produce the same result, that result is correct.

✒ TRAP

People tend to believe computer print outs more readily than hand written figures. The chances of a computer making a pure arithmetic error are so low as to eliminate any need to check. However, logic errors are far more likely, so computer data should not be trusted without checking. Some errors will be evident by the application of common sense, but others require making verification checks. **Do not automatically accept a computer generated data table as inherently accurate.**

FINDING AND USING ALLIES

"ALLIANCE, n. In international politics, the union of two thieves who have their hands so deeply inserted in each other's pockets that they cannot separately plunder a third." [Ambrose Bierce] During the American Revolution, Great Britain was our enemy. Today, it is our closest ally. Alliances shift, but they remain very important. Negotiations management includes finding allies and making use of their support in legally appropriate ways. In commercial negotiations, partnership alliances, and joint ventures between organizations, may be sources of support in negotiations with outside third parties. When negotiating with government officials, the support of lobbying and pressure groups may be valuable.

In labor-management negotiations, unions will seek the support of other locals of the parent union who have relationships with the employer at different locations. They may look to their international union for expertise, research, financial support, and strike funds; apply to the AFL or its international unions for assistance; seek help from community groups; and, may ask for aid from those religious groups who tend to favor organized labor's cause. Management may seek assistance from other companies by contracting out struck work (tolling) or by putting parallel pressure on other locals of the same union at distant sites. However, the practice once followed by the airlines of a "strike insurance" pact, under which a struck airline was given funds by the other operating carriers, based on their increased revenues from traffic diverted from the struck carrier, is now unlawful.

✒ TIP

When working with allies, remember that their interests and yours, although they may overlap, are not identical. Ask for support only on critical issues. If you request too much support, or ask too often, your chances of getting what you need will be limited.

PAYING IN ADVANCE OR FOR PROGRESS IN COMMERCIAL NEGOTIATIONS

"I don't like paying for the same real estate twice." [General George S. Patton] The question of making advance payments may arise when negotiating with builders, remodelers, and sub-contractors. Advance payments raise the danger that the receiving party may default on its obligations and may walk away with the other party's money, leaving the disappointed party with only the recourse of long and expensive litigation and facing a second payment to cover the same work. Good negotiation managers will resist demands for advance payments, unless:

- ◆ Advance payments are normal in the industry involved;
- ◆ Real performance benchmarks are tied to each advance;
- ◆ Sufficient safeguards against diversion are included; and,
- ◆ Sufficient "hold backs" provide incentives for completion.

The reputation and financial condition of the other party are also relevant as to whether advance payments may safely be made. A modified form of advance payments is the "progress payment" system, under which the customer pays for fractions of a job as it progresses, although the buyer has not yet received a fully completed or useable product.

Great Abodes is a well established building contractor which builds high end custom homes, no more than one or two at a time, in a middle sized community. As is common with construction contracts, Great Abodes seeks five progress payments during the course of a contract to build a new custom home. Each payment is contingent on the completion of certain work. The last payment provides for a "hold back" of several thousand dollars to insure that any follow up details are completed. Great Abodes and its master builder have a fine reputation in the community and one they wish to preserve, for in a community that is small or middle sized, reputation is a vital factor. Under these circumstances, provided the contract spells out the details of progress payments, a person negotiating with Great Abodes is likely to be relatively safe in accepting an advance payment requirement. Home builders are working with expensive materials.

🔥 TIP

When negotiating with builders and contractors, contact the local better business bureau to determine if complaints have been filed against the builder or contractor. Also check whether there are litigations pending. Verify how long the builder or contractor has been in business and do check references carefully.

ETHICAL CONCERNS

"The word 'ethics' is derived from the Greek word ethos (character), and from the Latin word mores (customs). . . . [Ethics] establishes the nature of the duties that people owe themselves and one another." [Cornell Legal Information Institute] The problem with ethics as applied to negotiations is that negotiations require you to hold back core information about your ultimate objectives and intentions. You cannot reveal your instructions. You may bluff at times or take moderately strong positions on issues where you know you will later retreat. Absent the legal disclosure requirements found in some states, if , for example, you were negotiating to buy a car or a house, you would be naïve to expect to be told all the facts, particularly any negative ones.

If you are a negotiator who happens to be an attorney, you may be under a code of professional ethics that requires you to avoid conduct involving dishonesty, fraud, deceit, or misrepresentation. The American Bar Association's Model Rules of Professional Conduct state that a lawyer "shall not knowingly make a false statement of material fact or law to a third person," a principle that is intended to apply to negotiations as well as litigation. The difficulty of applying this standard is evident from a further comment contained with the rule which says that "under generally accepted conventions in negotiations, certain types of statements are not taken as statements of material fact." Obviously, whether you are an attorney or not, dishonesty, fraud, and real deceit are unethical in negotiations. However, reality dictates that you must be able to overstate your case and therefore "deceit" at that level is simply recognized as "not material."

Ethical considerations (and legal ones in labor negotiations) require negotiation to be in good faith. "Good faith forbids either party from concealing what he privately knows, to draw the other into a bargain, from his ignorance of that fact, and his believing to the contrary." [Lord Mansfield] This suggests that in commercial negotiations it is unethical to withhold such a material fact from the other party that it would cause the other party to withdraw from the negotiation.

Green Water Developers is offering new homes at very low prices. Maria Hewball is interested in purchasing a home for herself and her two small children and is working out a deal with a Green Waters sales representative. That representative knows that Green Waters is built on the site occupied by a now defunct chemical corporation which had a chromium plant on the site in the early part of the twentieth century. During construction, Green Waters several times found deposits of chemicals and chromium in the soil. Green Waters never discloses this fact to Maria Hewball. Few would argue that Green Waters has acted ethically, even if the state in which the project is located has no disclosure rules.

There is no formal code of ethics that applies to negotiators who are not restrained by some form of independent professional code of conduct (such as attorneys, accountants, and physicians). What then may be defined as a negotiator's ethical responsibilities? In addition to the discussion of material deception above, my suggested code would include the following:

- Avoid improper information gathering methods;
- Turn over materials improperly offered to you;
- Never make a commitment you don't intend to keep;
- If possible, keep all your commitments; and,
- Honor your agreements even if it hurts.

While it is perfectly proper to gather information from a variety of sources including public records, research tools, and personal contacts, it is not ethical to acquire data by such methods as personal surveillance, snooping, spying, or industrial espionage. Common sense should tell you where the border lines are between legitimate information gathering and activities which, even when legal, are unethical.

Nero Holmes is employed by Montenegro & Baker. His job frequently takes him into the offices of Morse & Chan, where he often has conversations with various managers. Montenegro & Baker is about to negotiate an alliance with Morse & Chan and asks Nero Holmes to engage people at Morse & Chan in conversation about their business and its current success level. Nero Holmes does so and reports back what he has learned. However, at no point has Nero Holmes extracted information by pressure, coercion, or undue means. He has stolen no files, peeped at no records, and taken nothing from wastebaskets. People just like to talk with him and frequently volunteer information. Is his behavior ethical?

On leaving the negotiation room, John Alden, chief spokesperson for Mayflower Enterprises, leaves behind on the conference table a chart which contains Mayflower's bottom lines for settlement. Without knowing what the chart contains, a member of the other negotiating team glances at the chart, its meaning is instantly obvious, and the numbers are clear. What is the ethical thing to do?

A disgruntled individual once offered a major employer the internal documents of a union concerning a major national negotiation, which would have disclosed the union's bottom line positions. The employer took the employee's name and reported the matter to the union. Apart from the ethical considerations involved which seem clear, had the employer accepted the offer and been found out, a strike would have been almost inevitable and the employer's credibility and reputation ruined.

"The President has kept all the promises he intended to keep." [George Stephanopolous on Bill Clinton] A good rule of negotiation ethics is to make only those promises you intend to keep and then keep the promises you make. A negotiator's stock in trade is her or his credibility and reputation for good faith and fair dealing. Circumstances may make it impossible for you to keep a promise. The important thing is to do so to the extent practical and to make good faith efforts to carry out your promises. Keep in mind that a single failure to keep a promise will usually destroy credibility derived from keeping many prior promises.

Finally, a good sense of ethics mandates that you keep to your contractual commitments, even when carrying them out is to your disadvantage. That does not mean you cannot seek to renegotiate or reopen an existing negotiated arrangement, but until or unless there is a change, you will need to honor your agreement. Again, reputation and credibility are tied up in adherence to agreements. A party that breaks its agreements is a party that few will want to negotiate with in the future, whether or not a lawsuit is filed. Even in "one time deals," where there is no continuing relationship, you should ethically adhere to your commitments. Reputation is usually broader than any one negotiation.

Chapter 4

Getting Good Data

Why Good Data is So Critical

"What are the facts? Again and again and again—what are the facts? Shun wishful thinking, ignore divine revelation, forget what 'the stars foretell,' avoid opinion, care not what the neighbors think, never mind the unguessable 'verdict of history'—what are the facts, and to how many decimal places? You pilot always into an unknown future, facts are your single clue. Get the facts!" [Robert A. Heinlein, *Time Enough for Love*, G.P. Putnam's Sons (1973)] Why does good data matter so much to a negotiator? Information is one of the three elemental factors in negotiating (the others are power and time). The two central keys to success in negotiating are planning and having the right information. If your data is bad, your plan, strategy, and tactics will be of little or no value. Worse, they may affirmatively lead you down the path to significant error. Without the facts, you might as well go ahead and use a dart board for your decisions.

What complicates negotiations is that neither side is ever able to have a complete picture. Only God, and the professors in negotiations simulation programs, ever have all the facts, which temporarily puts those of us who run simulations in rather exalted company. Negotiations and military operations share a "fog of war." When you negotiate successfully, expect to put considerable time into obtaining data, analyzing your data, estimating the other side's objectives, goals, and bargaining power, and establishing your own side's willingness to take risk, or in military parlance, to take potential casualties. None of the estimates or projections will be solid if the information on which they are based is erroneous or contrary to the actual facts. Ignorance of the facts paves the road to negotiation failure.

Data collection and analysis is a key to negotiation success, but no matter how well your "intelligence function" operates, success at the table will be primarily bottomed on such aspects of negotiating power as economics, unity, and willingness to take reasonable risk. Although good data can never in itself substitute for negotiation power, correct information will greatly facilitate your ability to wring from a negotiation the most advantageous outcome reasonably attainable. Without good data, you should expect to have a miserable negotiations experience and come away feeling that you may have been victimized. Sometimes, good data may be devilishly hard to obtain. As a buyer, this is one of the reasons you may feel very frustrated when the time comes to bargain with an automobile sales representative. The consumer is far more in the dark.

Meg Magnum is interested in purchasing a new Packard Prometheus car. The Packard dealer in her area is the only one left in the state and the Packard is sold only in small numbers. She is unable to locate much information on the Internet or in books on dealer cost prices on the Prometheus. The one source she is able to locate says that too few of the cars are sold to offer a reliable average sale price. The manufacturer and dealership are also secretive about prices and the "stock on hand or in inventory" of the car. About the only information she is able to obtain are used car prices for the car and average dealer mark ups for similar "muscle cars." Magnum will be at a serious disadvantage when negotiating for the Prometheus.

Don't worry about overall "information overload." The problem will usually be a dearth of information, not an excess. As early in the negotiation process as practical, collect as much data as possible about both your own side, which is usually relatively easy, and about the other side, which will prove far more difficult. Planning, mission, strategy, and objectives, are all highly dependent on what you know or are able to reasonably estimate. If your assumptions are false, correcting actions based on them will be quite difficult after the negotiation process has begun and both sides have started to lock themselves into developed positions. In business negotiations, the results of decisions based on bad data may impact many people's lives and even company survival.

Josef Horner is executive vice president of Many Colors Paints. The company is about to enter into a negotiation in which it is seeking to become the sole source paint supplier to Home Deco, the premier national "do it yourself" firm. If successful in the negotiations, Many Colors would produce paint to be marketed by Home Deco using its private brand label. In preparation for negotiations, the Many Colors negotiating team assesses the capacity of the company's paint plants in relation to Home Deco's probable paint volume needs. They determine that the plants are collectively able to meet one hundred and ten percent of the customer's present needs over the next three years, without plant expansion. When they report this to Horner and outline a strategy based on this capacity, Horner has to be restrained from terminating the employment of the entire negotiating team on the spot. He says, "Didn't you do any research? Home Deco is growing at a rate of fifteen percent per year. You could have learned that from their annual reports. A recent magazine article said they plan a major sales campaign in the home finishing and decorating area. Our Thomas City plant is going to need extensive maintenance next year, decreasing our overall production capacity by twenty percent for six months. You could have learned that from our maintenance director. If we entered into this contract on the basis of your projections, in one year's time Home Deco would be suing us for failure to supply." Someone laughs. Horner becomes very angry and says, "This is no laughing matter. The decisions we make here impact thousands of people and millions of company dollars. How can we make them on incomplete or wrong data? You—or your successors, if you are no longer with us—will not bring me any more incomplete or unverified data." Horner is, of course, absolutely correct.

Bad data is not the only problem. Failure to obtain information may also cause difficulties. Personal negotiations are not exempt from this rule.

Paula Plug runs a small auto body and repair business which is outgrowing its current quarters. Plug is also looking to buy a house. She sees a property that consists of a three bedroom house with a huge garage and auto accessible basement space sufficient to hold five cars. She immediately sees this space as a useful annex for her business and this makes the particular and unusual house an ideal purchase. Enthused, she negotiates to buy the house and to get it, she pays a lot more than she intended. Plug justifies this additional spending because she will move some of her work operations into the basement. Only after she has closed on the new house does she check the zoning regulations. Plug is shocked to find out that the zoning regulations would absolutely prohibit the use of the basement in her business, that her neighbors would seek full enforcement of the zoning regulations, and that the town zoning board rarely grants any variances.

The sheer amount of information contained in even personal negotiations may be overwhelming. Consider the complexity of a house purchase offer or a contract to have a new house custom built. Construction contracts contain many detailed provisions and specifications about the concrete to be used in foundations; the dimensions and placement of lumber; lot grading; drainage systems; and even the number of coats of paint to be applied. This is necessary to avoid misunderstandings about the amount and nature of work to be done and what is covered under the purchase price.

Brook Greenstone is a general contractor and master builder of custom homes. Carlotta Acres is planning to have her first custom home constructed and approaches Greenstone about doing the work. Acres has up to $155,000 available for the project. Because Acres is a serious prospect, with land and an architectural plan in hand, Greenstone prepares a construction contract specifically for her, the terms of which are flexible and negotiable. Acres keeps her options open by simultaneously negotiating terms with Charles Cheapo, another master builder. Both Greenstone and Cheapo are willing to negotiate any of the terms of their proposed contracts. Both builders proposed agreements which contain large numbers of clauses concerning what materials and labor are included and excluded from the project. Site preparation, grading and excavation, masonry, framing, finishing, appliances, and kitchen and fireplace allowances are all specified in detail to avoid future potentially expensive misunderstandings. Acres finds these specifications somewhat incomprehensible and fastens exclusively on the one term she easily understands, price. When Charles

Cheapo offers to build the house for Acres for $149,000, she accepts, unwilling to spend the time to learn that Cheapo has cut many corners. Greenstone, who is offering Acres a much higher quality house for $150,000, which is only marginally higher than Cheapo's offer and well within Acres' budget, loses the contract. Acres, in ending her negotiation by making a decision based solely on cost, actually receives far less value for her money. Later, when the house is built and there are many problems, Acres realizes her mistake.

⚡ TIP

As a buyer, when negotiating a complex contract, take the time to do research, or obtain objective expert guidance, in order to understand each provision of a negotiation proposal, including those terms that may be either technical or unfamiliar. Because price is simple to understand, failure to understand other terms may result in a negotiation that is less successful in terms of "bang for the buck."

⚡ TIP

As a seller who wants to negotiate and close a deal successfully, recognize that in complex matters buyers outside your field may be thoroughly confused by terms you use every day and which are easy for you to understand. You may need to spend considerable time explaining terms other than pricing. Consider reminding your price centered potential customers that it is always possible for someone to undersell you if they produce a very low quality product or service.

When you have data but it is incorrect data, you may mislead both yourself and the other side. This has dangers of its own. In the King and I, the King of Siam observes that people very quickly fight "to prove what they do not know, is so." Remember that once an idea or a concept becomes fixed in someone's mind, even your own, it may be far more difficult to "unlearn" it than it would have been to accept reality in the first place.

RESEARCHING THE FACTS, HOW, WHERE?

"Judge a man by his questions rather than by his answers." [Voltaire] Before you can begin the relatively easy task of seeking the information you need for a negotiation, you will first have to face the more difficult task of framing the right questions to research. Because the right questions vary with the problem, it is impossible to make suggestions as to specific questions.

☞ TIP

Invest the necessary time to frame the questions to be researched for a negotiation. If you identify too many questions by including those of marginal importance, the research task will be onerous. If you identify too few, you may miss something important. So, once you have a list of questions you want answered, prioritize them.

The problem in researching hard copy published sources is that it may be very difficult to locate the information you need or to find a library or source which has the necessary material. The problem with the Internet is often "information overload," in that a search on a keyword may deliver thousands of irrelevant hits. Obviously, the sources of necessary data will vary with the nature of the negotiation and which side of the table you occupy. Frequently, necessary research will take you to a public library or an Internet site. While it is impossible to provide a complete range of data sources, some of the possible sources are:

Automotive negotiations: On the world wide web: auotbytel.com; autoquest.com; carquotes.com; carprices.com; and, edwards.com, will supply a potential buyer with price and other information. For trade in-values on your old car, see the automotive Blue Book, available at bookstores or public libraries.

House purchase or sale negotiations: To evaluate what else is on the market in order to do your own price estimates based on comparable properties see, on the Internet, era.com, or century21.com. Search the web for the names of leading realtors in your area. For the tax assessments on comparable homes, visit your county or town records office and ask your realtor to draw up comparisons from the realtor's data bank. For another source of price information, see realty publications which show homes for sale and their asking prices. For the actual value at which recently sold homes closed, visit your county or town hall of records where you may check on property transfers, as recorded. Remember that in real estate location is a critical issue. Do not make comparisons with an inappropriate geographical area. Your realtor will guide you in pricing a house for sale or making an offer, but remember that the realtor may have a personal stake in setting a price level. A low price facilitates both a quick sale and a quick commission.

Commercial negotiations: Sources will vary widely depending on the nature of the negotiation. The public library or an Internet search may provide considerable information on a commercial firm. Some library sources include: *Thomas Register of American Manufacturers; Hoover's, Guide to Private Companies; Hoover's, Handbook of American Business; Standard and Poor's, Register of Corporations;* and Dun and Bradstreet's, *Million Dollar Directory.* For large corporation financial news check the on-line service wsj.com. For legal matters, search the National Law Journal's ljx.com Internet site; lexis.com; and, the Cornell Legal Information Institute's site at www.cornell.law.edu. A good library and Internet search may provide considerable information.

Legal Negotiations: Attorneys will often be able to obtain data regarding past litigations from published case reports and on-line searches. Networking may provide information on the other side's advocate and its past history of willingness to settle outstanding matters short of litigation. Attorneys should be sensitive to an organization's vulnerabilities to adverse publicity. The primary on-line legal research sources are the fee carrying services, LEXIS and Westlaw. Although these services are relatively expensive, they may be the only source for some cases. There are now many free legal research sites on the Internet. For a good free source and links to other free statutory and case reporting legal research sources, see the Cornell Legal Information Institute's site at **www.cornell.law.edu.**

Labor-Management Negotiations: For unions, the sources in the commercial negotiations section above may yield data about a business. For employer research, financial reports known as LM-1 and LM-2 forms, which are public information, must be filed annually by unions with the U.S. Department of Labor. Copies are available through that agency or through the Bureau of National Affairs (BNA) (fee applies) on an expedited basis. Each side should search the Internet for news and information on the other, including information related to labor disputes elsewhere, their outcomes, and developments impacting the internal operations of the other party. Each side should check chamber of commerce, or union surveys, and economic data published by the government and private sources, such as those related to area trend settlements and cost-of-living.

LEARNING ABOUT THE OTHER SIDE (USING ALL LEGAL RESOURCES)

"An investment in knowledge pays the best interest." [Benjamin Franklin] In negotiations, knowledge often translates directly into power. The more you know, the better able you will be to realistically evaluate your side's strengths and its weaknesses. While knowledge does not inherently enhance your bargaining power and no one can ever be in possession of all the facts, the more knowledge you have, the better you will be able to apply whatever bargaining power you do have. In World War II, cryptanalysis provided advance knowledge of Japanese intentions at the Battle of Midway and helped turn the tide in the Pacific. The information obtained allowed Admiral Nimitz to place our less powerful fleet in just the right place at the right time. While this type of intelligence gathering is outside the pale of negotiations, the collection of information in legal and proper ways remains almost as critical in negotiations as it is in military planning and operations.

Apart from the publicly available sources, such as those outlined in the previous section, you are likely to have numerous informal channels for acquiring negotiation related information. One of the best sources may be your network, the web of personal relationships most of us develop with others through personal contacts and association or group memberships. Professional negotiators often maintain mutual personal networks of people who may be able to share with them inside information about the personalities and agendas of those they may face across negotiating tables.

Fleece Industries is in negotiations with the Amalgamated Fiber Workers union for a successor labor agreement. Fleece's negotiators are trying to estimate how well prepared its union represented employees are to strike. Many Fleece employees belong to the All Fibers Credit Union. One of the members of the board of directors of this credit union is the brother of a company negotiating team member. That team member asks his brother if, without revealing any particular names, there have been unusual deposits or withdrawals from Fleece employee accounts. Learning that employees have greatly increased their withdrawals leads the Fleece negotiators to conclude that employees are spending freely, are not likely to be thinking seriously of striking, and may think twice before striking. Further checks with area merchants such as travel agents, appliance stores, and realtors, confirm that employ-

ees are spending with confidence and are likely to face difficult financial circumstances if the union calls a strike or if they fail to ratify a tentative agreement.

Roger Morris, the spokesperson-designate for Lively Baseball Makers in an upcoming negotiation with the Professional Baseball Equipment Purchasing Cooperative, is trying to gather as much information as possible about Mike Mantel, spokesperson for the Cooperative. Morris sets up a business lunch with a knowledgeable source at the Baseball Writers' Association. From that source, Morris learns that Mantel has lost the confidence of some of the key team owners for causing too much controversy and being too confrontational. This gives Morris an insight that Mantel is likely to need a quiet and successful negotiation, so Morris decides to stir up things at the table if Mantel pushes too hard or tries to drive too hard a deal. He also knows that Mantel will be under serious pressure to settle. For the price of a lunch, valuable data is obtained.

The more you know about the other side and its negotiators, the more likely you are to get the best possible deal for your side. Keep in mind though that information is subject to change. Be sure to verify again from time to time.

⚡ TIP

Never totally discard the possibility that the information you have obtained has been deliberately provided in order to mislead you into believing that the other side is in a stronger position than the facts warrant (disinformation). If you are considering bluffing, you may want to provide similar disinformation to the other side. Remember, however, that there are ethical limits on materially misleading the other side.

UNDERSTANDING YOUR OWN SIDE'S NEEDS AND AGENDAS

"We have met the enemy and he is us." [Walt Kelly's Pogo Possum] As will be explored in greater depth in Chapter 6, negotiations with your own side to acquire internal information, get your negotiation plan approved, and to avoid waffling by your own side during negotiations, may be far more difficult than negotiating with the other side.

To be successful as a negotiator, you will need to know as much as possible about the factors that drive your own side economically, politics within your organization, and which individuals are concealing what personal agendas. To the extent you misjudge any of these factors, you risk considerably weakening your bargaining power and your chances for personal negotiating success.

Dynamic Power and Light is awakening to changes driven by deregulation in the power generation and distribution industry. Aware that in the future, the company will be unable to simply pass through to customers any increases in its costs, the chief executive officer is seeking to make the company more competitive and efficient. Tanya Tough has been offered employment with Dynamic as its first corporate director of productivity improvement, on terms still being negotiated. Before accepting the position, Tough explores Dynamic's real commitment to improving efficiency. She learns that most of the company's key managers are deeply opposed to large scale changes in the organization and would likely oppose her efforts. She also learns that the chief executive officer would expect her to be successful without causing any controversy and without taking any risks that might upset managers, employees, unions, the government, or consumers. She declines the job because her experience shows that significant productivity improvement requires change, overcoming opposition, and taking risks. Since those conditions are not present, the job formula is a recipe for personal failure. There are too many internal political and personal agendas at work. Not wanting to damage her career, Tough breaks off negotiations and declines the position.

Dwight Eisenhower was selected to command the Allied invasion of Europe during World War II not because of his skills as a field leader (Ike had never been a combat commander), but rather for his skills in coalition management. George Bush's major contribution to the success of the Gulf War was to hold together a coalition and refrain from micro-managing military operations. Similarly, many negotiations will involve you in cross functional or coalition activities. A negotiation may bring into play the interests of production people, maintenance experts, technical and quality controllers, finance representatives, buyers or marketers, the counsel's office, and human resources managers. No real life organization is likely to be free of some overlapping and conflicting agendas between functions. Negotiation planning and administration has much in common with building alliances. In hierarchical organizations such as corporations, only the president or chief executive officer has overall responsibility for the organization's goal as a unitary entity. In unions, different factions have to be made to pull together. Individuals negotiating alone have the advantage of avoiding these problems, although they may have to negotiate with a spouse or other partner about large expenditures. On the other hand, individuals lack the broad-based expertise that comes from having a variety of specialized functionaries.

Charley Brown has been designated as chief spokesperson for a variety of interest groups seeking to get the city council to institute a baseball league for children and to build an appropriate ball field. The group he represents includes people who know real estate, grading and outdoor construction, a PTA, and a sporting goods store. In lobbying the council (a form of negotiating), Brown will have to hold together this rather diverse group and try to get it to apply a coordinated approach and coordinated pressure on the council to get council approval of the baseball field.

⚡ TIP

Conduct surveys of your own side to determine what they wish to be accomplished in negotiations and to identify the major problems to be addressed. When preparing an internal survey be very careful in drafting the questions. How you shape the questions may well determine the answers you receive. Surveys of the "people in the trenches" often provide negotiators will valuable information.

⚡ TRAP

Remember that merely doing a survey raises expectations. The so called "Hawthorne effect," cautions that while surveys generally cause an immediate boost in morale, this boost is temporary and due largely to the fact that people react favorably to any attention. If the survey results are nor shared or are ultimately ignored, morale may well be damaged far more than if no opinion survey was done at all.

RESEARCHING THE PAST HISTORY OF NEGOTIATIONS WITH THE OTHER SIDE

"Those who cannot remember the past are condemned to repeat it." [George Santayana] On the other hand, money managers constantly remind us that "past performance is no guarantee of future results." Although both these lessons are correct, past negotiation history has great value in providing clues to the other side's likely methods and behavior in current negotiations. For that reason, it is important to both keep a record of current negotiations for long term future historical reasons and to consult the prior historical record when planning an upcoming negotiation.

⚡ TRAP

Don't accept the prior pattern of behavior of the other side as a likely barometer of current styles and methods if there have been significant changes in personnel, philosophy, or control of the other party. One of the most significant of changes is when the other side is an organization that has been bought by, or merged into, another organization. Once this happens, prior negotiations will be of little use as a predictor when the new organization has its own differing views and styles which have been imposed over the original organization's culture.

Dilbert Engineering has had three previous agreements with Dogbert Electronic Services to design new products for them. In the previous negotiations, Dilbert Engineering was an "engineering driven company," whose chief executive officer was an engineer and whose primary emphasis was on quality engineering designs. Six months ago, Dilbert Engineering was acquired by Mother Dilbert Associates (MDA). Now, the company is finance driven and is believed to be more concerned with prices than services. This change must be taken into account before negotiations for a renewal of the contract begin. Dogbert Electronic Services may need to stress the financial aspects of its proposals to MDA instead of emphasizing engineering and should expect to encounter more financially based proposals from the other side.

The best source of information on prior negotiations will be the minutes, diaries, and logs kept by your negotiators in prior years. When these are not available, the current negotiators should seek to interview their predecessors. The danger here lies in the fact that with modern career entrepreneurship, people frequently move between companies and may no longer be available, or willing, to discuss their prior negotiation experiences. On rare occasions, someone on the other side in the last negotiation may have joined your organization or someone may have left your side to join the other party. Under these unusual circumstances you, or your counterparts, will have an unusual window of opportunity to know and understand the other side's approach to negotiations.

Three years ago, Jim Burper, a laboratory technician at Big Blue Paint Company, was a union steward for the Pigment and Paint Workers union. Burper was then a member of the union negotiating team that was bargaining with the company. One year ago, Burper accepted a promotion and became Big Blue Paint's laboratory supervisor, a position outside the bargaining unit. The current Big Blue Paint Company negotiation spokesperson approaches Burper about participating on the management negotiating team this year. Burper is successful in his new role as a supervisor and his loyalty to the company is clear to both himself and the company. Accordingly, Burper accepts the offer and this time appears on the management negotiating team. The Pigment and Paint Workers union must now understand that whatever happened internally at the last negotiation will be an open book and that unless they deliberately change their style and methods, management will be privy to their internal operating practices.

☞ TIP

There is nothing unethical about recruiting onto your negotiating team someone who was formerly on the other side but is now a bona fide member of your side, even though that individual may bring considerable knowledge of the other side with them. However, the individual should genuinely have crossed over to your side, not just for purposes of negotiations. It would be unethical to promote a rank and file worker who was on the union team to management and place that individual on your team just as a means of acquiring information.

✍ TRAP

If you place on your team someone who was formerly on the other side but is not a part of your organization and that person retains ties of loyalty to the other side, information may be leaked or your vital negotiation secrets betrayed. Placing someone on your team who was once on the other side, even when ethically legitimate, carries risk. If you are not sure of the individual or if they are torn about their loyalties, do not place them on your team.

When it comes to looking at much older negotiations, consider that their relevance will usually decline as the years go by. Labor contract negotiations are an exception, for there the origins of a provision you may want to modify, even if decades old, may still be relevant. The only historical information that may be available on a twenty year old contract clause may be someone's personal recollection. Under these circumstances, unions often have an edge over employers. Union personnel tend to stay with a company for a long time because seniority is not transferable between companies. Management employees tend to be more entrepreneurial in their careers and to change companies freely, because they, unlike union represented employees, may be able to negotiate for themselves grants of service credit towards vacation and other benefits.

ARE THE NUMBERS ACCURATE AND IS THE DATA GOOD?

"[I]f you put into the machine wrong figures, will the right answers come out?" [Charles Babbage] Bad data is sometimes worse than none at all. The primary consequences of incorrect data fall into two categories: you will make mistakes and your credibility will erode or be destroyed. Without any data, you may be faced with uncertainty, but when you have been given bad data and rely on it, barring fool's luck, your very confidence may lead you into making major negotiation errors. Good data is essential for both internal and external credibility. Bad data fed to your organizational superiors is, when discovered, and in all probability it will be, devastating to obtaining and keeping internal support and respect for your positions, opinions, and advice. Externally, bad data may lead the other side to stop trusting anything you might say. In negotiations, credibility is an essential element for success.

Because the consequences of bad data are as potentially large as they are, it is worth time and attention to all numbers to be sure they are accurate and the data is good. But, how do you do this? As Ronald Reagan said, "trust, but verify." Verify not just external data but also information provided by your own side.

✐ TIP

Try to obtain the same information from two or more different sources, being sure that the parameters used are defined the same way. If the sources give different data, consider that a "red flag," warning you that the data must be re-examined. The differences may be due to slight definitional variances, to rounding error, or to bad assumptions. In any event, be sure you understand why the data differs and which data set is correct.

✐ TIP

Test the data you are given against reality. Don't assume that numbers are good because the source appears to be reputable or simply because the numbers have been prepared on a computer. One of the common mistakes people make when negotiating with numbers is failure to examine the figures to be sure they make sense. The fact that numbers have been supplied by your own side does not mean that you should accept them uncritically. While you will rarely be fed bad data deliberately by your own side, accidents do happen. Cross checking is even more important when the other side has supplied you with numbers.

WHO PREPARED THE DATA?

"Beware of false knowledge; it is more dangerous than ignorance." [George Bernard Shaw] Always ask, "who prepared the data?" Did they have stake in making the numbers come out a particular way? "A statement. . . contrary to [the individual's]. . . interest that a reasonable person in the [individual's] position would not have made. . . unless believing it to be true," [Rule 804, Federal Rules of Evidence] even if hearsay, may be admitted as evidence in court. Why? Given human nature, when people say something in their own interest, the information carries a real risk of being "self serving." When people say some-

111

thing against their own interest, we sit up and take notice. We tend to believe them. Knowing who prepared the information gives a vital clue as to whether or not the results are skewed by self interest.

Always question the source of data. "Facts" submitted by a party in support of its own position are particularly suspect. Data, such as economic data, prepared by "neutral third parties" should also be carefully examined as to the ultimate source.

Omni Foods Corporation is negotiating with Everywhere Food Stores to introduce a new line of food products featuring a new fat substitute invented in its labs. Omni assures Everywhere that the food products are safe and wholesome. The Omni spokesperson introduces a report from the "Independent Consumers Group" which reports no health problems from consumers during preliminary testing. The report contains numerous facts and figures. Everywhere then checks out the "Independent Consumers Group" and finally determines that it is funded one hundred percent by Omni Foods. The resulting report must therefore be approached as a possible self serving document. Faced with this, Omni now puts on the table a study by competitor Standard Foods complaining that its product share may well be eroded by the "safe and healthy" fat substitute made by Omni. This is a far more creditable report.

✒ TIP

When it comes to data, be a cynic. Trust numbers only with care. Test them for yourself. If you are given bad numbers by the other side, make sure that the other side knows you are aware of what was done. Keep in mind that the errors may well have been accidental and not deliberate. If you believe that the other side has supplied you with bad data deliberately one or more times, you must check all of their numbers and question all of their statements in the future.

Once you have good data in hand, you will be ready to move on to costing your own proposals and those anticipated from the other side, as well as to begin your negotiation planning. You are now ready to progress to the next phase of the negotiation process. The next two chapters address those concerns.

CHAPTER 5

COSTING YOUR PLAN
AND THE OTHER SIDE'S
PROPOSALS

"A billion here, a billion there, pretty soon it's real money." [Senator Everett Dirksen] Just how important is cost calculation? You wouldn't buy a product without knowing what you are going to pay or sell one without knowing if the sale is going to result in a profit or a loss. Although this chapter contains some material relating to personal negotiations, it is largely concerned with the cost analyses techniques used in commercial and labor negotiations. If you have ever wondered how the "big guys" handle cost problems or what goes on behind the scenes of large scale negotiations, you may find the material interesting. Many of the techniques may also be adapted and used in some degree for personal negotiations. Feel free to pick and choose what is helpful.

In individual and regular commercial negotiations, the importance of cost estimating varies in proportion to the size and nature of the issues to be bargained. In labor-management negotiations, merger negotiations, and large scale commercial bargaining, cost issues are often critical. Labor, energy, and materials are often the largest expenses in operating a business. With any high volume item, small changes in cost per unit, or per hour, may have significant aggregate results.

Tiny Gadgets produces products that sell at prices ranging from ten to twenty dollars per unit. In a typical year, the company sells ten million units. You are Tiny Gadgets' chief spokesperson, negotiating with Micro-Fabricators, to purchase a key part found in each unit Tiny Gadgets produces. Your two companies have agreed on a five year sole source arrangement and are only a nickel per unit away from a complete settlement. However insignificant that may sound, the impact of giving the seller that nickel per unit for the next five years will be an added two and a half million dollars in costs. Each one cent per unit you save is worth a half million dollars over the five years.

You may be able to negotiate the settlement of an issue in several different ways. When that happens, it will be important for you to know the cost consequences of each possible alternative, so you may pursue your least expensive option. Errors in costing, once embodied in negotiated agreements, may be very difficult to correct. It is impossible to control your outgo without first knowing your current cost levels and being able to predict your future costs with reasonable accuracy.

Costing is a numbers game and for many people numbers cause confusion. In the give and take of economic negotiations, things may become quite blurred. Lewis Carroll, a mathematician and the author of *Alice in Wonderland,* created such a numbers problem:

"They were standing under a tree, each with an arm round the other's neck, and Alice knew which was which in a moment, because one of them had "DUM" embroidered on his collar, and the other "DEE."

"I suppose they've each got 'TWEEDLE' round at the back of the collar," she said to herself.

"Two brothers were left some money, amounting to an exact number of pounds all in coins, to divide between them. DEE undertook the division.

"But your heap is larger than mine!" cried DUM.

"True," said DEE. "Allow me to present you with one-third of my heap."

DUM added it to his heap, and after looking thoughtfully at the now gigantic pyramid, he suddenly exclaimed "I am well off now! Here is half of the heap for you."

"You are generous," said DEE, as he swept up the money. "Two-thirds of this heap is the least I can offer you."

"I will not be outdone in generosity!" cried DUM, hastily handing over three-quarters of his property.

"Prudence is a virtue," remarked DEE. "Content yourself with two-thirds of my present wealth."

"One-third of mine is all I can now afford!" retorted DUM.

"And now, if I give you one pound," remarked DEE, "we shall, I think, be square?"

He was right. How much money was shared between them?"

Whimsy aside, no matter how baffling or complex the problem, one of your most critical functions when you negotiate is to cost your own objectives and plans and determine what the other side's proposals would cost, if agreed to in whole or in part. It is because of the importance of this form of "number juggling" that you, whether an individual bargainer, the spokesperson, or a finance member of a bargaining team, must be totally, and accurately, aware of the costs involved. The more money or economic resources at stake in a negotiation, the more essential it becomes to be completely numerate.

The amount of money at stake in relation to your tolerance for risk is also relevant. If you are the buyer of a new home or a new car, your costs measured in hundreds of dollars, or a few thousand dollars, may be quite significant. In commercial and labor negotiations, costs of this magnitude may be considered mere rounding error and you may be working with amounts rounded to thousands or millions of dollars ($K or $M), with no greater impact in relation to risk. When you purchase a car, an extra thousand dollars out of your own pocket may well be as meaningful as a million dollars is to a corporate giant.

The world of cost analysis has changed over the last several decades. In the past, simplicity in proposals was almost essential when complex negotiations were being conducted under tight time deadlines. You would have lacked the computational power to evaluate elaborate proposals containing many variables, when under time pressure. For that reason, most labor-management negotiations used to be resolved with either a fixed number of cents per hour increase for all or a simple across-the-board percentage raise, with perhaps a few minor variations or exceptions. Computers allow you to construct elaborate patterns of expenditures and to cost them out with a few key strokes. For example, today you may build a wage package featuring a combination of flat and percentage increases, one-time bonuses, and specific exceptions, using a formula in a spread sheet program. If you are the party on the receiving end of such a package without being given the formulas, you may have more difficulty in figuring out what the package is truly worth.

Through its attorneys, Discriminatory Inc., is in settlement negotiations with counsel representing the plaintiffs in a large scale class action lawsuit alleging sex discrimination. Discriminatory, Inc., puts on the table a proposed settlement plan. The plan distributes money differently among the plaintiffs using a formula based on each person's years of service with Discriminatory and skill level. There are also regional variations in the formula to recognize differing costs of living in various areas of the nation. Plaintiffs' attorneys make counter proposals to increase certain elements of the formula. Defendant's attorneys should be able to input the changes into their computer and determine the effect on cost. In some negotiations, the defendant may be willing to share the spreadsheet formula for costing with its negotiating opponents. If they do not, the plaintiffs' attorneys may need to take the time to analyze the formula and to build their own means of cross checking the information supplied by the defendant's attorneys. It may be a trap to simply take the cost information offered by the defendant as accurate.

You are likely to find costing difficult. Some issues are fairly easily quantified because hard data is available. Examples of this include the present cost of shipping per unit or the current premiums on group life insurance. Other issues such as the productivity improvement to be gained by purchasing and installing a vendor's equipment, or streamlining a job transfer system, are necessarily more obscure and may require you to use informed judgment. For these matters, the best possible cost figure may be nothing more than an educated "guesstimate." Even a "guesstimate," as long as it reflects thought and is reasonably conservative, is better than no estimate at all. Constructing a "guesstimate" is not always easy. Data must be acquired and it is sometimes obscure, hard to find, and those who control information may be reluctant to share it with others, whether inside or outside their organization.

✍ TIP

Avoid the appearance of precision in imprecise cases. When you are doing an estimate of something that will cost, for example, about $500,000 plus or minus ten percent, don't report the cost as $498,320, even if that is what your calculator reads after all your assumptions have been made. To do so will mislead those who must work with the figures. At appropriate levels of cost, work with thousands or millions of dollars ($K or $M), and round as necessary.

✍ TIP

When possible, cost the other side's anticipated proposals in advance, but avoid doing so when there are still a large number of open variables that could change before negotiations begin. Quantifying data that is likely to change drastically is wasted effort. Make only "ball park" estimates of these items. For items with fairly tightly defined parameters, cost early. The value to your organization of your own proposals should be determined in similar fashion.

Make sure you understand the basis on which cost figures have been computed. Is the auto dealer comparing its lease with only 10,000 miles included against another dealer's lease with 15,000 miles included, as though they are the same? Does the price of a heavy stone sculpture include shipping? In a sales contract, are your costs being figured for the next three years, using only today's costs, without estimating normal increases? In labor-management negotiations, are you calculating the hourly cost of a benefit per employee based on hours actually worked (productive time), or on the basis of hours paid, which include holidays, vacations, and other forms of pay for time not worked?

NASA lost a Mars probe because one team was working in English measures while another team was using the metric system. It is easy to turn what may have been hailed as a successful negotiation into an abject failure, should it develop that your cost estimates were inaccurate and too low. Instead of profiting on each unit, your organization may then be losing money on each unit it produces. If that happens, you may be paying a visit to an outplacement counselor to seek help in preparing your résumé.

COST SAVINGS AND COST AVOIDANCES

"Save $2,000 when you buy." [newspaper advertisement] Don't try to put your child through college on such "savings." What is the difference between a true cost saving and a cost avoidance? A negotiated cost saving is a reduction in outgo that would inevitably occur if a bargained change is not achieved. A negotiated cost avoidance is the elimination of incremental future costs, but costs which are not currently being actually incurred. Cost savings add to the current bottom line. Cost avoidances prevent future erosion of the bottom line.

Random Supplies has a negotiated agreement with Ordered Services under which Random ships products to Ordered. The present negotiated agreement calls for Random to ship via Confedex and to absorb Confedex's charges within its current contract price. As the current contract is about to expire, Random proposes to maintain its current contract prices but to add on a new shipping surcharge, equal to what it pays Confedex. Ordered accepts the new arrangement. Random will now actually be saving the cost of shipping on Confedex, which would have been inevitable, and out-of-pocket. Present shipping costs are clearly known, so ignoring probable future price increases from Confedex, it should be possible for Random to accurately predict its minimum out-of-pocket savings.

Assume the same facts, but Random is only successful in achieving a clause in the new agreement that provides that any increases in Confedex charges above present levels will be added as a surcharge, with Random continuing to pay current Confedex prices. Under this arrangement, Random has no cost saving over present costs but it will avoid the inevitable price increases in Confedex charges in the future. This is a cost avoidance. The amount of any Confedex fee increase is necessarily speculative, so this cost avoidance may only be estimated.

✐ TIP

Always estimate the value of cost savings and cost avoidances conservatively. The purpose of this is to insure that projected savings turn out to be real and reliable. If you make overly optimistic assumptions and cost savings or cost avoidances come in lower than you projected, you may lose credibility for your cost estimates in planning future negotiations.

VALUE OVER TIME

"Lottery Jackpot Now Ten Million." [Store sign] Would you rather receive ten million dollars today in a single lump sum check or get a million dollars a year for the next ten years? Although spreading out receipt of money may lessen tax consequences, there is a "time value" to money. Generally a given amount of money received today is worth more than an equal amount of money received later. This is because you get to put the money to work immediately at interest, or to seek investment gains, and because inflation is likely to erode the real buying power of money you receive in the future. Finance people refer to the value of an equal amount of money received now in relation to a larger future value as "net present value." This net present value for money received today will be smaller than the total sum offered for some future date.

Negotiators normally prefer to get their side's money "up front." Unions, sellers, authors, and governments, all prefer to get as much of what they are owed as early as possible in the period to be covered by an agreement. When you are figuring out the cost of money and how much may be available to settle a negotiation, the placement of that money during the contract term may well be critical. You may find yourself negotiating extensively over when payments will be made.

In a labor-management negotiation, the employer has placed on the table a wage offer which will increase wages on average by 2.5% over the previous year's wages at the beginning of each year of a three year labor agreement. The union counters with a proposal that the employer give 3.5% at the outset of the first year, 1.5% at the beginning of the second year, and 2.5% at the beginning of the third year. "You offered 7.5% over three years," the union chief spokesperson remarks, "and our counterproposal is also at 7.5% over three years." The fallacy in this is that the employer will have to pay 1% more during the first year and, while the second year percentage has been lowered by an equal amount, the employer will lose the use of 1% of payroll, which may be significant. In addition, the employer may have to pay for overtime and benefits at higher rates over the first year because base wages would go up earlier.

Hal Penman, an author, is negotiating a book contract with Print-All publishers. Print-All offers Penman a contract with royalties of ten percent on the first 10,000 copies and seven percent on copies thereafter. Penman is convinced the new book is another "Gone With the Wind" and demands the royalty schedule be reversed to seven percent on the first 10,000 copies and ten percent on all further copies. The new book sells only 9,500 copies. Penman has overlooked the value of receiving more money early. Of course, in the unlikely event that Penman has truly written the great American novel, his "back loaded" schedule would have yielded him larger royalties.

Costs added in a negotiation are termed "new money." Knowing how to calculate the cost of new money is essential in a negotiation. Just how do you calculate the cost of new money in a contract with payments spread out over time? To keep things manageable, assume that you are entering a three year labor agreement with wage increases of two percent each year on a current base wage rate of $15.00 per hour, for a bargaining unit containing 100 people. The average first year wage increase, at two percent, is thirty cents per hour.

The cost of the first year's wage increase is $0.30 (thirty cents per hour) times 100 (the bargaining unit population) times the number of hours in the year, 2,080 (this is arbitrary, based on a forty hour work week times fifty-two weeks per year and could vary depending on the actual facts), which comes to $62,400 ($62.4K). The employer will pay this cost for the entire three year period of the new agreement, so the cost of the two percent increase in the first year will be $62.4K, which must be multiplied by three to cover the three year duration of the contract. This is known as a "rollup cost," and in this instance the three year "roll up cost" for the first year wage increase is $187.2K.

After the first year increase, the average base wage rate became $15.30 per hour. For the second year, a two percent increase on this new base is $0.31 (thirty-one cents per hour, with rounding to the nearest full cent) times 100, times 2,080, which comes to $64,480 ($64.5K). The employer will pay the cost of the second year increase for the second and third years, so the "rollup cost" of the two percent second year increase will be $64.5K, multiplied by two, which comes to $129K.

After the second year increase, the average base wage rate became $15.61. Repeating the process for the third year's increase, we multiply two percent times $15.61, for an increase of $0.31 (thirty-one cents per hour, with rounding to the nearest full cent), times 100, times 2,080, or $64,480 ($64.5K). The final base wage rate under the agreement reaches $15.92. The employer will pay this cost under the agreement for only one year, so the "roll up cost" of the third year increase is simply $64.5K. The three year "roll up cost" for the entire wage package is the sum of the "roll ups" for each of the yearly wage increases, which comes to $380.7K. If you go through the calculations, you will discover that if the first year increase was raised to three percent, the second year remained at two percent, and the third year dropped to one percent, the three year roll up would change to $443.1K. This demonstrates how changing the distribution by year has a large impact on the cost of the package.

Items that you truly pay only once are rolled up without reference to which year they are to be paid. You do not multiply a true one-time payment by three simply because it is given in the first year of a three year agreement.

Keep in mind that for purposes of the example above, the wage rate increases for each year are "compound," that is they are based on the preceding year's wages. If all the increases were stated on "today's wages," rather than the preceding year's figures, the percentage increases would look higher in the second and third years. This would be a "non-compound" increase.

Although the example given is a labor-management one, exactly the same system may be applied to a commercial or personal negotiation. As with wages, price increases assumed earlier in time cost more than those assumed later. Benefits may be cost estimated in the same way. The example also assumes as a matter of convention that one stops costing a change at the end of the new contract term. The cost may, of course, go on and on indefinitely, but as the contract is likely to be negotiated again at its expiration, there is no certainty beyond that point. Remember that most new money granted is likely to be permanent.

☞ TIP

The concept and process of a "roll up cost," is not inherently difficult in theory, but people often have difficulty applying it. **"Roll up cost" is one of the most significant items in a** negotiation. It is well worth the time and effort to be absolutely sure it is done right.

✒ TIP

Have two or three members of a negotiating team do the roll up cost independently and then compare their numbers. If they don't all produce the same results, go back and determine what caused the differences. Take the time to understand the process.

If you are negotiating for a car, a house, or a mortgage, you should also be very aware that it is the total bottom line cost of the package being considered that is more important than any single individual item. For example, in a lease arrangement for a new car, the overall cost of the lease over its time frame has built-in elements such as the trade-in value of the old vehicle; the "residual value" of the leased car at the time the lease ends; a limit on the number of included miles after which the customer pays cents per mile; deposits; closing fees; depreciation assumptions; and a built-in cost (interest) for the time value of the money that the dealer is supplying until all payments are made. All in all, an auto lease is a very complicated instrument with many variables the sales representative can vary, using a computer to "low ball" you in one area and overcharge you in another, so as to maintain an overall target margin. Leases are an auto sales representative's dream. There is very little chance that you will understand how the money is being moved around. It is a game the customer rarely wins.

Edsel Olds is interested in leasing a car for a three year period for his business. The dealer has quoted Olds a lease price of $229 per month. For personal financial reasons, Olds wants to get as much of his costs into the current year as possible. So, he offers to pay the dealer "up front" the entire cost of the thirty-six month lease. The sales representative takes out a calculator and says that as a special favor to Olds they will accept his check for $8,244 ($229 times thirty-six months), at closing, to cover the entire thirty-six month period. Olds agrees. Olds has been taken to the cleaners. Built into the $229 per month quoted Olds is a considerable finance charge. The dealer now has that interest presently in hand, not spread out over thirty-six months, thereby reaping both the interest on money Olds has never borrowed and having the *opportunity to loan that money again to another customer for yet another round of interest. Any "single payment lease" should carry a reduction in price because the dealer is getting all the money up front and is not advancing credit. The "cost of money" is a considerable factor in the lease price of an automobile and is increasingly significant when interest rates are climbing.*

OPPORTUNITY, TRAVEL, AND OTHER COSTS AND SAVINGS

"Time is money." [Benjamin Franklin] Proposals submitted in negotiations, whether economic or non-economic in nature, often have an impact on the use of time, and paid time is worth money. Time used for one purpose is diverted from some other alternative purpose where the time might have been used more effectively. When negotiating, untrained people often fail to factor in costs related to the use of time and resources, such as travel. The value of time may be measured as the price (the wage and benefit cost) of time spent on an activity.

Armando Gonzales is one of twenty employees working as first line supervisors at the Pan American Ship Building Company in Shower, Maine. Production and maintenance employees at Shower are represented by the Sea Support Union. Times are good and the company is operating at peak production. Qualified employees are difficult to recruit. Rather than increasing staffing, the company is scheduling a lot of overtime. One of Gonzales' responsibilities is to canvass the work force to find employees who are qualified and willing to work voluntary overtime and, when there are none, as frequently occurs, to draft employees for mandatory overtime. The labor contract contains an antiquated and complex selection method requiring Gonzales to canvass the employees both in and out of the plant twice for voluntary overtime before drafting workers. Gonzales spends an average of forty-five minutes per day on simply securing people to work needed overtime. When the need for overtime first becomes known late in the day, Gonzales has to drop whatever else he is doing or the shift will end without anyone to cover the overtime work. The other nineteen first line supervisors each put in about an equal amount of time each day on the overtime selection problem.

123

*During contract negotiations, Pan American Ship Building propos-
es a change in the labor agreement to simplify overtime selection
by using a single canvass for voluntary overtime among qualified
employees actually on site, estimating that it will cut in half the
time spent organizing overtime. What is the value to the company of obtaining the necessary concession from the Sea Support
Union? The current cost of forty-five minutes per day for each of
twenty supervisor's time spent on overtime canvassing is currently estimated at $104,000 per year (salary including benefits), or
$520,000 over a five year contract period. The proposed simpli-
fied system of overtime canvassing will free up half the time currently spent by these supervisors on this problem to do other more
productive things, to the extent of $52,000 per year, or $260,000
over the five years.*

✒ TIP

Consider what will happen with recovered opportunity time.
Will the time, in fact, be used more productively?
Circumstances permitting, an alternative to filling newly available opportunity time with other productive work may be to
reduce head count in the group in proportion to the recovered
time. Staff reduction is usually feasible only in cases in which
the time saving achieved, spread out over the entire group
impacted, amounts to at least one full time position.

What about travel costs? Proposals from the other side that require
new, or increased, travel should be considered in light of the impact
they may have on travel budgets. Today, travel is often expensive.
When a proposal is unclear about who pays for travel, try to clarify that
it is the other side which will bear the travel costs.

When negotiating any agreement, whether commercial, labor, or
personal, there will likely be some aspects of a negotiation that are not
directly economic. These items may still be important.

*Gore City and Bush County are negotiating to establish certain
shared administrative services such as purchasing, legal, and
snow removal. Gore City voters invariably vote for Democrats,
while voters in the rest of Bush county invariably vote Republican.
The Gore City Council has five members, all Democrats. The Bush*

County Legislature has fifteen members, elected in districts, six Democrats, all from Gore City, and nine Republicans, all from Bush County districts entirely outside Gore City. Gore City has 50,000 residents. Bush County taken as a whole, has 120,000 people, including the 50,000 people who live in Gore City and another 70,000 who live in the rest of the county. Gore City's negotiator proposes to have all questions concerning shared services be determined by the City and County legislatures sitting jointly and voting together, with one vote per representative. Under this proposal, a majority, eleven of the twenty votes, would be cast by Democrats, five from the City Council and six from the County Legislature who represent Gore City districts. The Bush County Legislature (by a nine to six party line vote) counter-proposes that on shared service questions, the two legislative bodies vote separately, with the Gore City Council to cast five votes and the Bush County Legislature to cast seven votes, to proportionately reflect the county's population living inside and outside Gore City. They argue that their proposal is more in line with the Supreme Court's "one person, one vote" principle. Under this proposal, Republicans, all from outside Gore City, could expect to have a seven to five majority on votes concerning shared service matters. Resolution of this issue has no immediate economic value, but goes to the heart of who will control any shared service arrangements. It will be a hard fought negotiation issue and sufficiently critical that it may cause the shared services idea to fail entirely.

"Non-economic" items also need to be considered from a cost basis. While the current costs may be small, thought should be given to possible future problems, particularly the placement of any limits on your side's flexibility or freedom of action.

Garfield & Catburt, a dog biscuit marketer, is in negotiations with the Pet Supplies Distribution Workers Union. The union proposes a joint safety committee which is to have the final word on all safety issues. Management accepts the proposal which also provides for equal voting representation from each side. Because neither side has the votes to force the committee to act, the union perceives it has an effective veto over management's right to act. When management later wants to institute some work flow changes, the union sees safety implications, and the vote to declare the changes safe fails in the joint safety committee. A vote

125

> to declare them unsafe also fails to gain a majority. When management goes ahead with the changes on the grounds that the committee has not voted them to be unsafe, a grievance ensues, and ends in binding arbitration.

Remember that the other side will rarely propose items that are frivolous to them. If they have some value to the other side, consider what value the other side places on the proposed items. To do this, you will need to imagine yourself in their position and consider how their proposal furthers their needs and their interests. You should use their frame of reference and not your own. It is not always easy to place a dollar value on proposals. Some proposals will be placed on the table more to satisfy the other side's psychological needs than out of economic necessity. Other proposals may have no immediate economic consequences but may carry the potential for significant future costs. When you look at the other side's proposals, consider not only their impact on your present situation, but whether their proposals would impact your future freedom of action.

COST OF RESPONDING TO THE OTHER SIDE'S NEEDS

"One man's meat is another man's poison." [Proverb] The other side in any negotiation may desperately need or want something that costs you little. That is why you should do a cost-value analysis from the other side's perspective as well as your own.

✎ TIP

Consider that a proposal that carries little cost for you may be of incredible value to the other side. This makes the item an excellent vehicle for you to use to gain significant concessions from them. The single greatest mistake inexperienced negotiators are prone to make is to give away these "cheap to us" but "extremely valuable to you" items, without exacting in return something their side needs and which is extremely valuable if achieved. In a given negotiation, each side is likely to have one or more such items. Deliberately withhold granting the other side these items until one or more of your own similarly valued items is achieved, or offer them in a linked trade, similar to swapping queens in chess.

While in commercial and individual negotiations, items that are extremely valuable to one side and a matter of indifference to the other will vary considerable from negotiation to negotiation, in labor-management negotiations for a first contract (and sometimes in later negotiations) there is almost always a pair of such items on each side.

The Musical Instrument Workers Union (MIWU) is in a first contract negotiation with Magnificent Marimbas. Two proposals the MIWU makes are vital for union security. The first proposal would impose a "union shop" (union security) clause, which would require bargaining unit employees to become union members (at least to the extent of paying the union's uniformly required dues). The second proposal is that Magnificent Marimbas agree to a "checkoff" clause, under which the company would accept signed authorization cards from employees, authorizing the company to automatically deduct union dues from wages. The union argues that, for the employer, the sole cost of these clauses is the minor administrative one of adding a payroll deduction segment to a payroll system already run on a computer.

Magnificent Marimbas also has two key proposals, vital for management security. The first is the inclusion in the new contract of a strong "management's rights" clause, which makes explicit a number of things which management may do with minimal interference from the union, notwithstanding that the law is gray on this subject. The second management proposal is for a strong "no strike pledge," which would protect the company from wildcat strikes and most forms of labor based interruptions to work during the contract term. The company argues that these proposals will not be costly to the union, that many management rights are at least arguably protected by law, and that the grievance arbitration process replaces the need to strike while a contract is in force.

In the above example, if the management negotiators are inexperienced, they may yield the union shop and checkoff clauses before gaining union acceptance of the management's rights and the no strike proposals. If the union negotiators are new to the process, they may yield the management's rights and the no strike proposals before achieving the union shop and checkoff clauses. Professional negotiators will probably eventually set up a linked trade on these proposals, each of which is valuable to the side making the proposal and virtually without cost to the side granting it.

Never forget the value of a concession you make is not only what it costs you, but rather what the concession is worth to the other side, within its frame of reference. Always consider the other side's proposals in this light.

PAY FOR TIME NOT WORKED

"If all the year were playing holidays, to sport would be as tedious as to work." [William Shakespeare] Time on the job may be divided into two categories, time actually spent doing productive work and time that is compensated, but with no work required. The former includes time spent, for example, stamping out parts or drafting a report. The latter includes such benefits as vacations, holidays, paid leaves (funeral, personal, medical, military, jury, and union), release time for education, break time, wash up time, report in pay, and call in pay.

How do you cost the price of labor? The cost per hour may be viewed in relation to all hours paid, whether or not actually used for productive work, or be calculated only in relation to hours actually worked. Pay for time not worked is extensive in the United States. Out of a nominal 2,080 hour working year (forty hours per week times fifty-two weeks per year), many employees actually do about 1,700 hours of actual productive work. There is nothing wrong with using either costing method. What is important is that calculations are consistently done on the same clearly established basis.

The Shoe Workers Association is negotiating a labor agreement with Blister & Corn Shoe Company. The union has requested an improvement in health care benefits. The company determines that the cost of the benefit improvement will be $208 per employee, per year. As wage rates at the company are stated in hourly terms, the company's negotiator needs to determine what the cost of the benefit improvement is in cents per hour, per employee. Dividing by 2,080 (forty hours per week times fifty-two weeks per year), which arbitrarily represents time paid, yields a figure of ten cents per hour, per employee. Dividing by 1,700 (hours actually worked each year after deducting holidays, vacations, and other forms of time not worked), yields a figure of twelve point two cents per hour, per employee. The latter figure is a more accurate *reflection of the increased cost to the employer for hours its employees actually work, but the former figure is the measure more widely used.*

VARIABLE AND FIXED COSTS

"The real price of everything, what everything really costs to the man who wants to acquire it, is the toil and trouble of acquiring it." [Adam Smith] When the time comes, and it will inevitably come, for you as a negotiator to figure out what things really cost, you should be aware that costs come in two forms. Some costs are fixed (not subject to change with variations in production or labor) and other costs are variable (they rise or fall in relation to the ups and downs of production or work).

Williams Widgets operates a manufacturing plant at Fenway, Massachusetts. Real property taxes on the facility are ten million dollars per year. The plant has been running only a single shift. A dramatic increase in the demand for widgets results in the company adding a second and third shift for around-the-clock operations. The real estate taxes remain the same. They are a fixed cost. If the plant's throughput was formerly ten million widgets, one dollar of each widget unit's sale price was consumed by real estate taxes. If production now increases to twenty-five million widgets, the same fixed real estate taxes now consume only forty cents of the unit sale price of each widget. This may impact the price per widget the company is able to offer a buyer, although it does not impact the company's fixed real property tax cost.

Questions of fixed or variable cost may drive your decision as to which alternatives are acceptable in a negotiation. Variable costs are generally more acceptable than fixed costs.

Maris Manufacturing needs to increase its output and projects its employees will increase their average work week from forty-two hours per week to forty-six hours per week. In labor negotiations, the union has proposed that the company fill its need to cover the extra work by additional hiring, pointing out that if the company uses more overtime to cover the new work, it will have to pay the variable expense of time and one half for the overtime hours worked. The company rejects the proposal because each new hire requires the company to take on the fixed costs of health insurance premiums and other expensive fringe benefits for the new workers, which is calculated to be more costly than the variable overtime premium. The company agrees that when employees reach a level of overtime such that they will receive double time under the labor agreement (in this case, for actually working more than forty-eight hours in a week), then the fixed expense for employee benefits for new hires will be less than the double time overtime premium, and it will begin hiring.

If you are negotiating about the hours of operation of a business, fixed and variable cost analysis is often a factor. These questions may arise when a mall insists stores stay open during certain periods or when franchisers want to introduce new programs.

Tough Burgers, a nationwide corporation which franchises local outlets, is negotiating with an association of its retail store owners concerning adding a new breakfast line. One of the local owners complains that this will require being open for more hours, increasing payroll outgo. She complains that it is costing her a certain number of dollars now for every hour she is open. Tough Burgers points out that all of the business' fixed expenses will remain the same and that opening for breakfast will provide more hours of business to recoup those costs. "Our figures show," the Tough Burger spokesperson says, "that you will need only a small number of customers per hour for breakfast to cover your variable costs and come out ahead. Any hour you are open when you make more than your variable costs is worth doing."

Organizations do not always find ways to efficiently recoup their fixed costs. A classic example of using fixed assets at less than an optimum level may be found in school buildings. When school districts attempt to negotiate changes in the use of school facilities, politics and non-economic factors often defeat these efforts, leaving physical resources idle for a large portion of each day and year.

One of the three neighborhood elementary schools being operated by the Thatcher School District is in need of large scale maintenance to comply with safety codes. Making the necessary repairs would take two years, during which the school would be closed, and the cost is expected to be several million dollars. Each of the three schools is being utilized at slightly over two-thirds capacity. The Board of Education is considering creative alternatives to the repair bill, including reducing the number of schools to two and selling off the excess property for revenue, staggered semester full year operation, or a staggered school day schedule (to allow the two existing schools to accommodate more students). The Board is now "negotiating" these alternatives with parents and taxpayers. However, social factors such as the desire for neighborhood schools and the public's attachment to conventional school scheduling, probably doom any such "public negotiation" to failure. The school physical plants will continue to be operated inefficiently, while the taxpayers will be called on to either do major maintenance or build an additional physical plant. Economic logic is irrelevant.

🔏 TIP

When production warrants, adding a new shift to a facility greatly increases the utility of the capital invested in the facility. In capital intensive businesses, negotiating uses for buildings or equipment in off hours may have very high returns. Whenever possible, negotiate for increased use of existing facilities rather than the construction of new ones (unless a new facility's efficiency factors outweigh its costs).

WHEN YOU CANCEL CREDITS, YOU INCUR COSTS

"Nothing seems expensive on credit." [Czech Proverb] Suppose you have a credit balance in your account with the telephone company, a balance that you could demand as a check if you wanted the money immediately. The next month, your bill is paid by canceling part of your credit. Just because part of your credit is being cancelled does not mean your telephone service was free for that month.

Wormwood Forest Products has just acquired Termite Logging. In preparation for negotiations with the Wormwood & Termite Workers Association, you ask the benefits department of Termite Logging to provide the cost of the pension plan for Termite's union represented employees. The benefits department sends you a memo which says that the pension plan carries "no cost." That seems illogical. When you question the benefits director as to how this is possible, he answers, "Oh, we have a credit balance. We overpaid in past years. Now we are just canceling part of the credit each year. So, you see, it costs us nothing."

The idea that canceling a credit is cost free is akin to your having $100 in a savings account, against which the bank automatically deducts ten dollars a year for handling such a small account. Each year, some of your money is gone. In ten year's time, you will be left with *nothing*.

⚡ TIP

Anything which diminishes your assets is a cost, whether or not an out-of-pocket expense is required. Always check to see whether a proposal will raid your wallet in this indirect fashion. Keep track of all deposits others hold and be wary of authorizing automatic deductions.

WHEN TO ASSIGN COST ON CONTINGENT EVENTS

"For all sad words of tongue or pen, the saddest are these: 'It might have been!'" [John Greenleaf Whittier] How do you estimate, and account for, the cost of contingent events that might, or might not, come to pass? It is not unusual for a negotiator to be faced with a proposal that does not come into effect unless certain contingent events occur. For example, in a commercial negotiation, a proposal may specify that if the supplier ceases producing a specified product before a certain date, it will pay the customer cash penalties as liquidated damages. The supplier may have no current intention of leaving the business, but economic conditions may change. In labor-management negotiations, severance pay provisions are a contingent liability. If the employer does not close the facility, it pays no severance and incurs no real liability. But, if the employer does close, perhaps unexpectedly, the liability may be very expensive. How these contingent costs are handled is a matter of policy and preference.

Ticoa, a metals production company, is in labor contract negotia- tion with the Allied Titanium Workers union for its largest facility at Metalsville, West Carolina. The current labor agreement con- tains no severance pay clause. The contract covers 750 employ- ees. The Allied Titanium Workers union proposes a severance plan which would award one week (forty hours) of pay for each year of seniority (or part thereof), for each employee. The average employee has twelve years of seniority. The current straight time hourly pay rate, exclusive of all premiums and differentials, at Metalsville, is $21 per hour. As Ticoa's negotiating committee spokesperson, you calculate that if the severance pay clause was granted and the plant was to be closed, at current wage rates, Ticoa would incur a severance pay liability of $7,600,000. Under Ticoa policy, contingent liabilities must be "booked" in the year in which they are incurred. You respond to the union with the posi- tion that, "Severance is something we can discuss, but under- stand that the cost of your proposal is $7,600,000, if we closed tomorrow. If we were to grant any part of your severance propos- al, we would have to take that money from something such as wages or pension increases." The union objects, saying, "We don't understand. If you don't close, severance costs you nothing, so why should we pay for it out of our wage and benefit increas- es?" You counter this with the statement, "We don't plan to close, but we can't predict the future. You never know. We can't take on a liability such as you propose without paying for it. Let me explain. Suppose your bank said to you that to keep your mort- gage you had to agree to pay triple your current payments if cer- tain things, although unlikely, happened? Wouldn't you have to consider what that could do to your finances? Would you want that possibility hanging over your head?"

Notwithstanding the above example, many organizations do take on these contingent liabilities, casually dismissing them as unlikely, until the day comes when they materialize and someone asks, "How did we get into this mess? Why did we agree to this? Didn't anyone realize the cost?"

✐ TIP

Always calculate the cost of proposals that carry contingent liabilities. Whether to accept these liabilities will be a question of bargaining power and internal policy. The cost of the liability should be weighed against the probability of the occurrence of the triggering events. A professional negotiator will make sure that the organization understands all the implications of accepting the risk and is knowingly taking on potential liability.

ONE TIME PAYMENTS VERSUS ONGOING PAYMENTS

"God does not pay weekly, but He pays at the end." [Dutch Proverb] The way in which you pay an obligation is frequently negotiable and makes a difference in your costs. A "one-time payment" means literally that, a payment which, as negotiated, is to be made on only one date, without repetition. An athlete's signing bonus is an example of a one-time payment. Recurring payments are those that are made for every hour worked, every unit shipped, or in each month over a period of time, as with a home mortgage. What are the cost implications of making a one-time payment as opposed to building increased payments into a recurring system?

A disadvantage of a one-time payment is that when you make such a payment, you lose the use of your money for investment or interest bearing purposes by paying it out early. The time value of money has been discussed in a prior section of this chapter. If the one-time payment is "back end loaded" (comes at the end of the negotiated agreement), this factor does not apply. An advantage of the one-time payment system is that any surcharges, fees, premiums, differentials, or benefits, based on normal rates, do not apply to the amount in the one-time payment. The one-time payment is kept out of permanent recurring costs.

Employees at Fagin Pocket Pickers receive vacation pay for the hours permitted them at their "regular straight time hourly rates of pay on the day the vacation period begins, not including any premiums or differentials." Oliver Twist earns fourteen dollars per hour and, because he works on the second shift, receives an additional premium of fifty cents per hour. Two months ago, Fagin completed a negotiation with the Miscreant Service Workers. The *employees were awarded a one-time bonus. For Twist the bonus amounted to $2,184, which was stated to be the equivalent of a thirty-five cents per hour wage increase over the three year term of the contract. However, when Twist goes on vacation, his vacation pay will be based on fourteen dollars per hour, not fourteen dollars and thirty-five cents per hour. The shift differential will also be ignored in calculating Twist's vacation pay. Many of Twist's other benefits will be impacted in a similar way.*

Why then would Twist and his co-workers be likely to favor the one-time bonus over a wage increase? A check for $2,184 in a lump sum (before taxes) may be more psychologically and economically satisfying than a fourteen dollar a week wage increase before taxes ($0.35 per hour times 40 hours). Also, if Twist leaves the company within the three year contract period, he will be better off having received all of the value of the increase up front. One-time payments are far less attractive to labor organizations because they fail to build up a permanently higher wage base.

One-time payments have become popular with labor relations management because they hold down costs keyed to the wage structure. They are also useful when an employer's wage scale is much higher than its industry average and time is needed for the other employers to reach wage parity. Remember that many costs such as holiday and vacation pay are calculated from wages. The usefulness of one-time payments is more limited in commercial and individual negotiations where the costs of paying in advance and the risks of non-performance are greater.

COST OF LIVING PLANS AND INDEX CLAUSES

"In spite of the cost of living, it's still popular." [Kathleen Norris] You have probably heard of cost of living adjustments being negotiated into various agreements. These arrangements are sometimes called "escalator clauses." There are analogs in which other indices are used to adjust negotiated financial arrangements. If you are a home buyer, you may be offered an adjustable rate mortgage which will slide up or down on the basis of some published index, such as the prime rate. Since the adjustments in individual contracts with these provisions take place based on future events that cannot be predicted with certainty, it is difficult to estimate the eventual price of a cost of living arrangement, or other indexed item.

Why do negotiators use cost of living and other index clauses? In short term agreements, economic and other conditions are generally either known or quite predictable. However, as the time horizon for a proposed agreement lengthens beyond three years, it becomes increasingly difficult to commit to locking in your prices, wages, or rates. An index system is a way to protect both sides' vital interests over a long term, while maintaining the general intent of a level that was originally negotiated.

Cayuga Airlines is a major trunk carrier, operating thousands of flights a day. The airline's requirements for jet aviation fuel are substantial. Cayuga is negotiating a sole source supply contract with Mobexxen, under which Mobexxen will supply all of Cayuga's jet aviation fuel needs for the next five years. Because of the volatility of the petroleum market, each of the parties is deeply concerned about how to price the fuel Cayuga will purchase. If a fixed price is used, one side may be benefited and the other hurt, but it is impossible to know in advance which side will gain. That would require knowing the price per barrel of raw crude oil several years in the future. This means a fixed price arrangement over the contract term is too risky for either side. The parties agree to set a price based on today's jet aviation fuel cost levels to be fixed for two years, and thereafter to adjust that price on the fifteenth of each month, using a formula based on a well known published index reporting the average price of a barrel of oil on the first of each month. This protects each side against wide swings in market price.

In the late 1970s, the United States was undergoing an economic phenomenon known as "stagflation," a condition which combined economic stagnation with double digit inflation rates. In 1981, while stagflation was still present, a large chemical manufacturer operating a works on the Gulf Coast negotiated a three year labor agreement with a union representing certain chemical workers. At that time, the area pattern wage settlements were averaging about ten percent per year. The 1981 negotiations were resolved without a labor dispute and with the company obtaining some truly significant productivity improvements in a three year contract. Accordingly, the wage settlement was a fixed one at thirteen per cent in the first year, ten percent in the second year, and an additional ten percent in the third year. What the parties did not anticipate was that in the next few years econom-

ic conditions would change radically for the better. By the third year of the agreement, wages had moderated everywhere and many companies, including the one discussed here, had frozen wages or had cancelled large increases that had been previously planned. Because a labor agreement is a contractual commitment, the company, which had granted the large fixed contractual increases, found itself saddled with unavoidable costs that were no longer relevant to current labor market conditions.

✍ TIP

Use caution in selecting indices and constructing formulas. The conventional consumer price index (CPI) is actually a series of different indices for different groups of people and is available using several different base periods. The "market baskets" used to calculate these indices are for typical consumers in specified categories and may not be appropriate for indexing a commercial or labor contract. The formulas for using an index to partially or completely cancel out inflation are also quite complex. The possibility of expensive mistakes means that expert advice should always be sought.

✍ TRICK

Consider proposing a hybrid fixed and indexed price when negotiating long term agreements. Short term agreements, or agreements covering the highly predictable near term portion of a long term contract, are good candidates for fixed prices or wages. In longer term agreements, consider negotiating terms that adjust the fixed terms up or down only in the later years of the agreement, depending on the movement of a chosen index.

✍ TRICK

If an index adjustment is being used for the later years of a proposal to control costs, consider adopting a fixed level for those years, using an adjustment factor which becomes effective only if there is a wide swing, up or down, from stability. Under this system of "economic protection," both parties receive the general benefits of a predictable fixed cost negotiated price, but both are protected against catastrophic swings up or down from historical norms. Once the parties have this form of protection, much longer term agreements become feasible. Keep in mind though that your side will probably not want a long term agreement if it would lock in a number of other unfavorable conditions.

⚡ TRAP

Be aware that if you negotiate for variables controlled by published indices, the indices may be discontinued during the life of your agreement. Published financial indices are also subject to change. For example, the companies in the Dow Jones stock index are changed from time to time. If you are considering using an index, or accepting an indexed proposal, you should obtain competent professional help. There simply isn't room in a general evaluation of negotiation techniques to explain all the ins and outs of using indices, but do understand that **mistakes made in negotiating index based adjustments may turn out to be very significant and *very* costly.**

PENSION PLANS

"You always say 'I'll quit when I start to slide,' and then one morning you wake up and realize you've done slid." [Sugar Ray Robinson] Retirement issues (pension plans and retiree health insurance) are a routine part of both many labor-management and business acquisition negotiations. Determining the cost of pension plans, designing plans, and writing plans, are extremely complex tasks. Private sector pension plans are governed by the federal Employee Retirement Income Security Act (ERISA). Normally, pension issues should be left to very experienced human resources managers, in-house counsel, and outside pension experts. However, many organizations negotiate pension plans and their negotiators must know enough to analyze costs and be able to present and explain pension plans to the union and employees, if on the management side, or to evaluate pension offers, if on the union side. Many of these concerns also apply to organizations negotiating in a commercial context with pension plan administrators and consultants, regarding the pensions of employees who are not union represented or who may be acquired in a merger. Organizations in an acquisition or merger process will need to negotiate whether or not to assume the pension plans of the other employer, and under what conditions. This book offers only a superficial look at pensions. Be sure to consult competent experts before trying to negotiate these items.

There are basically two types of pension plans you may encounter in negotiations. The first variety is known as "defined benefit" plans and the second is termed "defined contribution" plans. In a defined benefit plan, the employer guarantees the participant a benefit of a fixed amount, as specified by the plan, and usually determined by a formula. The employer is required by ERISA to fund the plan, over time, to a level sufficient to provide the guaranteed benefit. In a defined contribution plan, the employer agrees to pay a fixed amount or percentage of contribution, but what the participant receives at retirement is not guaranteed and varies based on investment experience. Defined benefit plans are more highly regulated and far more complex to fund and administer than defined contribution plans. Consequently, they are less common today than in the past. An employer may also operate a "thrift savings plan," often called a 401(k) plan. While these plans are subject to ERISA and are often used by their participants for additional retirement savings, they are not true pension plans.

✦ TIP

When negotiating increases in a defined benefit plan, distinguish between proposals that provide pension increases for past service and those that make the increases applicable to future service only. Granting increases for past service means funding for back years of service and is vastly more expensive than providing increases that operate only in the future.

Another basic variation is between the typical single employer pension plan and the more unusual multi-employer pension plan. Multi-employer plans are usually jointly administered by a union and a number of companies, with management and labor each appointing an equal number of members to each plan's board of directors. Multi-employer pension plans present very complex issues and should never be negotiated by anyone other than a professional with expert knowledge, or without the help of a specialist attorney or consultant.

✦ TRAP

When negotiating for an employer, whether in labor negotiations or merger and acquisition talks, never sign a multi-

employer pension plan agreement without counsel on all the legal and financial ramifications. Resist signing any agreement which gives the plan trustees a "blank check" to set the rates in the future and to bind you to pay them. Don't be fooled by the "joint" nature of the program. In practical terms, such "jointly administered plans" are, in practice, usually controlled by the union. You may also find it difficult to get financial information about a jointly administered plan. The negotiating local union will not have the data and the plan fiduciaries will have no direct relationship with the negotiating employer. Should you eventually wish to withdraw from a multi-employer plan, you may be liable for your pro-rata share of any vested unfunded liabilities of the plan. This may be extremely costly and, if unanticipated, a shock to your organization's financial controllers. Further, unions tend to very strongly oppose such withdrawals.

Pensions are likely to be a major issue for any group of employees or for an employer which has an older work force. Younger work forces are generally more interested in wages than pensions. However, employers should not let a pension plan, particularly a defined benefit one, lag too far behind their industry. To do so will mean high "catch up" costs at a later date.

𝆺 TRAP

Unless you are a professional negotiator with developed expertise in ERISA and how pension plans are designed, administered, and funded, do not attempt to negotiate about pensions. Get professional advice and guidance. Make sure that your experts examine all the documents supplied by the other side for legal compliance and for cost implications. In some cases, you may wish to take your pension advisors to the table with you, or to have them immediately available in a caucus or back room.

HEALTH INSURANCE PLANS

"After you're older, two things are possibly more important than any others: health and money." [Helen Gurley Brown] Health insurance is something which is frequently negotiated, whether in a labor-management negotiation, or between an employer and a health care provider, or between health care providers themselves. The assumption of health care obligations should also be carefully considered in merger and acquisition negotiations. As is the case with pension plans, costing, negotiating, understanding, and administering health insurance programs is also a very complex task. Health and welfare plans are legally regulated by the federal Employee Retirement Income Security Act (ERISA). This summary will barely scratch the surface of the issues related to negotiating health care plans.

There are a wide variety of health insurance plans in use today. Traditional "fee for service" plans leave patients with complete freedom of choice in selecting their doctors and place most medical decisions in the hands of their physicians. These plans are usually the most expensive to fund and are increasingly being replaced by "managed care" programs. Managed care systems, including health maintenance organizations, preferred provider organizations, and point of service plans, while offering health care marked by reduced patient choice and greater organizational and carrier control over what is "medically necessary," often have the virtue of lower costs. Whatever system is used, the adoption of, and changes in, health care programs will entail issues that are frequently negotiated, are a major cost for employers, and constitute a major benefit for employees and unions.

Health care plans may take the form of true "at risk" insurance, under which an insurance carrier bears the risk of loss; pure self insurance with self administration; an ASO (administrative services only) approach, under which the employer pays all costs out-of-pocket (self insurance), plus an administrative processing fee to a carrier for handling claims processing; or, be under a multi-employer plan (generally jointly administered by union and management trustees).

✍ TIP

Employers may wish to seek a negotiated clause reserving the right to unilaterally change health care carriers, without negotiating this change with the union. The rationale for such a clause is that the employer is left free to shop for the most economical deal in order to minimize the amount of money spent on administration, as opposed to health care benefits. Union negotiators will, at a minimum, wish to secure a specification that a change of carrier will result in no decrease in any benefit.

Employers try to reduce their costs in health care by assigning employees a share of current costs, assessing employees a share of future premium increases, increasing deductibles and co-pays, or raising the out-of-pocket limit (after which the plan pays a hundred percent of costs). Naturally, employees and unions resist such changes and these issues may become serious impediments to reaching negotiated agreements.

✒ TRICK

Paradoxically, it is sometimes possible to reduce an employer's costs for health care coverage, while according employees what may be presented as a new benefit. For example, an employer might offer to pay the full cost of a second surgical opinion (while moving to requiring one), on the grounds that it will help the patient avoid unnecessary surgery. Such a program also has the effect of saving the employer money when some surgeries are avoided.

✒ TRAP

Without an extensive background in the design and administration of health care benefits, do not attempt to cost or negotiate these programs without professional assistance. The costs of an error in a health care plan may be very significant. Recovery from these errors is also extremely difficult as health care program recipients are likely to be very emotional about any negative changes in their benefits.

FLAT AMOUNT VERSUS PERCENTAGE CHANGE

"The worst form of inequality is to try to make unequal things equal." [Aristotle] Sometimes things which are superficially equal are, in fact, unequal. Method matters. For example, in recurring negotiations, there is a difference in value between an increase in a benefit offered via a flat amount and a proposal offering the same current benefit outcome by using a percentage formula. A percentage formula will yield automatic future increases and avoid the need to bargain over and over again for advantage on the same item. Even if the flat amount and the percentage have the same current value, the percentage will be more valuable to the party obtaining it.

Those employees of Marsupial Airlines who are represented by the Koala Association of Machinists (KAM) have average yearly base earnings, before overtime, of $40,000. Under the current agreement between Marsupial and the KAM, employees receive forty thousand dollars of fully company paid group term life insurance. Marsupial and the KAM are negotiating a successor labor agreement. Marsupial has offered a five percent increase to wages in each year of a proposed three year agreement. This would raise average base earnings to $42,000 in the first year, $44,100 in the second year, and $46,305 in the third year. They have also offered to increase group life insurance from the current level of $40,000, to $42,000 in the first year, $44,100 in the second year, and $46,305 in the third year. KAM accepts the wage offer, but counters with a proposal that reads, "the amount of group term life insurance provided each employee under this agreement shall be set at 100% of the average yearly base earnings of the employees in the bargaining unit, adjusted each time employees receive a general wage increase, to be paid for entirely by the company." Marsupial's chief spokesperson refuses this proposal, although the union's proposal and management's proposal both have precisely the same effect on the group term life insurance level during the term of the new agreement.

An employer who agrees to a percentage formula is locked into automatic increases in the future. The burden then shifts to the employer to affirmatively modify or negotiate the provision out of the labor agreement in the next round of bargaining. If it fails to do so, its costs for group term life insurance will automatically escalate with each general wage increase. Further, in future negotiations, automatic upward moves in group life insurance would deprive the company of the chance to take credit for conceding increases in life insurance. So, equal results does not mean that proposals are equal.

🖋 TIP

If you are a party to a long term or recurring agreement under which you regularly seek to gain on a particular issue, you will be better off obtaining that gain through a percentage or other formula than a fixed amount. The party which is giving ground will usually be better off insisting on yielding a flat dollar amount. Of course, this does not apply to transactions which are strictly single occasion negotiations with no prospect of needing a subsequent agreement. When formulating your proposals or reactions to proposals, consider the form in which your proposals are presented and not just the results to be immediately obtained.

SURVEYS AND CHARTS

"There are two kinds of statistics, the kind you look up and the kind you make up." [Rex Stout] However you obtain statistics and data, they have to be presented in some readable form and, human nature being what it is, you will want to present the information in the way which is most favorable to your position. This will lead most negotiators to display information using selected surveys or charts in both internal and external bargaining. For example, any survey you are likely to introduce in support of your proposed price point on an item you are trying to sell will show your price as comparatively quite low, or you will discard that survey. The desired result may be achieved by only including on your survey of "selected representative companies," those competing companies that charge about the same or a higher price than you demand. Sometimes survey bias is unconscious and sometimes it is deliberate. Surveys and charts should be taken with a grain of salt. They are sometimes selected and prepared in a self serving manner.

Jaded Products is in labor contract negotiations with the Industrial Chemical Operatives Union (ICOU) for its Anytown plant. In preparation for negotiations and to provide a basis to support their respective wage proposals, each side has made a survey of wages at organizations it considers comparable. Compare the following surveys:

WAGE COMPARISONS IN DOLLARS PER HOUR (Prepared by ICOU)

Company	Jaded	DuPaint	Big3Auto	PittsGlass	Harvastraw
Location	Anytown	Anytown	CA	MI	PA
Union	ICOU	CEU	UWA	UWS	Unorganized
Unit Size	250	210	460	330	275
Mechanic I	14.00	14.00	17.83	16.04	20.00
Mechanic II	11.45	11.03	17.21	15.21	15.00
Operator I	13.45	14.06	17.12	14.63	20.00
Operator II	11.45	12.51	16.34	12.12	15.00
Quality Cont.	12.75	13.22	16.99	14.63	20.00
Specialist	12.75	NA	16.21	NA	NA
Production	11.45	11.38	16.21	NA	NA
Warehouse	11.45	NA	NA	NA	NA
Generalist	09.05	11.04	15.76	10.26	10.00
Probationary	08.05	10.60	NA	NA	NA

NA means not applicable.

WAGE COMPARISONS IN DOLLARS PER HOUR (Prepared by Jaded)

Company	Jaded	A	B	C	D	E
Union	ICOU	CEU	BCE	ITB	UWS	CEU
Unit Size	250	148	186	321	137	200
Miles From Jaded	0	5	45	28	71	46
Mechanic I	14.00	14.91	13.71	15.03	15.69	14.03
Mechanic II	11.45	11.98	11.33	12.25	12.82	11.05
Operator I	13.45	13.99	13.71	13.02	15.03	14.03
Operator II	11.45	12.97	12.66	10.97	13.44	12.02
Quality Control	12.75	12.97	12.83	13.03	14.55	13.23
Specialist	12.75	NA	NA	NA	NA	NA
Production	11.45	11.95	12.22	09.65	12.82	11.39
Warehouse	11.45	NA	NA	NA	NA	NA
Generalist	09.05	09.94	08.42	08.51	11.45	11.02
Probationary	08.05	09.50	NA	NA	10.99	10.67

NA means not applicable.

These two surveys demonstrate completely different approaches. These parties are likely to be headed for a serious misunderstanding. The union has selected for comparison, and chosen to survey, a sampling of companies geographically widely spread throughout the United States and not necessarily in the same industry as the employer. The employer considers the proper comparisons to be with facilities in the same industry and located within about a one hundred mile radius of its plant site. The differences in the two survey results will be used by each side to justify its position. The employer's negotiators will face union expectations molded by the high wage companies the union selected for its survey. Not considering itself in competition for labor against the companies chosen by the union, the company will likely resist wage demands based on those expectations.

Some surveys and charts are made and prepared by outside third parties such as employer associations, trade union groups, or publishers of economic news. The source of a survey or chart, and who paid for the research, should always be taken into account before accepting the survey or chart as a good reflection of the real world. It would be surprising to find a published survey which produced data adverse to the party who commissioned the survey. It is also quite possible to slant a survey by how the questions on the survey are worded.

✒ TIP

Don't be fooled by your own surveys. If you conduct a survey, keep in mind whether you are doing so to try to obtain accurate data, regardless of whether it favors your position (for private use by your side), or whether the purpose of the survey you are conducting is to present favorable numbers to the other side. There is nothing inherently wrong with the latter, but under these circumstances, don't be fooled into believing your own numbers. Also, be aware if your survey is slanted too far, you may hurt your credibility with the other party. Always be sure you understand the criteria used to report a specific item so that any comparisons you make are on a common base.

✒ TIP

Use charts to illustrate your negotiation presentations, preferably large, and in color. People tend to ascribe more reliability to numbers when elegantly presented and may not be as ready to question their validity.

✍ TRAP

The eye is sometimes quicker than the mind. Charts may be displayed with their scale or axes manipulated in order to diminish or magnify differences. Use of this technique may translate minor differences into graphics with large visual impacts.

Cost estimation is something you will do throughout most negotiating processes. It is singularly important in the planning phases because if you don't understand your own costs or the costs of the other side's proposals, you will find it very difficult to establish a position or to react to the other side intelligently. Without cost data, you are likely to make a number of expensive mistakes and to negotiate either unsuccessfully or less successfully than otherwise possible. Once you've done your cost estimation homework, you will be ready to move on to getting necessary approvals from your own side for your posture as a negotiator. That is the subject of the next chapter.

CHAPTER 6

WINNING APPROVAL FOR YOUR STRATEGY, INTERNAL NEGOTIATIONS

THE HARDEST NEGOTIATION IS WITH YOUR OWN SIDE

"God defend me from my friends; from my enemies I can defend myself." [Proverb] When you are working with your own side, you are "among friends." Suppose that you want to be successful and work long hours to prepare for negotiations, creating a well thought out plan. No matter how much high quality staff work you put into the preparation of a negotiation plan, if your plan is not blessed by those with the necessary authority (whether your boss, your spouse, or a key stakeholder), it becomes worthless. You must convince those whose approval you need that your plan is the plan that should be used. In a personal negotiation, the approval process, if any, is relatively simple, but it is still important.

At the outset of World War II, the Germans were seeking to finalize a military plan to invade and defeat France. Hans Guderian, one of Germany's most brilliant tank commanders, came up with a creative plan to defeat the French. His immediate superiors did not like the plan, but ultimately Hitler did. He adopted Guderian's war plan over the objections of many of his most senior military officers and it worked so well that France fell within a few months. But, suppose Hans Guderian had been unable to sell his plan? All his brilliant planning would have been left to gather dust and the course of World War II might have been quite different.

Let's assume that you have done a thorough job of preparing for negotiations. Your research is impeccable, your numbers are unassailable, and your proposed negotiating plan white paper contains a complete analysis leading to carefully framed and defensible objectives. Are you ready to go ahead and start negotiating with the other side? By no means, for unless you are the sole owner, leader, president, or sole stakeholder, your first and sometimes your most important negotiation will come when it is time to secure approval to implement your plan.

You, as a negotiator, will seldom hold ultimate power in an organization or have such high level support with stakeholders that your plans and objectives will be adopted automatically. Even if you are negotiating for a house, a car, an antique, or a rug, you may need to obtain someone else's approval or concurrence before bargaining.

Victor Brenner is a coin collector. Brenner has located a coin dealer who has available for sale a brilliant uncirculated specimen of the rare 1916 Denver Mint Mercury dime. Brenner wants to negotiate to buy this coin. However, Mrs. Brenner would strongly prefer to use the money to do some work on their house. Because Mr. Brenner wants to preserve domestic peace, before he begins negotiating with the coin dealer, he first negotiates with Mrs. Brenner, to secure her agreement to the coin purchase. They negotiate a compromise. She gives her consent to his trying to secure the coin, provided that he is able to do so for not more than seventy percent of the coin dealer's asking price. Brenner's research shows this is a low, but reasonable, offer. In turn, he agrees that if he is unable to negotiate the price down to the agreed level, he will walk away from the deal and the available money will be used entirely for Mrs. Brenner's project. Having completed his internal negotiation and secured approval, Brenner is now ready to begin his external negotiation.

In organizations, those who have high level executive authority seldom go to bargaining tables. Indeed, people at the highest level should not negotiate, as doing so tends to make the other side believe that it and its needs are more important than may actually be the case. In international negotiations, the top level person only enters the negotiations picture at a "summit," when virtually all the work has been done by subordinates. This keeps the risk of failure relatively low.

Students in negotiation simulation programs are often frustrated when they find that their negotiations must be conducted entirely within the bounds of limited authority and subject to fully binding and often quite restraining instructions. Although negotiators are often allowed flexibility in designing systems that implement bargaining objectives and may even have proposed the parameters for their own negotiation instructions, they must usually work within controlled or absolute pre-approved limits on such items as spending, contractual terms, and permitted commitments. Time after time in simulated negotiations, students and even experienced bargainers who come close to settlement, but who cannot reach it without violating their instructions, go ahead and grant unauthorized concessions. For a negotiator, operating outside instructions may well be a "career decision," culminating in an unemployment insurance line or placement in a dead end job which carries no hope of promotion. A personal negotiator who goes further than even self imposed limitations allow, may suffer from guilt or incur financial problems.

As negotiators are usually bound by their approved instructions, a critical portion of the negotiation process for a successful negotiator is framing and getting a negotiation plan approved. One thing that differentiates these internal negotiations from the later external ones is that the people you are negotiating with during the approval phase, whether business executives, spouses, or stakeholders, are likely to have the advantage of being aware of every weakness in your case. They have access to facts and information external negotiators on the other side probably lack. They may want to be assured that you have a cogent response to probing questions about how you will minimize your side's weaknesses and maximize your strengths. You are also apt to have to deal with internal politics or delicate personal relationships. In organizations, you will probably need the approval of high level people. These people do not normally reach these levels without being unusually bright and highly analytical. They are not likely to bless or approve negotiation plans that you are unable to justify completely.

✐ TIP

Think of internal negotiations as a "play within a play," the device used by Shakespeare in Hamlet and A Midsummer Night's Dream. Prepare for your internal negotiations with the same or greater rigor that you use to prepare for your external ones. Many of the techniques for bargaining with the other side may also apply to bargaining with your own side, with the difference that your own side is entitled to clearer answers and will be likely to have a better understanding of what your are proposing. Try to keep agreed upon approvals clear, unambiguous, and mutually understood. The clearer your approval, the easier it will be for you to stay within agreed upon limits.

COMPLETED STAFF WORK

"I have offended God and mankind because my work didn't reach the quality it should have." [Leonardo da Vinci] Completed staff work is another way of saying "quality work." Individual or personal negotiators will not have to produce the same type of staff work as business or labor negotiators. This discussion of completed staff work may be interesting to individuals to learn what is "best practice" in organizations, but it is less relevant to personal negotiations.

In organizations, if you find yourself faced with a high level review of your negotiation plan and want that plan to be approved, you will need to meet or exceed your organization's quality standards for accuracy and completeness of work. It is this ability to produce "completed staff work" that often separates those who do reach executive rank in organizations from those who do not. Those who have reached upper management tend to insist that work presented to them is of the highest quality. Keep in mind that for people at high levels, time may be a precious commodity. A terse, crisp, presentation is normally in order. For example, you would not waste the time of the President of the United States by using extraordinarily valuable presentation time less than wisely, omitting necessary information, and being unable to respond to questions.

What is "completed staff work?" Consider the following definition:

---

*Completed staff work is defined as work that is suitable for presentation to organization executives, that is: work that is well thought out; materials that are presented tersely, logically, and coherently; work which is internally consistent; work in which positions are justified by providing supporting numbers which are consistent, accurate, and defensible; work containing correct spelling and grammatical usage; and, work which contains **specific recommended courses of action for executive approval and*** *supporting rationale (not alternatives for organization leaders to decide themselves).*

Failure to present completed staff work may make it far more difficult to obtain approval of your proposed objectives, strategies, and authority. Completed staff work will also bring you greater credibility with those who not only have the power to grant you negotiating authority but also the power to take it away or to interfere with the course of a negotiation, which will result in embarrassment for the negotiator.

RISK ANALYSIS

"Take calculated risks. That is quite different from being rash." [General George S. Patton] All negotiations, personal, business, or labor, involve some form of risk taking. Risk taking in negotiations closely parallels risk taking in the stock market. If you buy stocks without analysis, you risk major losses. If you take too many risks or none at all in negotiations, you limit your success. Really successful negotiators propose and take risks all the time, but they prepare reasonable estimates of the percentage odds concerning the risks they are suggesting or taking. They are comfortable because they have thought through a "risk analysis" to use in responding to the questions that may be expected from an approving authority or stakeholders. A risk analysis is the weighing of the probability of success in achieving your proposed negotiation objectives within the requested authorization. There are several levels of risk of a proposed course of action:

HIGH RISK, HIGH REWARD

A high risk, high reward negotiation is one in which the chances of an unfavorable outcome are high, but this is offset by obtaining significant gains if the negotiation is successful. For example, a high risk, high reward, negotiation might take place when a prospective purchaser wants very much to acquire a shopping center but is unwilling, or unable, to close a deal if the center cannot be obtained at a very low price. Offering a low price may mean that the probability of not closing the acquisition is high, but the reward from closing at the acceptable price is also high. For a car buyer, high risk, high reward, may mean offering the dealer what has been discovered by research to be dealer cost and refusing to go any higher, which risks rejection, but in which the reward for success (a great buy) is high. In labor-management relations, there may be a high risk of a strike when management presses for significant change to make a plant considerably more profitable, but a high reward is obtained if goals are achieved without a labor dispute. High risk, high reward negotiations should only be undertaken when your risk tolerance and willingness to accept the consequences of being unsuccessful fall within your acceptable range. It is important that all stakeholders understand that an unsuccessful negotiation is likely.

LOW RISK, HIGH REWARD

This is the ideal situation for a negotiator. This case exists when the party is not in material need of the arrangement being negotiated and can therefore afford to hold out tenaciously, while the reward for success is significant. An example of this is when a company is considering closing down a facility which is merely breaking even and is seeking large scale changes from a union which will bring in significant profit. In this scenario, the company simply closes the plant if it does not get what it wants. For a company in such a scenario all alternatives are good. Closing such a business carries neutral effects, while the alternative of turning the business into a profitable one carries positive ones. The employer has nothing to lose and is free to seek high reward. A negotiator in this scenario will enjoy considerable bargaining power. For an individual, a low risk, high reward negotiation may occur when you are bargaining for a piece of jewelry you might like to own, but when you are fully prepared to walk away if you are not able to obtain it at a bargain basement price.

LOW RISK, LOW REWARD

Many negotiations are low risk, low reward. Some individuals and organizations set their negotiation objectives so low that there is little probability of negotiations resulting in clear failure. On the other hand in such scenarios, there is little gained out of success. An example of this type of negotiation would occur when one party to a sales agreement has as its only primary objective some minor modification in terms. Since that party seeks little, the other side may have no difficulty granting these minor items, but success will be essentially meaningless. Low risk, low reward negotiations often occur from fear of setting more challenging objectives out of lack of appreciation of bargaining power or from insufficient knowledge of negotiating techniques. These are "lost opportunity" negotiations. The negotiator has achieved a settlement, but has not obtained the rewards that the organization's bargaining power warranted its receiving.

HIGH RISK, LOW REWARD

This is the worst possible situation for a negotiator. This type of scenario is most likely to occur when a side lacks relative bargaining power. High risk, low reward negotiations should be avoided whenever possible. If a side must settle for low rewards, it should develop a strategy that also involves minimal risk.

Risk analysis is one way to make clear to a negotiator's approving authority or stakeholders the scope of the opportunities and liabilities of a given negotiation. The important thing is that your organization or stakeholders understand what you are attempting to do and the probability of various outcomes. For organizations, a risk analysis should always be accompanied by a plan as to what the organization will do if the negotiation does not achieve its primary objectives. For individuals, you should work out your course of action if the negotiation does not achieve your aims, although there may be no need to put your ideas in written form.

NUMERICAL ACCURACY

"The creator of the universe works in mysterious ways. But he uses a base ten counting system and likes round numbers." [Scott Adams] Although the question of numerical accuracy has been discussed before in Chapter 4, it is worth repeating here that in the process of obtaining internal approval of a negotiation plan, for organizational negotiators, numerical accuracy is absolutely critical. One of the worst fates that may befall you if you are a business or labor negotiator is for the reviewing authorities to find significant computational or mathematical logic errors in your negotiation plan. Such flaws destroy the vital credibility and confidence factors which secure your "home front."

Every number in a business or labor negotiation plan should be checked and rechecked, preferably by at least two people acting independently. In addition, tables of numbers should be checked for internal consistency and flaws in computational formulas. You simply cannot afford to have your numbers shown to be inaccurate.

DEFENDING YOUR PLAN ORALLY AND IN WRITING

"If you see a defense team with dirt and mud on their backs they've had a bad day." [John Madden] Individual or personal negotiators will seldom have a formal written negotiating plan they must defend, but should be prepared to answer orally the questions of any internal stakeholders. Some negotiation plan "white papers" may be reviewed without a formal oral or written presentation, but actively playing defense will often be necessary. Business presentations must be made in keeping with your organization's culture and cultures do vary, but some suggestions to consider are:

- Keep your presentation brief and to the point;
- Use the types of charts and graphs that are normal in your organization;
- "War Game" answers to difficult questions in advance;
- Provide reviewers with completed staff work, in advance;
- Offer concrete proposals, not alternative courses of action;
- Have supporting facts and figures available; and
- Know as much as possible about those reviewing the plan.

Probably the best way to prepare to defend your negotiation mission, objectives, proposals, and authorization request is to do a simulated run through in which other members of your own team play "devil's advocate," ask you difficult questions, and probe your plan for weaknesses. This will enable you to safely work out responses that justify and defend your positions. If you must go through a top level business review of your negotiation plan, it may well prove to be the most challenging part of the entire negotiation process. At the same time, an excellent presentation may be rewarded with firm authorization, firm support, and enhanced credibility. Should your negotiation later become difficult, or should your organization be on the verge of panic, a good impression previously made in a top level review may help prevent your own higher authorities from pulling the rug out from under you in the middle of negotiations.

ANTICIPATING OTHER PEOPLE'S AGENDAS

"To be prepared for War is one of the most effectual means of preserving peace." [George Washington] Anticipating the other party's moves and agendas is an important part of preparing for negotiations. Internal negotiations, whether personal, business, or labor, are no exception. Being prepared for internal discussions requires being attuned to the politics of your own organization or your stakeholders. To win approval for your negotiating plan, you will need to anticipate the motivations and needs of key players. Some organizations or groups will be far more fractious than others. Individuals may have vested interests in the status quo or a personal or political reason to support change.

Toys and Dolls was, until last year, Dolls Limited. The president and chief executive officer of Dolls was persuaded by one of her two executive vice presidents to acquire the toys line and to rename the company. The other executive vice president opposed the diversification. Recently, the president/chief executive officer announced that after thirty years with the company she would be retiring late this year. The two executive vice presidents are both hoping to be her successor. The toys division has been marginally profitable. The company has been compelled by the upcoming expiration of a major buyer's contract to reopen negotiations with that buyer. The executive vice president who supported the toys acquisition wants to keep the toys division going and knows that if the buyer pulls out, the division will probably have to be sold off or closed. Accordingly, he does not want a risky negotiation. The other executive vice president knows that if the toys division fails, he will likely become the new president. So, he prefers a high risk negotiation. Whichever stance the negotiating team recommends to the president, it is likely one or the other of the executive vice presidents will oppose that program. The negotiating team must be aware of the problem and be fully prepared to defend whatever recommendations it believes are best for the company.

Not all personal agendas will be as glaring as the one in the example above and most executives do not want to see their companies in serious trouble, even if that means personal promotion. However, almost everyone has some form of personal agenda. For example, a husband may agree to his wife's bargaining for some good jewelry with the idea that later on it will be hard for her to argue against his negotiating to buy a boat. A negotiating team may be able to draw support from individuals whose personal agendas coincide with the proposed negotiation plan.

In organizations, splits in levels of support or opposition are most likely when the best interests of the overall organization requires that one or more of its components be placed at risk in the proposed negotiating strategy. When one operation must subsidize another in the event negotiations are not successful in bringing about a settlement, it will generally be necessary for the common superior of the affected units to make a decision. Negotiators can expect some opposition from any unit that may have to make sacrifices, particularly if the head of that unit has a compensation package based on the unit's separate performance.

Once you've won approval for your plan, you will be able to move ahead with its implementation. Resources tentatively assigned or designated may now be formally committed. However, unlike your external negotiations which may conclude with a settlement or an agreement, internal negotiations never really end. Next, we will take a look at the types of resources you may need to apply in negotiating.

CHAPTER 7

COMMITTING NECESSARY RESOURCES

"Pray calculate the volume of Champagne, whiskey and other spirits I have consumed in my entire life and tell us how high it would reach if poured into this room." [Winston Churchill] Informed that the alcohol would reach his knees, Churchill then glanced up at the ceiling and sighed, "How far to go. . . how little time remains." Among Churchill's many talents was an amazing capacity to absorb alcohol. It is the nature of economics that time, resources, (and, in Churchill's case, liquor) are rarely as extensive as needs. However, if you are going to get a successful return on your negotiating efforts, for other than the most casual personal negotiation, you will usually have to invest at least some time, material, and money to set up the negotiating process.

Charlie Brown has always wanted to add a rare autographed Joe Shlabotnik baseball card to his collection. Charlie learns that three baseball card dealers will have autographed Shlabotnik cards for sale at a local show next month. Since his financial resources are limited, Charlie wants to get the card at the best possible price and knows he will have to negotiate with the dealers. To prepare for this, Charlie begins saving his money. He goes to the public library and gets some catalogs of recent baseball trading card prices. Charlie also spends several hours on the Internet, searching for data on the current value of autographed Shlabotnik cards. He calls several people who collect baseball cards to ask how they would value the Shlabotnik card. Charlie arranges for tickets to the show and for a ride to get there. Even his simple personal negotiation requires marshalling some preparatory resources.

Having strategically planned a negotiation, set out goals, and won approval, your task is to assemble the resources required for day-to-day success. A personal negotiation, such as that for a car, a house, or a collectible baseball card will profit from the labor spent in gathering information, but a personal negotiation rarely mandates the ordered assembly of people and equipment that is warranted for a large scale commercial or labor negotiation. When negotiation stakes are high, as in many business related negotiations, failure to commit the resources needed for success may translate into costs that could have been avoided and lost profit opportunities. **One of the most significant ways to cause any negotiation to fall short of optimum goals is to allow "penny wise, pound foolish" attitudes to result in a failure to commit sufficient resources to get the job done.** This chapter is about the tactical use of these resources, budget, language writing, and negotiation skills training.

NEGOTIATION BUDGETS

"Though wisdom cannot be gotten with gold, still less can it be gotten without it." [Samuel Butler] To secure success in negotiations, you may need to secure a commitment of people and money to staff and finance the bargaining process. In commercial or business negotiations, the costs of negotiating may be assigned in a number of different ways.

- Costs may be made a part of the overall negotiation authorization expenditure package approved by your organization's leaders.

- Costs may be defined as a separate budget item for negotiation expenses.

- Costs may be paid out of ordinary budget lines (covering such people as professional negotiators on staff who incur negotiating expenses in the ordinary course of business).

- Costs may be charged to the account of the chief executive officer or to the organization leader whose organization is most impacted by the negotiation.

Which of these methods is used is a matter of organizational preference. Placing the cost of a negotiation inside the negotiation authorization itself means that any overrun on negotiation cost must come out of your substantive negotiation authorization. A separate budget for negotiations isolates negotiating expenses from the negotiation package and treats those expenses as a cost of doing business. If you are a professional negotiator, you may have independent budget lines for such expenses as travel and lodging, established as a routine part of your home function's budget. In some organizations, your chief executive officer funds negotiating expenses directly from the CEO's own budget lines, while in others, executives, such as vice presidents, who have divisions or operations impacted by negotiations, have their business operations charged.

However it is done, your negotiations may require resources which need to be budgeted. Some of the items that may be part of a negotiation budget include:

◆ Travel;
◆ Meals;
◆ Lodging;
◆ Negotiation meeting room;
◆ Caucus and/or war room;
◆ Telecommunications;
◆ Counsel fees;
◆ Computer consultants;
◆ Security; and,
◆ Office support services.

If you will be bargaining at a distant and neutral site, travel may be a considerable expense, particularly when you may be going to the table for a significant number of meetings, broken by time intervals. Short notice and same day commercial air fares mount up quickly. Don't forget to budget not only for inter-city transportation but also for such matters as mileage to the origin airport; parking at the airport; local transportation on arrival, such as a rental car or taxi fares; and tips and other travel incidentals. All of these considerations may also apply to personal negotiations.

⚡ TIP

While first class travel is usually not necessary, it is generally a mistake to deny yourself or those involved in significant negotiations comfortable business class travel at reasonable hours. Avoid "red eye" specials. Whenever possible, book your negotiators in business class. This will facilitate getting work done during flights. Tired, jet lagged negotiators may more easily be goaded into a legal or negotiating mistake that will cost vastly more than the price of providing more comfortable travel.

Budgeting for meals for your negotiators should include personal meals while away from home, working meals which may involve room service charges, and entertainment meals for side bar and internal consultation meetings. Armies supposedly move and fight best when well fed. The same may certainly be said of negotiators. Accordingly, keep your meal budgets generous. Don't forget to budget for the occasional need to supply the other side with refreshments, particularly when things are going well. As with trying to save money on transportation, poorly fed and surly negotiators will be far more prone to making expensive mistakes. This may be even more important in personal negotiations than in business ones, for in personal negotiations the cost of errors comes from personal funds, not from a business budget.

Tomasina Kovich is a plant manager who is negotiating a six million dollar contract related to her facility through her five member negotiating team. In Kovich's company, the negotiation cost budget is assigned to plant managers and Kovich is an extremely cost conscious manager. She decides that it is not necessary for her to "pamper" her negotiating team by providing generously for meals or using top tier hotels. She has the out of town members of the team stay at the "Lumpy Mildewed Mattress Inn" and suggests the team members dine at the "Greasy Spoon Diner," with an occasional upgrade to "Burger Heaven." In the caucus room, she generously supplies the team with bulk purchased peanuts, but nothing else. Her negotiating team is tired, surly, and irritable. Pressed by the other side on an issue, they lose patience, blow up at the table, and lose a six million dollar deal on which the company stood to make a profit of over two million dollars—and that isn't peanuts.

Out of town negotiators need a place to stay and often this will be the same neutral site hotel at which negotiations are to be conducted. Good lodgings are a key to effective negotiations. Consider selecting a hotel that offers those on site services that a negotiation may require, such as room service (so you may work through lunch or may continue negotiations instead of taking a meal break); duplicating and copying services; a public stenographer; and, very significantly, wiring for computers. The same hotel may be used for negotiator lodgings, a negotiating room, and for a caucus room.

Elephant Industries, headquartered in New York City, and Rhino Manufacturing of San Francisco, are in multi-million dollar negotiations in Chicago over the possible merger of their two organizations. Negotiations are being held at Significant Towers. A series of meetings is scheduled about every third day for three weeks. Elephant arranges for its chief spokesperson to have a two room suite connecting to a room normally used as a hospitality room. The second room of this suite is used during working time as a caucus room and informal team work room while the hospitality suite is converted over into a war room with charts and graphs on the walls and with the in-room refrigerator stocked with food. To maintain continuity, Elephant retains the rooms throughout the six week period of intensive negotiations, even when its negotiators are back at headquarters. This allows them to leave things in their rooms and permits the uninterrupted use of the war room. Because the stay is relatively long term, the hotel permits special security locks on the rooms, installs telephones bypassing the hotel's switchboard, and offers reduced room rates. With sufficient and comfortable working space, the Elephant negotiating team is able to put forth its fullest efforts to win the best possible merger deal.

Sally Diamond owns and operates several jewelry stores in Miami. She travels to New York's diamond district to buy stock for her shops at wholesale prices. She takes the "red eye" flight in a jam packed coach compartment, sleeps in a noisy, low priced hotel, eats some fast food, and arrives at her supplier half asleep. Sensing she is not as attentive as usual, her supplier takes advantage of Diamond when she misses some flaws in the stones and successfully charges her four thousand dollars more than his bottom line. For the cost of a better airline seat at a better time, a good hotel, and decent food, Diamond would likely have caught the flaws in the stones and have come home ahead.

During your negotiation, telecommunications may be very important. You may need to acquire information about prices, wages, benefits, production, or a host of other items on short notice and sometimes at two or three in the morning. A meeting location which lacks sufficient telecommunications capacity to assure an outside line for data or voice at critical times is an inadequate location. If you use cell phones, be sure that you have chosen a location for your meetings which is not in a dead spot. Consider that cell phones pose more of a security risk than land lines. To avoid information leakage, avoid hotels where all calls go through a switchboard and which do not allow you to install a direct line to bypass that board.

AB&O Vampire Supplies has been negotiating with the City Council of Blood for tax abatements, in return for building a new processing plant in Blood. City council members are scheduled to meet this evening with Peter Abneg the chief spokesperson for Vampire. Three hours before the meeting, Abneg calls headquarters for a strategy discussion. He does so on a telephone running through the hotel's switchboard. The switchboard operator, Laura Opos, a partisan opponent of tax abatements in Blood, listens in on the call. During the conversation, Abneg is instructed to try hard for the abatements, but is directed that if they cannot be obtained he is authorized to commit to build in Blood anyway. Opos tips off a friend on the Council that she has reliable information that the plant may be obtained without granting abatements. That evening, a majority of the council, who were previously ready to grant the company's hoped for abatements, denies them. Abneg never learns that sloppy telephone security cost his company large amounts of money. Of course, Opos' action was unethical (and probably unlawful), as was the Council's in making use of information obtained in this way.

Tawana Williams' church has delegated to her the responsibility of recruiting a new minister and negotiating an employment offer. The church board is highly impressed with Jonathan Edwards, an out of state candidate who is also being considered for the ministry of several other churches. Williams has been negotiating terms with Edwards, who asked her to call promptly at 6:00 P.M.

with a final offer. Williams, who is attending a church retreat at a mountain lodge which has no telephones, takes a cell phone with her. She places the necessary call to Edwards right on time, but the lodge is in a dead spot and the cell phone gives a "no service" message. Williams makes her way down the mountain to the nearest phone, arriving there twenty minutes later. When she reaches Edwards, he tells her that since he did not hear from her as scheduled, he has accepted an offer from another church.

Almost all significant negotiations are impacted by the law. Almost any arrangement you reach at a negotiation will ultimately need to be reduced to a legally binding writing. When the stakes are significant, both sides may want their proposals and final agreement quickly examined by a lawyer (privately, not in view of other side). Legal review is particularly important in labor-management negotiations because if an employer commits an unfair labor practice and there is an unfair labor practice strike, the employer may be compelled to pay huge sums in back pay to striking employees. While your home purchase negotiations may be resolved without an attorney by using standard forms available to most real estate agents, an attorney's expertise may sometimes result in tax savings or winning purchase or sale terms out of the ordinary. Unfortunately, in auto and consumer appliance purchase negotiations, the seller usually produces a form contract and then obstinately refuses to negotiate changes to any of its terms.

What should you budget for an attorney? If you are part of an organization with in-house counsel with appropriate expertise, you may not have to budget anything. But, if you are in a specialized area of the law (e.g., mergers, acquisitions, anti-trust, civil rights, or labor) or are in a personal negotiation, you may need an outside attorney who has particular expertise in that subject. The cost of counsel varies widely in different areas, by specialty, and by whether counsel is an associate or a partner. Expect to spend a bare minimum of one hundred dollars per hour for every hour worked and possibly several times that in high cost areas such as New York City. In addition, you will pay disbursements and counsel's out of pocket costs, other than normal office expenses. You will pay for certain travel time, although the rate for travel time may be reduced from the regular hourly rate. Higher priced expert counsel may actually prove to be more cost effective when they know the answers to questions from experience, without having to spend billable time on research. Personal negotiators may be shocked at the cost of counsel, while business organizations are generally more familiar with legal rates and anticipate these costs as inherent in doing business.

𝄢 TIP

Don't scrimp on legal advice. The cost of counsel, while seemingly high, may be quite modest if counsel saves you from doing something unlawful or suggests a method of accomplishing your end with less legal risk. Legal errors are cheaper to prevent than they are to cure. Also, make sure counsel are limited in number to those necessary to handle your problem. You will not want to pay for an excess number of associate attorneys who are being trained by the law firm and billed to you.

It is very difficult to conduct a modern complex negotiation without computers. Under normal circumstances, properly programmed and tested computers will work and take you through a negotiation. However, particularly if you are engaging in a time critical negotiation, remember that when a machine fails it may do so at the worst possible moment. Just in case, have an internal computer expert on call who is knowledgeable on the programs and systems you use or make similar arrangements with an outside computer consultant. On-call rates for outside computer consultants will vary widely and cannot specifically be predicted for your area.

You may well say that my concerns about security are almost paranoid and you would not be far off the mark. The more money that is involved in a negotiation, the more vital security becomes. You may know that you are a reputable person who would not use any form of snooping or espionage to obtain information, even if that information would give you a vital edge. But, you never really know about the other guy. Further, even if the other guy doesn't intend to root through your wastebaskets or look at your notes while you are in the restroom, if you leave something vital behind, it may be difficult for the other side to resist temptation and return it to you unread. Further, once you leave something behind during a break or after a meeting, you will always wonder if the other side did actually read it. If your negotiation is a large stakes one, use common sense security precautions and consider also bringing in a security expert. The following is not hypothetical:

A labor agreement was being negotiated at a hotel in the Detroit area. An engineer on the negotiating team heard clicks on the telephone line. Being curious, the engineer traced the lines to an employee cafeteria on a service floor where it was found that a group of employees, using alligator clips in a telephone junction box, were listening in on guest telephone calls. Whether they were eavesdropping for amusement or to find ways to blackmail guests is unknown. Could information obtained by these employees have been offered for sale to the other side in the negotiations? Certainly. Was it? We never found out.

The cost of budgeting for security is also difficult to estimate. It will vary with location, the expertise required, and the frequency with which the security expert will be needed. But, if you have millions at stake, be cautious, and spend what it takes to be secure. For a personal negotiation, just be careful with your notes and papers.

Office support services may be only an indirect cost if you are negotiating on your site. But, if you are not, then the person, or persons, providing those services will either have to be from your organization and transported to the meeting site with their expenses covered, or you will have to use an outside service, such as a public stenographer, or a copy and graphics service. If you are negotiating for yourself, you will seldom have enough at stake to bring in support services and will always be at risk of a security error by the third parties you use for help. **Any time you use an outsider for office support services, you risk an expensive security breach, whether deliberate or accidental.**

Vikki Chen works for Understaffed Office Services which has a location in the Tromp Towers Hotel. She has just finished a rush job her boss assigned her "from the Elephant Industries and Rhino Manufacturing negotiations." When the job which was Rhino's was finished, Chen's boss said, "take that upstairs to that negotiating room." Chen hurried to the negotiating room and handed the copies, fresh from the printer, to the chief negotiator for Elephant, who had also sent a job down to the same copying service a few hours before. "At last," she said, and glanced down at the papers she had been handed. They were labeled, "Rhino Manufacturing—Management Confidential, Final Bottom Line." There on the first sheet, bulleted, in large bold print, was Rhino's bottom line. No matter how ethical Elephant's negotiator is, the copy service's mistake meant that Rhino's bottom line had now been prematurely and completely revealed. Any advantage that Rhino might have gained in a lower cost settlement is gone, lost because Rhino did not bring its own support services personnel with them. This is not a far-fetched example. Mistakes happen.

Generally, parties do not cost, or budget for, lost opportunity time during negotiations. For example, a finance manager who spends time on a negotiation team may not have time to perform all regular duties. Some of this regular work may be delegated to a subordinate. When negotiations peak and are very time consuming, some negotiators must temporarily become entirely divorced from their regular work. That work often must be covered by another employee or be left undone. For a large team taking part in a lengthy negotiation, the shift of work may be disruptive. Nevertheless, few parties take into account the costs which are related to lost opportunity time. Whether or not to cost opportunity time is a question of financial policy for each organization. For individuals, consider that the time you spend negotiating must be taken from other activities, whether money making or leisure.

LANGUAGE WRITING

"When I use a word," Humpty Dumpty said, in a rather scornful tone, "it means just what I choose it to mean—neither more nor less."

"The question is," said Alice, "whether you can make words mean so many different things."

"The question is," said Humpty Dumpty, "which is to be the master—that's all." [Lewis Carroll]

Once you reach beyond small scale personal negotiations, one of your most essential negotiation resources will be the availability of someone capable of competently and legally drafting the detailed language you need to formalize your agreement. Excellent skill in this type of writing is a difficult talent to teach and few people have a natural talent for this work. Your language writer may be an internal person or you may need to go outside to find a labor relations professional or a labor attorney with the specific ability. Don't assume that all lawyers are good wordsmiths. Many do not write creative or novel language well. Be careful in your selection. Individuals negotiating with organizations will have particular language problems. The institutional party will often "solve" this for you by offering you ready-made language. Be wary. That language will be written to favor their interests. If you have enough money at stake, retain an attorney or a person skilled in writing out negotiated agreements.

Words are important. In an age in which a president, testifying under oath, quibbles about the meaning of the word "is," you will need to exercise care in putting your agreements into writing. It is possible to seem to achieve your primary negotiation objectives at the table during the "agreement in principle" stage and then to lose all your gains during the "working out the detailed language" phase of your negotiation. Language bargaining may be viewed as either a problem or as an opportunity. The problem stems from the risk of making a major mistake in the substance of language or which may make the agreement invalid; a mistake which is then embodied in a legal document. Apart from simple consumer agreements, auto purchase contracts, stock brokerage agreements, and the like, where the purchaser is rarely accorded any right whatsoever to negotiate language, the opportunity stems from the ability to use language creatively. Even in your dealings with those who thrust form contracts in front of you with the attitude of "take it and sign or go somewhere else," you should at least try to negotiate about the items that concern you. Occasionally, you may achieve at least a modest success.

Sula Safe, an individual home owner, is offered a five year home security monitoring contract by KeepEmOut Security Services. The contract provides a reduced annual rate in return for a five year commitment. Ms. Safe, who is nearing pension age, knows that there is a good probability that she may sell her house in two to three years. The printed contract sent to her contains a simple, unvarnished, five year monitoring commitment. Ms. Safe calls the Service's customer service agent and says that she will sign the contract if she is allowed to add a clause stating, "Should I sell my home within the term of this contract, I have the right, as of the closing, to cancel this agreement. From the day I cancel, I won't have to make any further payments for future monitoring services. I will also be given a pro-rata refund for the rest of any annual payment I've already made." Services, not wishing to lose its customer, agrees. Ms. Safe writes in the change, initials it, and sends it back to the company with a note that they should also initial the change and send her back a copy. They do so. Three years later, when Ms. Safe actually sells the house, she avoids a problem with the security company. She has won a rare small victory. However, realize that many companies will not consider negotiating any changes to their standard language.

Think of the language embodying a negotiated agreement as your road map. It should be clear, easy to read, and define the major routes and points. You will rarely be able to create language to cover every possibility, but at least address the issues which are mostly likely to occur. In negotiations, written language has two major purposes.

- Language guides the parties themselves as they administer their negotiated agreements.
- Language sets down the agreement for the benefit of attorneys, judges, or arbitrators in the event of a later dispute over what the negotiated agreement means.

There are several basic principles to guide you in writing language:

- Don't lightly borrow language from other people's agreements;
- Think of the negotiated agreement as a seamless whole;
- Seek to control the drafting process;
- When possible, write in clear, simple, easy to read, language;
- When you can't win clear language, make ambiguity work for you;
- Be aware there is danger in proposing and failing to obtain language;
- Keep good negotiation minutes or notes;
- Use statements of intent;
- Use examples;
- When time permits, verify how the language really works;
- Prepare language ahead of time, whenever possible;
- Cost the language you write and receive;
- Use extra-contractual documents when appropriate;
- Don't limit your options through your own language;
- Watch out for (or create) language with unacceptable conditions; and,
- Read every word of proposed language.

One of the things that may cause your negotiations "to go bump in the night" is to borrow language from other people's contracts or agreements. Adopting someone else's language without careful scrutiny is a very common mistake. When they are not themselves borrowed clothes, other people's agreements are drawn up to meet their specific needs. Your particular case may not easily fit into their pre-cast mold. Further, if you borrow language rather than create it, the danger exists that neither you nor the other side will fully understand what it is that you are agreeing to do.

Potent Chemicals is in its first labor contract negotiations with the Substance Workers Union. A critical issue in the negotiations is the bidding process, under which employees are to be placed in open positions. The parties do not reach agreement in principle on a bidding system until the last hour before a threatened strike. It is close to midnight and the parties need detailed contract language to flesh out this agreement in principle. The union produces a contract used by a sister local with nearby Strong Chemical Products. They show management the bidding clause which contains the language, "All successful bidders shall be transferred to their new classifications within three (3) calendar days of their successful bids. Employees who do not qualify on their new classifications within ten (10) calendar days may be returned by the company to their prior classifications." The union says, "If our sister local can live with that language, so can we." The management negotiating committee, comprised of a human resources manager, a finance manager, and an attorney, but acting without an operations manager, looks at the clause and also accepts it because, "Strong has adopted it, so it must work in our industry." The two parties shake hands and a contract is reached. Later, the parties learn that because the work at Potent is vastly more technical and complex than at Strong, it is impossible for Potent to transfer successful bidders within three days and that no employee will be able to qualify on a new classification in less than a month. Both parties are responsible for the problem. Neither understood that what is good language in one place may be wrong in another place.

Don't be enamored with "boilerplate," or form, language. Unfortunately, attorneys tend to be very "conservative" people about drawing up language, preferring the tried and true standard language to new and creative solutions. However, to resolve problems, negotiators may need to apply unique or unusual solutions which are particularly suited to their environment and culture. Once you are comfortable with your language writing capability, feel free to create language solutions, but do run them by counsel. If you don't feel competent to write language yourself and are unhappy with the language you are offered, consider hiring an expert, provided the value of your negotiation warrants. Boilerplate language does have one advantage. It has frequently been interpreted by the courts or in arbitration and therefore has been tested for validity and enforceability. There are certain fields in which tampering with boilerplate may be dangerous. It is unwise to negotiate major modifications in house sale, or house purchase, boilerplate language without consulting with counsel.

A negotiated agreement may often contain a number of paragraphs or items, some of which may cross reference or depend on other parts of the agreement. Think of the entire agreement as a seamless whole, although this may be difficult with a very long or complex negotiated agreement. Be sure and consider to what extent, if any, a change in negotiated language in one place will impact the agreement in another place. Try to avoid language that creates internal conflict within an agreement. **Actually read the fine print. If necessary, read it over and over and ask questions until you understand what you are being asked to sign.**

Paragraph 10 of an agreement between a buyer and seller of a large piece of land, with a house and a storage building on it, refers to "all that property known as 1 Main Street, Anytown." The parties later agree that the storage building in one corner of the property will not be part of the conveyance. But, they forget to modify paragraph 10 to reflect the exclusion of the storage building. Conflict of this sort may come back to haunt the parties or their successors years later.

Winston Churchill said, "History will be kind to me for I intend to write it." If you actually write most of the language of a negotiated agreement you will have a great advantage, for it is the drafter of language who largely shapes the ultimate agreement. Because it is more work to write language than merely to receive proposed language from the other side and because people tend to be lazy or to find writing difficult, your offers to write language will frequently be gratefully received. Only a part of what you then write will be debated. Many of your words and their nuances will survive and become part of the final agreement. For the receiving party it is important to remember that the party writing the language is not doing so to give away advantages. **Caveat: If you are writing language in a complex field you do not understand, get professional help.**

✒ TIP

For tactical reasons, it is often a good idea, even when accepting the other side's proposal in principle, to write the implementing language yourself or, if the other side offers you language, to work up your own substitute for it. However, be aware of the legal principle that if you drafted the language of an agreement, any ambiguities are to be construed against you, on the theory that when you drafted the language you had the opportunity to clear up the problem and failed to do so.

Skilled language writers draft clear and simple language. The purpose of language is to provide a kind of guide that is easy to read, outlining how the vast majority of cases or issues will be handled. One way to check the quality of your language is to test it on a person unfamiliar with what you are trying to accomplish or with the systems your language describes. If the other person understands the language clearly and interprets it as you intended, the language meets the quality test.

Quiet Person Recliner Manufacturers and the Relaxing Furniture Wholesalers chain are negotiating a commercial agreement for Quiet Person to supply Relaxing with several thousand recliners over two years. Relaxing is worried about interruptions to supply. The parties write a clear and simple clause that states what will happen in the event Quiet Person cannot deliver the committed number of recliners. The clause reads: "If for any reason whatsoever Quiet Person is unable to meet the delivery commitment dates specified in this agreement, Quite Person shall: 1) Substitute an alternate supplier of recliners which meets Relaxing's quality standards and is satisfactory to Reclining, at a price no higher than specified in this agreement, and using Quiet Person's own brand label; 2) Failing this, Quiet Person will supply Relaxing with recliners made by its competitors, which are acceptable to Relaxing, under the competitors' own brand labels, and at a price *no higher than specified in this agreement; or, 3) Failing this, shall pay the sum of $50,000 to Relaxing in lieu of litigated damages.*

✒ TIP

If several steps are involved to carry out a process outlined during a negotiation, in your detailed language you should spell out each step in chronological order. Your language should anticipate major problems and provide a resolution for them through evident application of the language itself.

Ambiguity is a problem when you have drafted the language. The legal principle is that doubts about what language really means are to be construed against whoever wrote the language. However, sometimes you must leave language ambiguous or your negotiations will flounder. If this is the case, and it is tolerable, some ambiguity may be better than no agreement at all. You may make ambiguity work for you when you use it to avoid a problem that cannot be resolved at the table, but as to which you are willing to risk a later dispute. If language must be left ambiguous, you may want to get the other side to write and propose that language.

Anderson Snow Removal and Noel Yule are negotiating an arrangement under which Anderson will clear snow from Yule's property throughout the winter for a single flat rate. Yule would like to have a clause that requires Anderson to clear snow during and after all storms that leave at least one inch of snow on the ground, but cannot get Anderson to specify what it means by "Anderson will clear snow from Yule's property after each significant snowfall." There are few snow removal services in the area and none are accepting new customers. Yule agrees to the language, although it is ambiguous. Yule will get snow removal services. If Anderson uses the clause to avoid snow removal in too many borderline situations, Yule will resort to legal action.

Another language principle is that if you propose something, do not achieve it, and later claim the right to do what you once proposed, ultimate silence on the point in the final agreement is to be construed against you. The presumption is that you failed to obtain your suggested enabling language in bargaining and hence should not be allowed to achieve by interpretation those aims which you were not able to achieve by negotiation. Before you put language on the table, think about worsening your situation by making a proposal that may be difficult to achieve. Be cautious, but don't be deterred from making serious language proposals.

During negotiations between Anderson Snow Removal Services and Noel Yule, Yule proposed modifying Anderson's standard language, "Anderson will clear snow from Yule's property after each significant snowfall," by replacing it with, "Anderson will remove snow from Yule's property, during and after all storms that leave at least one inch of snow on the ground." However, Yule signed Anderson's contract as Anderson originally proposed it. During the winter, Anderson performed snow removal only when storms left at least six inches of snow on Yule's property. Yule protested and sued. The court found that as Yule had proposed a more restrictive clause and not obtained it, Anderson would prevail.

Humpty Dumpty's statement that words mean what he wants them to mean applies to negotiations. After a negotiated agreement is in effect, parties will often try to reinterpret the words, sometime torturously, to favor their respective sides. One way to counter this problem is to take good notes, or minutes, during negotiations.

In a labor negotiation, the parties agreed that former employees who had worked for the employer in the last five years would be given preference for employment in a new plant which is to be built as part of an expansion. When a number of former employees were recruited for the new facility, the company gave them a new seniority date based on the date they began work in the new plant. The union insisted that these employees were to be "reinstated," that is given their original seniority dates from their prior employment. The union was able to win this argument before a labor contract arbitrator because during negotiations they took good notes and had a record that the company negotiator assured them that the preferentially hired employees would "not break seniority." This example also illustrates how ambiguity (the nature of reemployment as a rehire with a new seniority date or a reinstatement with a continuing seniority date) leads to disputes.

You will find that you cannot cover all possible future cases with reasonably concise negotiated language. Some events are too unlikely to occur to warrant taking valuable negotiating time to work out detailed language. One way to cope with this problem is to secure agreement on a statement of intent which provides guiding general principles for applying less than detailed language to those unlikely situations which actually do arise. These statements are useful benchmarks and guidance for informing judges or arbitrators as to the overall intent of the parties at the time they wrote the language. Because the statements were written at the time of the original negotiation, they are free from the implication of self serving bias that flows from a position taken only after the facts are known. If on a given negotiation issue, you stand to profit from ambiguity, you may want to resist agreeing to a statement of intent.

*The following clause appears in a labor agreement: "The parties intend to provide a means through a bidding system for **employee** initiated transfers to occur between classifications in an orderly manner, with the least possible disruption to the existing work force." Subsequently, a dispute arises over an **employer** initiated transfer. The union maintains that once an employee has successfully bid to a position, the company has no right to transfer the employee, other than as expressly stated in the agreement. The company argues that the words "**employee** initiated transfer" in the intent clause means that the entire clause has no impact on **employer** initiated transfers. Other issues about the details of bidding which are not spelled out in the agreement result in an employer claim that it is entitled to use the least disruptive method of movement. In both these instances, the intent clause will be helpful to management.*

Written examples you hand across the table are sometimes useful in building a record on how proposed language would actually be administered. Examples, while rarely placed in the formal written agreement negotiated, form part of negotiation history. Testimony or negotiation notes showing the examples may be introduced in court or in arbitration to support claims. Examples are particularly useful for complex matters such as the application of employee health care benefits or when there are complex contingency provisions to be included in commercial agreements.

On the surface, the language you create to embody your negotiated agreements may appear to be "just right." However, there are no guarantees that systems that look good on paper will work well in the real world. Provided time permits, before using new language, take the opportunity to ask those who will be impacted by the new language if they see any problems with it. This process accomplishes two things. First, it may bring to light errors in proposed language that are not obvious, particularly if you are not an expert in the function which the new language covers. Second, if something does later go wrong with the application of the language, the people who are impacted by the problem will have had the opportunity to identify the problem when the language was first considered. Remember that no one can be an expert on every function and aspect of a business transaction.

You have set up a new business and just negotiated your first contract with a major customer. Among the terms on which the customer insisted was that all your shipments to them go via UniFed. Happy to get your first contract, you agreed. Under time pressure, you did not check with the individual who handles your shipping activities. You are surprised to find out that UniFed does not serve your town and has no plans to establish an office there. To use their services, you will have to truck your product sixty miles to their nearest drop-off site, at considerable expense.

In end stage negotiations there may be a time deadline. When time is of the essence, pressure and the risk of error increase greatly. Circumstances permitting, draft language for your proposals well ahead of time and carefully check with those who will live under the system as to whether it will work. This "prepared in advance language" may be trotted out and modified as necessary, but its existence may save you time when time is precious. Most things that diminish the possibility of significant error are worth doing.

Whenever possible, cost the language that you are proposing or language that has been offered by the other side and which you are accepting. Very few "non-economic" proposals are entirely cost free, whether the costs are direct or indirect (such as opportunity time, which is paid time that could be spent on other productive activities).

⚡ TRAP

As a matter of practice, many proposals which carry low or only nominal direct costs are termed "non-economic." However, a proposal that has little economic impact today might well have significant impact in the future as times change.

In 1979, Best Buggy Whips negotiated a successor labor agreement with the Stable and Livery Workers Union. The union proposed, and the company accepted, language that read, "any employee who uses a digital computer at any time during a work week shall be paid double time for that entire work week." Company financial people estimated that the clause would impact only those few employees working on mainframe computers and would therefore be a low cost item. With the advent and growth of personal computers, the company negotiated repeatedly to modify this clause. But, the union was adamant that it must remain in the agreement.

Ivan Nash completed a personal negotiation by purchasing a new car. The papers Nash signed contained a clause that, "Customer wishes to have the new vehicle sprayed with a special rust resistant compound and agrees to pay the cost of this process on taking delivery of the vehicle." Nash assumed that the clause might add fifty or a hundred dollars to his purchase. The dealer told him, "It's not a big deal. Don't worry about it." When the new car is delivered, Nash learns that he must now pay almost six hundred dollars extra for this unwanted service, because he failed to insist on knowing the cost in advance.

Not every negotiated agreement must be reduced to writing and placed in the basic signed agreement. For political reasons, it may be desirable to place certain items in side letters, or to supplement the basic agreement with written understandings that do not fall within the agreement itself. In keeping with the principle that the negotiated agreement is a seamless whole, exercise caution about such extra-contractual understandings. Be sure that they are not in unintentional conflict with your basic agreement and that they contain defined expiration dates.

Alpha Manufacturing and Beta Wholesalers have a long term negotiated relationship under which Alpha is required to submit a certain percentage of its production for Beta to an independent outside laboratory for quality control purposes. Years of experience have shown that Alpha's quality is excellent. Alpha wants to switch to in-house quality testing. Beta is willing to let Alpha make the change on an experimental basis but does not want to change the extant contract, which still has three years to run. Alpha and Beta enter into a side letter of understanding which reads, "Notwithstanding the provisions of our sale and purchase agreement, on an experimental basis, Alpha may conduct in-house quality control testing in lieu of an independent outside laboratory. This agreement shall expire one year from its effective date, unless extended by the parties by a signed mutual agreement."

Limiting your own options through language you write is a frequent mistake. This is often done in response to internal political pressures exerted by those who want to lock in current policies by making them contractual commitments to third parties.

Invisible Products has a current internal policy under which they do not release the names of their direct customers to any third party, including their own wholesalers. In entering into a contract with a new wholesaler, the wholesaler has asked for a list of Invisible's current direct customers in its franchise area. Invisible Products not only refuses the request but writes into the contract the following language, "Invisible shall not make direct customer lists available to the wholesaler." Note that the use of the word "shall" makes the policy of not releasing customer names an enforceable contract term. A year later, when someone inside Invisible Products decides that wholesalers should be co-opted to advertise to customers, an opponent of that course points out, "We can't do that. We have contracts with third parties that bar that policy." The contract clause limits the freedom of the organization. Contract language reading, "Invisible has the right to release or withhold customer lists from wholesalers," gives Invisible just as much power, but leaves it with an option. The wholesaler cannot require the release of customer names but the second clause does not limit Invisible from changing its policy without renegotiating or changing its agreements.

There is a significant difference in negotiation agreement language between "shall," and "may." The former is mandatory while the latter is permissive. Consider the world of difference between the following two clauses:

"Company A *shall* acquire Company B no later than the January 1 next following the effective date of this agreement," and "Company C *may* acquire Company D within one year of the effective date of this agreement." Under the first clause, Company A has no choice in the matter and a legally enforceable obligation to make an acquisition. Under the second clause, Company C has a choice and an option. "Will" and "shall" are essentially the same although "shall" has a stricter nuance.

"Poison pill" language consists of wording that ties some desirable thing to an unacceptable condition. The idea of a poison pill is for you to be able to say in public relations releases "we offered that and they refused," when you know full well that the way the language was offered made its acceptance impossible.

Board of Zoning Appeals chairperson Azbug is firmly opposed to granting Stonemart a permit to build a "big box" store on certain land. She arranges for the Board majority which she controls to offer Stonemart the desired building permit, with the condition that Stonemart build a new school for the City. The cost of a new school is disproportionate to the opportunity for Stonemart and they decline to build in the City. Azbug tells the press, "We were willing to have them here, but if they create jobs there may be more people coming in with children, so it is not unreasonable to expect them to bear the costs. We tried to work with them." A spokesperson for Stonemart says, "The City's conditions for the permit were totally unreasonable. The new jobs could hardly generate enough additional school population to require us to build a whole new school." The condition on the offer was clearly designed to kill the deal.

Finally, with regard to language, very carefully read any proposal or counterproposal given to you by the other side. A counterproposal may look very much like your original proposal but have a totally different meaning. Consider:

A company proposes, "Our company may discontinue manufacture of large widgets without your agreement." The other company responds with a counterproposal, to reword your clause, "Our company may discontinue manufacture of large widgets only with your agreement." At a quick glance the language appears the same. Only a few words have been changed but the meaning is one hundred and eighty degrees different. In a long clause, the language may appear identical until compared word by word. This comparison must be done. Changes are, of course, sometimes more subtle than the one in this illustration.

SIMULATION TRAINING

"Training is everything. The peach was once a bitter almond; cauliflower is nothing but cabbage with a college education." [Mark Twain] To learn negotiations skills, you might take a negotiations theory course or you might read a book such as this one. But, there is no substitute for on-the-job experience and, unfortunately, the price of gaining experience in real time may be paid in costly mistakes. The alternative way to hone your theory skills is to participate in realistic simulation training, in which failures and mistakes, from which we all tend to learn, exist only in a simulated world, free of real time consequences.

The value of simulation training is increasingly being recognized. If you are a commercial airline pilot, you will receive much of your training in sophisticated flight simulators. Flying real military or commercial jets for training purposes is simply too expensive to be done with the frequency necessary to build high skill levels. Simulators make it possible to test reactions to unusual and dangerous situations, without risking an airplane that costs millions of dollars. In the hands of a trained instructor, social science situations may also be simulated at relatively low cost. For this reason, national leaders and government officials who may have to cope with security crises or disasters are often simulation trained.

181

One of the single best ways to maximize your possibility of success in large scale commercial or labor negotiations (or for smaller scale but frequent negotiations) is to practice and train for negotiations using simulation. You may receive some useful negotiation theory review at the outset of a simulation program, but you'll find that negotiation theory is not terribly complex. Rather, it is the practical application of theory that usually proves more difficult. Because simulation is a controlled process, a single simulation may be packed with experiences that would take you years to acquire in the real world.

How does negotiations simulation training work? You learn by doing, by carrying out a programmed series of tasks and challenges designed to parallel, as closely as possible, the real world in which your negotiations are to take place. A custom simulation program sets its challenges within the world of your own business culture and that of your negotiation opponents, so that your experience can be made truly life-like. The real world is a dynamic place, so your simulation leaders will invoke unpredictable variables and events that could arise and present you and your team with unexpected problems.

Alchemy Chemicals is in a labor negotiation with the Chemical Alchemists Union for a successor contract. Alchemy has taken a very strong position at the table because it has the advantage of considerable surplus capacity at a plant where employees are not represented by a union. The company plans to shift work to that plant in the event of a strike. During the mid-negotiations phase of the simulation training exercise preceding the opening of the real negotiations, the simulation leader informs the management and simulated union teams that the other plant has had a fire which has wiped out half the surplus capacity for at least three months. As the company negotiating team attempts to cope with the impact on their strategy and tactics, the simulation leader observes and later on invites the two teams to critique the management team's performance.

The purpose of simulation training is to prepare and ready you and your negotiating team for what may take place during your actual negotiation. For this reason, a good simulation must be constructed within the real cultures and personalities of the parties. That is why you will find that a "canned" simulation, or a public "one size fits all" simulation with people present from many organizations, is not nearly as useful as a custom designed program.

⚜ TIP

Choose someone to lead your simulation who has extensive negotiation experience and the ability to facilitate and teach. If that person is from outside your organization, select a leader who is willing to take the time to learn the culture in which the actual negotiation will be performed.

Your simulation leader will set up a number of situations which test the negotiating skills and cohesiveness of you and your team. For example, you may find yourself faced with a walk out by the opposition, a public relations disaster, or with personal attacks launched by people on the other side of the table. The events chosen may include a mix of those that are highly probable and those that may be unusual. From time to time during the program, the leader will stop the process, take you out of role, and have you discuss what was going on, how it was being handled, and what could and should have been done. You may then be asked to do the sequence again, learning as you go along. From this process, you will gain confidence in your ability to handle problems and use your skills. Should the simulation incidents actually occur during the real negotiations, you will already know what to do.

Should you participate in simulation training? This type of training is useful for an identified negotiation team working as a group, whether or not any, or all, team members have negotiating experience. Simulation will also be useful for you, even if you are not currently scheduled to take part in a negotiation, if you hold a position where it is likely that you will, at some future point, become involved in bargaining. If you are already an experienced negotiator, simulation will refresh your skills, provide you with the opportunity to learn new things, and will give you the chance to share your capabilities with others who have less experience. To provide a simulated "opposition," others from your organization who are not on the current team, but have either been on prior teams, or who are likely to be on future ones, may be assigned to role play.

Simulation training should be done very soon after your negotiating team is identified and your organization's general objectives for the negotiation are known. Doing a simulation early will allow you and your team to adjust for, and to correct, any weaknesses which may appear during the simulation. Further, should any team member emerge as unable to perform an assigned role, it is likely to become clear during the simulation and before any real harm is done.

Simulation training may be done at your normal work location, but it is likely to be more effective when done away from your work site. An off site location will tend to minimize interruptions from routine day-to-day work. A good negotiation simulation may consist of a half day to a day of negotiation theory and tips, followed by two to three days (including work into the evenings) of role play negotiations against an "opposition" team. The total time you spend in simulation work should run about twenty to thirty hours, be intense and demanding, and so realistic that you tend to forget the training is an exercise.

Why should your organization use simulation training? If a negotiation involves large sums of money or is complex, simulation training provides an ideal way to prepare you and the team for the real thing. You may then handle the negotiation with a much greater chance of avoiding miscues. You will have more confidence. If you or your team doubt your own abilities, or become intimidated by the other side, you will tend to underestimate your side's real bargaining power and to accept a less satisfactory settlement than might be available.

The benefit to cost ratio of simulation training may be astonishing. The cost of simulation training, a few days time for the negotiating team and its "opposition," including travel and logistical expenses, and the cost of a qualified instructor is often relatively trivial in comparison to the sums that may be won or lost in an actual moderate to high stakes negotiation. It may be "penny wise and pound foolish" to send a negotiating team to the table in a complex negotiation without simulation training.

You have probably heard a great deal about such negotiations concepts as "win-win" bargaining, "interest bargaining," and "mutual gains sharing" negotiations. Having planned, set up resources, and simulation trained, in the next chapter we will consider what you may do to establish a sense of mutual victory while still gaining an edge for your side.

CHAPTER 8

ESTABLISHING A
PERCEIVED "WIN-WIN"
OUTCOME

"The object of war is not to die for your country but to make the other bastard die for his." [General George Patton] Since this book is about winning "game, set, and match" for your side in negotiations, it is logical to ask why you should be concerned with having the other side come away from negotiations with the perception that it has achieved at least modest success. The answer lies in enlightened self interest. Successful negotiations generally end in some form of written agreement. Whether in a business or personal context, these agreements often require each side to perform a series of on-going acts over a period of weeks, months, or years. You are far more likely to actually receive the full benefit of your negotiated bargain if the other side has played a meaningful role in reaching agreement and has truly committed itself to the agreement's success. When the other side is satisfied with its bargain, it is far more likely to freely do what it has legally committed itself to do. This is the "principle of legitimacy." Unless you are certain that you will never negotiate or see the other party again, legitimacy is important.

Laura Lotus is on the trip of a lifetime. She is exploring the casbah in Casablanca. Laura locates a fine Moroccan leather pouch and begins negotiating with the vendor over a price. She knows that she is extremely unlikely to ever return to Morocco or to do business with the vendor again. She need have no concern over any long term relationships or the vendor's perception of the deal. Given the vendor's greater knowledge of prices, it is, of course, Lotus, who will probably emerge with only a perception of having bargained well.

It is important that the other side has the *perception* that it has achieved at least some progress through negotiations. That what the other side gains from you is of low value to *you*, or objectively is of no real import, *does not matter.*

In a commercial negotiation, the manufacturer offers a price per unit, exclusive of shipping charges. The buyer insists that the manufacturer include shipping within the offered price. The manufacturer is quite surprised by the importance that the buyer is placing on shipping, so instead of yielding early on that point, holds its planned concession back. The manufacturer's negotiating team therefore continues to resist the proposal that it absorb shipping, until virtually all other terms of the agreement have been reached. Having achieved excellent terms on other issues and since it had always intended to include shipping within the offered price, the manufacturer "capitulates" at the last minute on the shipping charges. When the seller makes this concession, the buyer's negotiating team feels that they have won a major victory. The manufacturer's team knows that the buyer's "victory" is objectively meaningless, but they say nothing to undercut the buyer's feeling that it has accomplished something of great value in negotiations.

In establishing a "win-win" negotiation outcome, we are talking about subjective perception, not objective reality. If the reality of bargaining power demands it, you may be forced to permit the other side to achieve something critical for itself, with your side paying the cost by yielding something meaningful, short of a primary objective. Ideally, if your bargaining power permits, your concessions will be made on things that are not truly significant to you. However, if you leave the other side with absolutely nothing that they may claim as a victory, your chances of success in a negotiation will likely vanish in a personal or commercial negotiation (when the parties are free to walk away) and markedly decrease in a labor negotiation (where the parties must reach an agreement or risk a labor dispute). You will find it difficult to reach agreement if you leave the other side with no choices and with a loss of face.

---

*Smoke Signal Telecommunications is in a negotiation with the Smoke Workers Union for a successor labor agreement. Due to fierce competition in telecommunications from more modern means of information exchange, Smoke Signal is under pressure to lower its staggeringly high labor costs. Smoke Signal's negotiating team is considering whether to recommend primary objectives for its negotiation plan involving wage concessions from the union or to seek changes in work rules and work practices that will yield significant productivity savings. A member of the team suggests that Smoke Signal seek **both** wage concessions and work rule changes as cost cutting primary objectives. A member of the team who argues that Smoke Signal should seek either wage concessions or work rule changes, but not both "guns and butter," is overruled by the negotiating team. Top management then approves the team's recommended strategy. Four months later, this high risk strategy results in a major labor dispute. Negotiations were probably doomed from the outset for the union was denied any possibility of perceived victories. The union might have swallowed wage concessions or accepted work rule concessions in return for a continuation of jobs, but could not live with losses in both. There was no face saving avenue open. Such negotiations are usually doomed.*

An additional reason for not pushing an opponent too far when you have a dominant position is that you may want the other party to remain in a long term relationship. Imagine an amateur playing chess with a grand master. The amateur loses every game very quickly. The usual result is that after a short time it becomes clear to the amateur that it is time to find a better matched opponent.

Last American Shoe Manufacturing has been purchasing leather soles for many years from Soles for Sale, under the terms of a negotiated agreement. Soles for Sale is under enormous financial pressure and desperately needs to retain customers, a fact known to Last American as they begin renegotiating their agreement.

Last American uses its bargaining power to make sure that it is getting a reasonable, somewhat below market, price from Soles before reaching agreement. Last American could have pushed Soles further to force Soles into a sales contract on which Soles made virtually no profit. However, Last American values the long term relationship for many of its intangible benefits and does not wish to risk forcing Soles out of business. They stop short of using all the bargaining power they have available, accepting a slightly higher price than they could have achieved had they pushed bargaining to an extreme.

UNDERSTANDING THE OTHER SIDE'S VITAL NEEDS

"Leadership should be born out of the understanding of the needs of those who would be affected by it." [Marian Anderson] Regardless of the type of negotiation, if you want to be a truly successful negotiator it is very important that you understand the other side's needs and methods and how to address them, always at the least cost to your own objectives. After the North African battle of Kasserine Pass in World War II, General George S. Patton won some notable victories over the brilliant German Afrika Corps leader, General Erwin Rommel. He did this, in part, because he had read Rommel's book on armored warfare and understood Rommel's needs and methods.

Armed with an understanding of the other side's interests, it will be easier for you to estimate the things the other side will vigorously push to obtain and which proposals they may be willing to abandon. If your information were perfect, you would merely have to line up your own primary objectives against the other side's primary objectives and you would then immediately know if any settlement would be possible.

In our less than perfect real world, no matter how straightforward the other side is with you, and whether or not they are engaging in some form of "win-win" negotiations, you should realize that the other side is unlikely to ever present you with its true bottom line. Problem solving may suggest different methods of allowing both sides to meet their primary objectives, but if those objectives are infringed, regardless of method, then no settlement is possible. Good, clear signals from the other side should help you to work out the other side's needs, but signals come fairly late in the bargaining process.

✍ TIP

People have "wish lists." Don't confuse the other side's "wish list" with its vital needs. A vital need is something which is so at the heart of negotiations that the other side must achieve it or it will leave the negotiations (or to cause or take a labor dispute in labor negotiations). In essence, the other side's vital needs are the "flip side" of your own side's primary objectives. Ask yourself the question, "If we were sitting where they are sitting, how vital would this issue really be for us? Would it be worth breaking off negotiations (or striking, or locking out)?" To make this determination you must have the empathy to place yourself in the other side's shoes, although you can never do so with all of the information the other side possesses about its own situation. There are always some clues as to the other side's vital needs. A press report may tell you something about the other side's internal problems. Required government reports may contain significant useful data. People who are on the other side may make the mistake of talking too much.

Once you understand the other side's vital needs, you will be able to consider whether your side is able to bend enough to create ways to meet those needs, without compromising your own vital interests and primary objectives. This is a process that needs to continue throughout negotiations, as more data becomes available. Keep in mind that the other side's statements should not necessarily be accepted at face value. People do sometimes purposely supply disinformation.

Maria Villa has been trying to sell her house without using a realtor. After a long wait, Harold Home, a potential buyer showed interest in the house. Home has made a number of offers, the last at $147,000, just three thousand dollars below Villa's real bottom line of $150,000. Home has not moved from that level. Villa thinks she may lose Home as a buyer, but is simply unwilling to let the house go at $147,000. However, during the last three negotiation sessions held at Villa's house, Villa has noted Home's repeated attention to the large riding tractor with snow blower she uses to clear the five hundred feet of her driveway. Despite Home's comments about the tractor's "sad condition," the way Home keeps looking at it makes it clear to Villa that Home is very interested in the tractor. Villa is moving to a condominium where *the owners' association will do all necessary snow clearance. Grasping Home's deep interest in the tractor and having no further use for it herself, except to sell it in the open market, where it is worth perhaps a thousand dollars, Villa "reluctantly" offers to throw the tractor in as part of a deal at $151,000. This is four thousand dollars above Home's previous offer. Home rationalizes that the addition of the tractor makes a price of $151,000 reasonable and tenders an offer at that level for the house and the tractor. The deal is closed. Home has the perception he has won something, because his negotiation skills obtained the tractor. By understanding that for Home, the tractor had become a key objective, Villa netted her bottom line of $150,000 for the house. The additional $1,000 Villa offered represents the value of the tractor she "threw in." She is pleased to allow Home to think he "won" the negotiation.*

GAMES, TACTICS, AND TECHNIQUES FOR LETTING THE OTHER SIDE THINK IT "WON"

"We don't see things as they are, we see them as we are." [Anais Nin] There are a raft of devices that skilled negotiators use to give their opponents the idea that they have "won" something significant during a negotiation. Of course, you may actually yield something which is truly important to the other side, but which represents a compromise of your own vital interests. That, it hardly needs to be said, is not a preferred method for comforting the other side. Short of that, what techniques might you use to create a perception of victory for your opponents? A summary of some examples is listed below, followed by more detail on each item at the conclusion of the list.

+ You may hold out on something that the other side really wants and which you eventually intend to yield, then capitulate gracefully at the last minute ("OK, you've fought hard for it, we'll concede on that issue").

+ You may secure language on a point written in such a way that your side retains a full option to do, or not do, something at a future date (for example, "we may, at our option, permit you to reduce the number of required inspections"). This commits nothing.

+ You could establish a joint study committee to consider the troubling issues after the agreement is reached, with equal party representation, and a majority vote required for any action. This commits conversation, but not ultimate concession.

✦ You could praise the other side for "forcing" your side to yield something ("you guys sure are tough negotiators").

✦ You may give the other side something of great value to them, but which is of little or no cost or consequence to you.

✦ You may permit the other side to achieve an impressive, numerically long, list of "successfully negotiated items," each of which represents very little actual value.

At first blush, this list may sound quite manipulative, but these devices are frequently used, often with the knowledge and understanding of the party on the receiving end. For political and career related reasons, negotiators who lack bargaining power may knowingly receive these devices favorably because they allow the weaker party to save face. These ploys also allow the parties to remove potentially unsolvable items from current negotiations, to defer them to some future time, or to effectively abandon a position. Now, let's look at each of these devices in more detail.

Sometimes the other side will give you a clue early in negotiations that some item on their list is disproportionately important to them (perhaps for political reasons) and which is an item which your side has no problem in accepting. Once you are convinced that the other side has a disproportionate need for the item, hold your agreement in abeyance for a considerable time, or trade it only for something of real significance to you. **Granting an item of high value to the other side early in negotiations merely because it is of little value to you, instead of getting something of high value to you in return, is one of the most frequent mistakes made by inexperienced negotiators.** When you hold out an item, the other side is likely to perceive that it has won a "victory" when it finally achieves a gain for which it has fought long and hard. We appreciate what we pay for more than what is given us free.

Think about a negotiated agreement clause that says that your side "may do [something the other side wants done] at its sole option." Because it actually commits you to nothing, such a clause has no real meaning. However, it will allow the other side to publicly overlook the discretionary nature of the clause and to "point with pride" to having won a concession from you. An option of this type does not legally bind you to actually do anything. However, keep in mind that frustrating expectations may cause problems in the next negotiation. There may well be at least a moral obligation to seriously consider in good faith doing the thing the language suggests. So, this device is not risk free.

"Joint study committees" are an excellent way to allow the other side to at least claim a victory, while obligating your side only to a study, not to an action. Study committees are usually face savers for the other party. If you are the party offering a study committee, be sure to structure the study committee so that it may only make recommendations or act by majority vote. Divide representation equally between the parties. Committees of this type are almost always adopted for political reasons or to get embarrassing items off the table, with no real intent of executing future change.

One of the least expensive devices in a professional negotiator's arsenal is praise for the other side. Even in an adversarial negotiation, perhaps even more so than in a relatively cooperative one, a kind word to the other side may greatly improve its perception of how it is doing. A more secure other side is an other side that may be more willing to compromise. So, telling the other guy that "you were very convincing on that point and sold it to us," or, "you sure outdid us on that one," may go a long way toward creating a perception on the other side that it is doing well.

Often the other side will demand something from your side that it is relatively easy for you to give and possible to yield at low cost. Sometimes they will try to embarrass you about your positions. Remember that initial positions are often overblown to leave yourself room to make concessions and move toward agreement. Don't let embarrassment about your positions lead you into premature concessions made without getting anything in return. **Self made concessions (bargaining against yourself) give away your stock in trade, the capital with which you trade and get the other side to move. Negotiating against yourself is a very common mistake for inexperienced negotiators.**

Allen Advocate is an attorney and partner in a small plaintiff side law firm. The firm has won a large contingency lawsuit which entitles them to recover legal fees from the defendant. These fees are submitted by the firm and reviewed and adjusted by the court. Fees are also charged for travel time. Concerned that travel time may look too extensive to the judge and that they are frequently reduced by the court, Advocate voluntarily gives up half the travel fees. Defendants attack the reduced amounts. The court ignores the original voluntary reduction and applies a fifty percent reduction to the remainder. Advocate receives only twenty-five percent of travel time billing. Advocate was negotiating against himself with the first reduction. It seems likely that had Advocate submitted the original travel charges, the judge would have cut that in half and Advocate would have received fifty percent, instead of twenty-five percent, of the billing.

Finally, a useful device is to give the other side a lengthy list of concessions and movements that look impressive in their number, but have little or no real impact on your side and which carry minimal cost. For example, in a labor-management negotiation, an employer may concede moving the limits on lifetime major medical insurance from one million dollars per employee to unlimited (cost effect usually zero), or add a few thousand dollars to employees' accidental death and dismemberment insurance (an extremely low cost item). It may even be possible to cast something that saves an employer money as a benefit to employees (requiring a "second surgical opinion" saves some employees from unnecessary operations, but also saves the employer considerable costs from these operations).

🏷 TIP

It is usually a good idea to allow the other side to "save face" when it is making a major concession. Some of the methods outlined above may be utilized to allow the other side to retreat with dignity. There are exceptions. If the other side has run a rude, contentious, negotiation and quality long term relationships are not a particular issue, your side might consider delivering a lesson by forcing a settlement without room for much face saving, so that the other side is not likely to risk a similar problem in the future. Be cautious about this and stay away from its use unless you are virtually certain the balance of bargaining power will not later turn against you. Otherwise, you run the risk of a return engagement with the tables turned.

USING HUMOR AND ICE BREAKING TECHNIQUES

"The human race has one really effective weapon, and that is laughter." [Mark Twain] In any negotiation, there will be moments of tension, anger, or frustration. Humor, sometimes self deprecating humor, may be very effective in getting stalled negotiations moving again.

Deadpan Publishing and Studs Deadfish, the sole author of a text Deadpan wishes to publish, have bogged down in negotiating the specific language to implement their agreement in principle. The parties have been having a tense afternoon. Deadpan has placed language on the table stating that the "the author will defend certain claims against the publisher at his or her own expense." Studs, who is a 250 pound former professional football player, decides to lighten things up when the parties reach this clause. Wearing a large grin, Studs says, "This says his or her. I hope you are not suggesting a sex change operation." He laughs. The other side joins in and the tension is broken.

Another humor related device is to utilize a single slide made from some popular cartoon, such as the late Charles Schulz's *"Peanuts,"* or from Scott Adam's *"Dilbert."* Often negotiators take themselves too seriously. Part of establishing a "win-win" atmosphere in negotiations is establishing a casual, non-confrontational mode. Humor can serve a very important role in helping the parties learn to relax together, even when they are discussing issues which are important to them.

Another icebreaking tool is food. When progress is being endangered at the table, one side may alter a negative tone by bringing in coffee, donuts, hamburgers, or other food or beverages. This should not be done often enough to become expected. Breaking bread with other people is a way to help cement civility and to lower aggressive behavior at the table.

Admitting error may also cause a thaw in a stalled negotiation. People are naturally reluctant to own up to mistakes. But, if you have made a minor error, admitting it may go a long way toward establishing trust. Particularly in relationships which have previously been marked by suspicion and adversarial behavior, an admission can be startling and helpful. Of course, it helps if the error is institutional rather than personal.

The Paint Manufacturers Union (PMU) has been in negotiations for a labor contract with Newco. Newco purchased the plant a short while ago and is negotiating its first labor agreement with

PMU, which had a long history of fractious labor negotiations with the predecessor company, Stanley Steamer Paint and Varnish (SSPV). One of the members of the union bargaining team tells the Newco management bargaining team stories about how SSPV abused and mistreated good employees when they had a death in their family and needed time off. These stories are verifiably true and were one of the factors causing deep distrust. Newco's negotiating team wisely does not defend SSPV, nor does it accept responsibility for its predecessor's acts. "I've heard those stories," the Newco spokesperson says, "and it seems to me that SSPV was completely off base. An employee who has a death in the family and who has a creditable record with our company will be treated with special concern and helped at a time like that. The former owners were wrong. We won't be like that." Newco thus disassociates itself from SSPV, and it does not take a "management, right or wrong stance." This type of change may greatly facilitate the development of a "win-win" mood.

A word about the concept of "win-win" negotiations. Relaxing the atmosphere does not make the other side your partner or any less your adversary on ultimate issues. What it does do is to open the door to developing more creative solutions to problems. In devising these solutions, the other party's needs are examined and addressed so they may perceive success, but **"win-win" negotiations should never be an excuse to unnecessarily compromise or undercut your own side's primary objectives or vital interests.**

If you have taken the steps outlined to this point, you are almost ready to begin negotiations. Next, we will consider the circumstances under which it is best to bargain individually or with a team, before moving on to a discussion of essential preliminaries to your first bargaining session.

Chapter 9

Team Bargaining

"The way a team plays as a whole determines its success. You may have the greatest bunch of individual stars in the world, but if they don't play together, the club won't be worth a dime." [Babe Ruth] When should negotiating be done by a team and when should it be done individually? In some circumstances, negotiations tend to be an individual activity. If you are buying or selling a single car, a house, or a Persian rug, these negotiations are almost always conducted by one or two people on each side. However, if you are buying or selling a fleet of cars, a shopping mall, an e-commerce business, or when significant commercial or labor-management negotiations are involved, team bargaining is the norm. The size of a team may depend on what is at issue. For example, in negotiations between attorneys or accountants and the IRS, the negotiations may be conducted by either individuals or by small teams.

Once a situation warrants team bargaining, teams have several virtues.

- Teams combine a variety of expertise.
- Teams tend to cut down on mistakes, as one team member may often head off a problem about to be created by another team member.
- Teams allow for the division of a wide variety of often complex tasks which overlap in time and could overwhelm a single individual.
- Teams allow the "on the job" training of junior team members, to prepare these individuals for later senior negotiating assignments.

On the other hand, teams may suffer from an inability to make quick decisions, particularly when time pressure is a factor. A committee has been described as "many stomachs without a head." In the public arena, purely from an efficiency standpoint, consider how much faster and how much better focused a single person President can be than a multi-person Congress.

HOW MANY ON A TEAM AND AT WHAT LEVEL?

"What counts is not necessarily the size of the dog in the fight—it's the size of the fight in the dog." [Dwight D. Eisenhower] If you are negotiating as an individual, team operation won't be of concern to you. Once you have decided to bargain using a team, the question naturally arises about the size of your negotiating team. A small team may not be sufficient to cover all necessary expertise or provide enough people to handle all the required tasks. A team that is too large is likely to be inefficient. For a less complex negotiation, two or three team members may suffice, but for a large complex negotiation, five to seven team members may be desirable. Groups of more than nine on a side may be difficult to focus and to handle.

What level personnel should be used on a team? The spokesperson should preferably be an individual with negotiating experience and have reached a senior level. However, the spokesperson should ordinarily not be chosen from the very top levels of an organization (president or vice presidents) because this implies too much importance for the negotiation. It will also be difficult for a top level person to spare the necessary time to conduct a lengthy negotiation. Apart from the spokesperson, other team members may range from fairly senior, to intern, or note taker level.

There are circumstances under which you might want your team to be headed by two equal co-spokespersons. For example, in labor-management negotiations, the management team might be jointly led by a plant manager with line responsibility for the facility in negotiations and a senior labor relations manager with functional responsibility for that site or a number of sites. A commercial negotiation team might be led by a purchasing manager and an attorney. Co-spokespersons should only be used when the individuals chosen are compatible and are able to work closely together, deferring to each other in their respective areas of expertise.

Titanic Shipping Lines is in negotiations with the Ship and Lifeboat Workers Union for a successor labor agreement to cover its Olympic Shipyards operations. Because of the complexities of ship-building and because the labor agreement covers a wide variety of work practices, Titanic decides to have co-spokespersons heading its negotiations team. The Shipyards' general manager provides senior level line expertise on the team and specializes in questions concerning operations. Titanic's corporate manager of labor relations, who is also a labor attorney, serves as the other co-spokesperson and specializes in questions concerning collective bargaining techniques, labor relations law and practices, contract language, and human resources issues. This division of responsibility between senior managers reduces the possibility of serious negotiating errors being made.

The number of people ultimately chosen for a team may depend on the expertise required and will sometimes be driven by your organization's internal politics. It may not be possible to leave a particular function without a representative on your negotiating team. For example, a team that includes a representative from maintenance, but does not include one from operations, may provoke internal political difficulties.

✐ TIP

For most applications when a team is indicated, a team size of three to five members per side is probably most efficient. In very large teams of ten or more members, consider using sub-teams to discuss various subjects. Sub-teams should rarely be empowered to make binding commitments. Smaller teams may find the use of sub-teams useful on occasion, when the work load remaining is too extensive for the number of meetings available.

HOW TO SELECT A SPOKESPERSON AND TEAM MEMBERS

"Almost every man wastes part of his life in attempts to display qualifications which he does not possess." [Samuel Johnson] Who qualifies to be on your negotiating team? Few people are professional negotiators. Indeed, deliberately setting out to become a professional negotiator is usually a futile quest. People without negotiating experience are rarely chosen to negotiate, so how does one get selected? One must be in the right place, at the right time, with needed skills. For your organization, selecting the right spokesperson is often a key to negotiating success. What are the characteristics that make for the best spokespeople? There is no one formula or check list that works in every situation, but generally an ideal spokesperson should have as many as possible of the following traits (but no one is likely to have all of them):

- The respect of superiors and peers;
- Patience and perseverance;
- The ability to command masses of data;
- Multi-tasking ability which is the ability to juggle many issues at once;
- The ability to think quickly and under stress;
- The leadership skills to coordinate and manage a team;
- Listening skills, in relation to other team members and the other side;
- The ability to persuasively articulate positions;
- The emotional stability to deal with reverses;
- Numeracy, that is the ability to understand and manipulate numbers;
- The flexibility to achieve goals without bogging down in details;
- Clock management skills, to fit negotiation to the available time line;
- Training skills, for teaching junior team members how to negotiate;
- Decisiveness, when time constraints require quick decisions;
- The willingness to take reasonable risk;
- Acting skills, including the ability to maintain a "poker face";
- The ability to subordinate all personal agendas;
- Knowledge of the applicable laws;
- Knowledge of human psychology;
- Public relations sensitivity;
- Dedication, including a willingness to work long hours;
- Good health, as negotiation can be very stressful; and,
- Prior negotiation experience.

The chances are that the average individual negotiating for a car or a house won't be able to bring to bear a large majority of these skills, nor will they be required. Indeed, few professionals negotiators have them all. Some skills are less important than others. **Among the most critical abilities in complex team negotiations is the capacity to maintain emotional equilibrium at all times. Negotiations can be an emotional roller coaster, as the prospect of success or failure ebbs and flows.** For the same reason, the spokesperson must be able to deal with stress and this generally requires good health. In practice, many professional negotiators are middle aged. Also extremely important is the ability to juggle a lot of issues at the same time without being overwhelmed.

An ideal team spokesperson should perform both as a leader and as a trainer. This means that the spokesperson must have the ability to switch styles as negotiations move from phase to phase. In early and mid game negotiations, the spokesperson should be able to take the time to train others and to allow the team to function in a moderately democratic fashion. In end game negotiations, which are conducted under time pressure, the spokesperson must shift into more of the old line authoritarian manager mode. When there is little time, as General Ulysses S. Grant said, "Someone must decide." The person who must be able to be decisive under time pressure is the spokesperson.

From what function should the spokesperson be selected? In labor-management negotiations, the spokesperson is often either a senior labor relations manager or director, or a senior line manager, such as a plant or division general manager. For unions, the spokesperson might be an international union representative, or the local union president. In commercial negotiations, the spokesperson might be chosen from the function being impacted most heavily by the negotiation. A buy and sell negotiation for "widgets" might be led by a purchasing manager, assisted by the widget production manager. A negotiation to acquire land might be led by an in-house counsel, or by a real estate manager. A particularly complex and critical negotiation might be led by an organization's professional negotiator, regardless of that person's normal function.

Overlord, Inc. has recently acquired Juno, Sword, and Gold, Inc. At the Juno site, employees are represented by the Tank Armor Employees union. Juno is an aging site with an outdated labor agreement that must be changed if the plant is to survive. This will required the replacement of the entire current labor agreement and significant change in the work culture at the Juno site. A spokesperson is required to head the Overlord negotiating team. Overlord, Inc. normally conducts routine collective bargaining using the local site labor relations manager, or the local site works manager, as chief spokesperson. However, because of the complexity of a negotiation of the type contemplated, Overlord names as a spokesperson the corporate manager of labor relations, who as a senior labor relations manager, attorney, and a professional negotiator, is generally assigned only to non-routine negotiations. For political reasons, the site works manager (general manager at the site) is also assigned a spokesperson role. These two managers are officially designated as co-spokespersons. They agree that the labor relations manager will have primary control of table tactics, labor law issues, and all labor relations related issues, while the works manager will have primacy on maintenance and operations questions.

Wooly Mammoth Clothing is negotiating with Mastodon Stores over a wholesale contract for Wooly Mammoth to sell huge quantities of winter fashion clothing to Mastodon. The contract must be closed quickly if the factory is to have the fashions ready for delivery on time for the winter selling season. Wooly Mammoth decides that speed is of the essence and that the negotiation is reasonably straightforward. Accordingly, it decides to dispense with a negotiating team and to allow its sales chief to conduct the negotiations alone. Wooly Mammoth provides support for its negotiator by having a finance person and an attorney on call to answer any questions the sales chief might have that are likely to require specialized expertise.

TIP

One way to test the abilities of a first time spokesperson-designate, or to hone the skills of a professional negotiator, is to hold a pre-negotiation simulation session. To make this as realistic as possible, other people who know the organization should be selected to play the roles of the expected opposition team and assigned to probe and challenge the spokesperson and the negotiating team. A spokesperson who does badly in the simulation should be removed before being allowed to enter a real negotiation where mistakes can have costly results.

For a full discussion of simulation training, review the third and final section of Chapter 7.

🦖 TRAP

Automatically assigning the role of chief spokesperson to the person on the team with the highest rank may be a serious error. The highest ranking individual may not be either temperamentally suited to lead the team, or may lack the necessary expertise. Sometimes, for political reasons, the ranking individual must be formally denominated as a co-spokesperson, but in such instances, the individual should have only limited powers and be overseen by a more experienced senior negotiator.

Apart from the spokesperson, how should other members of a negotiating team be selected? One method is to assign people to the negotiating team so as to provide well rounded expertise. The spokesperson cannot be expected to have strengths in all the necessary competencies. While some gaps may be supplied by having experts available for consultation on the telephone or in caucuses, significant areas may best be covered by appointing a negotiating team member with the required competency.

Market-Garden is interested in acquiring Einhoven-Arnhem, a large tulip growing and marketing operation headquartered in Holland, Michigan. The acquisition will be a large scale one for Market-Garden and a considerable portion of its capital will be required for the purchase. Market-Garden appoints an acquisition team to negotiate the terms. Bernard Montgomery, Associate General Counsel, is named spokesperson. On Montgomery's recommendation, to assist him, Market-Garden adds to the team: Shan Hackett, Finance Director; Pip Hicks, Marketing Director; Charles Mackenzie, Director of Human Resources and Benefits; and, Maxwell Taylor, Chief of Operations. The team is rounded out with a personnel assistant and a secretary to serve as note taker. Hackett is to serve as the principle keeper of the numbers, Hicks to advise on Einhoven-Arnhem's marketing requirements, Mackenzie to look at questions of staffing and of merging the two organizations' employees and personnel systems, and Taylor to evaluate the strengths and weaknesses of Einhoven-Arnhem's operations. Their special expertise will help Montgomery avoid mistakes. The personnel assistant is assigned to the team primarily as a training device to develop her for a future negotiation leadership role.

⚜ TIP

When additional expertise is needed on a team, but the size of the team would become difficult to manage, assign people with low priority expertise to the negotiation "back room." The "back room" is the home base at the negotiating site for the negotiating team and is sometimes used as its caucus room. For those needed less frequently, arrange to have them "on call" during negotiating sessions.

DELEGATION AND WORK ASSIGNMENT

"We accomplish all that we do through delegation—either to time or to other people." [Stephen R. Covey] One of the key tasks of the spokesperson is to delegate work and assignments to other members of the team. During a complex negotiation it is usually difficult or impossible for all members of the negotiating team to take the time to work together on all aspects of the negotiation. Having the full team working together on a single subject is generally most appropriate during the planning stages, when the team must decide on questions of strategy and tactics. By the time the mid-negotiations phase is reached, team members chosen for their special skills will need to be focused on the projects that are germane to their specialties. In the end game negotiations, every team member may be needed to handle separate assignments. The spokesperson's responsibility is to coordinate all these efforts and to insure that all work meets the quality standards for "completed staff work" (see Chapter 6 for a definition of completed staff work).

Meade, Inc. is negotiating a very large land acquisition with the Lee Holdings Corporation. Lee Holdings (the seller) is currently also simultaneously negotiating with another prospective buyer. Because of restrictive changes to land use laws that become effective in a few days, but which do not apply to owners already in possession, the parties to the negotiation have determined that any deal must be wrapped up by the end of the day today to allow adequate time for the legal formalities of a change of title. Meade's spokesperson has assigned various tasks to Meade's negotiating team members. One company team member is writing contract language to support an agreement in principle on an important point which was reached at the last table session. The second Meade team member is putting the finishing touches on the company's next purchase offer to Lee Holdings. The third Meade team member is costing out a Lee Holdings counterproposal placed on the table at the last session. The fourth Meade team member is talking with the company's public and governmental relations director about how to respond to press and government inquiries. Meanwhile, the spokesperson is preparing to review all of the open issues still on the table to be sure the parties agree on which proposals are still be considered active. On the Lee Holdings side, the spokesperson is examining a Meade proposal to see if it contains any hidden problems. A second Lee Holdings team member is preparing a counter offer to the company. The third Lee Holdings team member is working on closing logistics. The fourth Lee Holdings team member is on the telephone with the corporation's legal counsel on some easement issues. The fifth Lee Holdings team member is fending off a reporter.

🖋 TIP

If a team is of sufficient size, the spokesperson should avoid taking on any direct substantive work assignments. The task of coordinating the work of the other team members and of preparing for the next session may well consume all of the available time of the spokesperson. Spokespersons should not allow themselves to take on more direct work than they are able to successfully handle.

Not only work may be assigned, but also authority. When work is delegated to sub-committees which meet with the other side, the sub-committee head may be delegated the authority to make commitments. If this is done, the problem is to delegate just the right amount of authority. Too little authority and the individual is perceived as powerless. Too much authority and the individual may make a serious and binding mistake. Generally, unless time is absolutely critical and the sub-committee head is experienced and very trustworthy, delegation of binding authority to anyone other than the overall spokesperson is dangerous and should be avoided.

BACKWARDS PLANNING

". . . I have to live backwards from the front, while surrounded by a lot of people living forwards from behind. Some people call it having second sight." [Merlyn] Backwards planning is a borrowed military concept that was described by James C. Burris, former Vice President Human Resources, BASF Wyandotte Corporation, as a method where you look ahead to the crucial point in time and ask yourself what objective you want to achieve by then. You identify each step that precedes attaining your objective and set a time target for that step, so that you may reach your final goal on time. In a commercial setting, the objective may be to obtain a three year sole source sales agreement, within budget, by a certain date. In labor-management negotiations, the objective may be to obtain a three year contract, within budget, preferably without a strike, by expiration of the current agreement. For an individual buying a car, the objective may be to obtain a Land Rover SUV, or equivalent, by a certain date, at not more than a certain price. Backwards planning requires that you assume a final date for attainment of the objective.

The concept of backwards planning may best be understood by looking at an example. The following is a backwards plan that has actually been utilized for a labor-management negotiation. For commercial negotiations, the principles are the same and only the items listed would differ. No two backwards plans would necessarily be identical.

(1)	Contract expiration	D-Day
(2)	Final negotiation preparation paper approved	D Minus 45
(3)	First negotiating session held	D Minus 50
(4)	Negotiation objectives formalized	D Minus 70
(5)	First draft of strike plan due	D Minus 70
(6)	Wage and benefit survey completed	D Minus 80
(7)	Negotiation simulation training held	D Minus 85
(8)	First (internal) meeting of negotiating team	D Minus 90
(9)	First meeting of strike plan team	D Minus 100
(10)	Wage and benefit survey commences	D Minus 125

(11) Strike preparation team appointed   *D Minus 170*

(12) Negotiation team appointed   *D Minus 180*

(13) Steering or coordinating committee named   *D Minus 190*

(14) Business mission adopted   *D Minus 200*

The above backwards planning chart assumes that there is a well defined target date, as there usually is with a labor contract expiration. In commercial negotiations, the target date may be self-set, or circumstances may not allow for as wide a time spread as reflected in the backwards plan shown above. The purpose of the illustration is not to show any invariable time line or check list of items, but rather to demonstrate how the backwards planning concept works.

Backwards planning is a device of great usefulness. It is often difficult to determine how much time the various aspects of a negotiation may require for planning and implementation. A good backwards plan should allow sufficient time for each element to be done thoroughly and to sift out any mistakes. Having time targets will also facilitate each negotiation related function in meeting its requirements for input and information by the necessary date.

✐ TIP

Think of a negotiation process as analogous to the assembly of a complex piece of machinery, such as a computer. The various parts needed must be on hand at just the right point in time, without delay. For your parts manufacturers to be able to perform, they need to know the latest date by which they must produce and deliver the parts. In the case of negotiations, what is needed is generally information. That information cannot be prepared too far in advance or it will be obsolete. The data cannot be provided too late, because if it is late it may no longer be of use or a mistake may already have been made. A backwards planning chart is a tool that allows the process to flow smoothly and on time.

✐ TIP

Look at prior comparable negotiations to determine how much time they required in each phase. Then, consider any factors that would make the current negotiation different from the previous one. If there is no prior comparable negotiation to use as a benchmark, err on the side of caution by allowing more time than you conservatively anticipate is likely to be required. It is far easier to shorten a schedule that is too long than it is to try to cram things into a tight schedule that doesn't allow sufficient time.

THE TEAM AS A TRAINING VEHICLE

"Knowledge exists to be imparted." [Ralph Waldo Emerson] Negotiation teams are very useful training vehicles. The best way to acquire competent negotiation spokespersons with good negotiating skills for the future is to grow them within your own business culture in the laboratory of current negotiations. For this reason, people such as purchasing managers, international union representatives, and labor relations managers who lead negotiations should consider taking more junior people with them in all stages of the bargaining process. When possible, these individuals should be exposed not only to one negotiation, but to many, and in a variety of contexts.

People do not all learn in the same way. Some individuals, particularly those exposed to ineffective negotiating the first time they witness the process, may attend several negotiations and emerge with poor skills or skills that must be "unlearned" in order to do well. Don't take experience in prior negotiations at face value. Some people may have been through several negotiations but have really experienced only "one negotiation repeated many times." Good negotiators are likely to have experience in a wide range of situations involving complex and varied problems.

A negotiation spokesperson who is working with a team should have the express duty to train other team members. This may be accomplished by giving inexperienced team members selected assignments requiring presentations and speeches at the table. However, inexperienced people should be limited to issues on which, if mistakes are made, the consequences will be small and easily correctible. Whenever possible, junior members of the negotiating team should be permitted to observe every aspect of the negotiation. When time permits the spokesperson should be explaining to the inexperienced people exactly what is happening, why it is happening, and what to expect.

Apart from the on-the-job training that takes place by participation in an actual negotiation, the next best way to learn negotiation skills is through negotiation simulation training. Simulation training provides both new and experienced negotiators with the opportunity to learn and hone their skills in a close analog of the real world, but in a context in which mistakes are useful for learning and do not have practical consequences. A complete description of simulation training is provided in Chapter 7.

Clark Kent graduated from the M.B.A. program at Cornell last May and has been hired as a marketer by Krypton Industries. Krypton is a young company seeking to open space exploration through the private sector. Krypton has been in frequent negotiations with NASA over access to certain government technologies. Krypton's marketing director, Cap Marvel, invites young Kent to become a junior member of Krypton's negotiating team. Kent takes part in negotiation simulation training. Kent is permitted to accompany Marvel throughout the process, even being permitted to quietly sit in on a side bar meeting between Marvel and NASA negotiator Lois Lane. During a meeting of the two teams, Kent is permitted to make a presentation on access to certain minor technology items. Marvel evaluates Kent's performance and determines that Kent should be considered for a full team member's spot on the next negotiation team formed, depending on Kent's performance at the next negotiation simulation exercise. After three or four such experiences, Kent turns out to have considerable negotiating talent. As the company expands, it may look at Kent for future chief spokesperson roles, because the company now knows it can trust Kent at the table.

⚡ TRAP

An organization that sends a team made up entirely of inexperienced bargainers to a negotiation must expect some serious and possibly costly errors to be committed. When no one in-house has been trained as a negotiator, this trap may be avoided by either hiring an outside consultant, or attorney, who has solid negotiating skills to lead the team, or by putting the entire team through negotiation simulation training. When difficult and complex negotiations of any kind are involved, there is no substitute for experience and training.

THE TEAM AS CONTROLLER OF THE TIMING OF DISCRETIONARY EVENTS

"You win battles by knowing the enemy's timing, and using a timing which the enemy does not expect." [Miyamoto Musashi] In the course of a negotiation, each side may have control of certain events it has the ability to trigger in order to try to influence negotiations. The question may be just when to make things happen. Controllable events may include such items as: announcing the opening or closing of a facility; announcing a new product or discontinuing an old one; changes in personnel; price changes; press releases on foreign competition or other matters; or, opening negotiations with others (in commercial negotiations).

Some events will always be beyond your control or the control of your organization. For example, in the middle of a negotiation, the governor or president may propose legislation (or it may be enacted) which will change the negotiation context. Not all the events that are controlled by an organization will be within the reach of your negotiating team. For example, a union negotiating team may be impacted by the decision of the International Union to continue, or end, a long standing strike at a competitor to the employer. For these events, the negotiators must be able to be flexible and to adapt.

When the organization has discretion over the timing of events and is willing to listen to the input of the negotiators or grant them timing authority, control of discretionary events may have a powerful impact on the course of a negotiation. This is not to suggest that the organization will make the underlying timing decision solely in reference to negotiation factors, but rather that it may be willing to bend a bit on timing.

Dynamo Power, an electric generation (but not distribution) company, now finds itself in the world of deregulated energy prices. Dynamo is one of the largest energy generating companies in the northeastern part of the United States. Dynamo is negotiating with Cayuga Electric, which distributes (but does not generate) electric power in the region, to sell power to Cayuga. Assume that current generation capacity in relation to demand is approximately balanced. Dynamo Power needs to take Ontario IV, one of its large nuclear power generation plants off-line for maintenance sometime in the next six months. Operations managers are relatively indifferent to when this down time is scheduled during this six month period. Because of the potential size and value of the contract with Cayuga, Dynamo's negotiators are given control over the timing of the Ontario IV maintenance shutdown. They judge that Cayuga is now fairly deeply committed to resolving a deal with Dynamo. They then order the Ontario IV maintenance shutdown to be announced. The impact is that the supply of available power is decreased. This facilitates Dynamo's negotiators' position in holding out for a higher price. (This example assumes that out-of-region power, although available, would be more expensive).

Large Widget Corporation is negotiating with the World Wide Widget Workers Union for a successor labor contract for its Kramerston plant, which manufactures only a medium size widget line. Assume that small, medium, and large widgets each constitute a distinct product line. Because operation of the Kramerston plant under current labor conditions is not profitable for Large Widget, it opens secret negotiations with Small Widget Company to sell it the entire medium size widget line. Small Widget Company wants to add this medium size product line to its existing small widget business. Assume that labor rates make up fully three-quarters of the cost of producing widgets. With a lower paid work force and excess capacity at its existing factory, Small Widget has no interest in acquiring the Kramerston plant. They would manufacture the transferred medium size product line at their existing factory. Large Widget Corporation would prefer to retain its medium size line and operate the Kramerston plant, but has determined that to do so it must considerably lower its labor costs. Large Widget assigns control over the announcement of the existence of negotiations with Small Widget to its labor contract negotiation team. Finding the union very resistant to its proposals for cost lowering work rule changes, the Large Widget Corporation negotiation team decides the time is ripe to publicly release the fact that there are product line transfer negotiations in progress between the two widget companies. Small Widget then announces that it is not bargaining for the acquisition of the Kramerston plant. Realizing that there will be no product to manufacture at Kramerston if the product transfer goes through, the union feels that it is under enormous pressure. They become more amenable to making changes in the work rules. When the union makes sufficient concessions to reduce Large Widget Corporation's labor costs at Kramerston to an acceptable level, a contract is

> *reached and ratified by the union membership. Large Widget Corporation then breaks off its product line transfer negotiations with Small Widget Company. Control of the timing of the announcement has increased the bargaining power of Large Widget Corporation's negotiation team. Large Widget was careful throughout the negotiations to avoid any threat of plant closure, which is an unfair labor practice.*

The timing of events may also be very important on a tactical level. Keep in mind that negotiations often involve the development of pressure on the other side. Remember that negotiations involve three key elements: power, time, and information. Pressure is an element of power. The timing of the release of information is sometime convertible into bargaining power.

✐ TIP

Pay real attention to the pace and timing at which you trigger any events within your control that will place pressure the other side. Events of this type are not common. If you release them all at one time, there will be nothing left to do should a later, more critical, point develop. On the other hand, if you have a number of events that will create pressure, don't dole them out a little bit at a time. Slow escalation can lose much of its effect. You will have to balance these concerns in determining timing.

Having reached this point, planning and preparation are essentially over. You are now ready to get into the "nitty-gritty" of negotiations. That process starts with setting up your first negotiation meetings, the topic of the next chapter.

CHAPTER 10

NEGOTIATION PRELIMINARIES— THE FIRST BATTLES

"A journey of a thousand miles begins with a single step." [Confucius] When you've finished your negotiation planning and reached this stage, you will be just about ready to begin the actual journey through the negotiation game. You will be prepared to step out onto the "negotiations tennis court" and play for game, set, and match. Just one last set of tasks remains. You need to check out the game environment and see how it helps or hurts you. In sports, you may check out the playing field. Military forces seek the high ground. In negotiations, you will also want to scout out tactical advantages.

The simplest personal negotiations may occur on the spot. More complex ones and most business negotiations go through a number of preliminaries that must be resolved, such as where the negotiation meetings will take place, the shape of the table, who will pay for the facilities being used, negotiation logistics, and establishing a meeting schedule. Complex personal negotiations, such as real estate transactions, may also be influenced by where you negotiate.

Do these preliminaries really matter? Sometimes they have little or no substantive impact on the outcome of a negotiation, but occasionally they have a disproportionate importance. An experienced bargainer will often secure these preliminary advantages from a less experienced negotiator by default. In a close and difficult negotiation, seemingly small successes in winning the preliminary skirmishes may ultimately yield large dividends in the negotiation's later critical stages.

Why is the issue of negotiation venue important? Consider the example below.

In a labor contract negotiation being conducted against a contract expiration deadline, carrying serious consequences for each side, Edward Tudor is the International Representative for the Union and Jane Grey the Chief Spokesperson for the employer. The negotiation is being held at the "Top Dollar Luxury Hotel," selected by the employer, who has agreed to pay the entire cost of the meeting room. As Grey anticipated, the Union, with more modest resources than the employer, has declined to pay for a sleeping room for Tudor at this luxury hotel, despite the fact that in their latter stages, the negotiations have, as anticipated, been going virtually around the clock. The employer has provided Grey with a comfortable sleeping room at the hotel. In the last hours before contract expiration, at 2:00 A.M., only one issue remains, a cap on a cost of living formula. A very tired man, Tudor has dozed off on a hotel lobby couch. Grey, who is reasonably well rested, wakes Tudor and asks what cap level would bring a contract settlement. An exhausted, bleary eyed Tudor, without thinking, blurts out, "Half a buck, we would settle for a cap of fifty cents per hour." Grey, who has been authorized to accept a cap of seventy-five cents per hour now knows the contract will be settled, but Grey says to Tudor, "Ed, a half dollar cap is too high. I can't do that. But, since that would settle all the issues, I'll call the president to see if we can get authorization." A half hour later, without making the unnecessary phone call, Grey informs Tudor, "Ed, it wasn't easy, but we have a contract with the fifty cent cap." A week later, when Tudor has gotten some sleep, Tudor asks Grey, "Was there more? Could I have gotten more on the cap?" Grey laughs and says, "Ed, I won't answer that. If I said there was more you'd be disappointed you didn't get it and if I said that you got all there was, you wouldn't believe it." As the contract later unfolds, economic conditions result in the fifty cent cap being reached and prove that if the cap had been at seventy-five cents, the formula would have taken wages there. Tudor's tired, sleepy error of revealing his bottom line has resulted in the union represented employees losing many dollars in wages. This costly error was probably due almost entirely due to Grey's successful selec-

tion of an expensive hotel for the meetings and the union's failure to allocate sufficient resources to its negotiator.

SHAPE AND LOCATION OF THE NEGOTIATING TABLE

"Man should be master of his environment, not its slave. That is what freedom means." [Anthony Eden]. The immediate physical and mental environment of a negotiation is manifested in, of all things, the shape and location of the bargaining table. In a complex negotiation, this is one of the first issues that must be resolved. Each side is seeking home court advantage. But, more fundamentally, each side is trying to determine and establish relative psychological dominance. The way you handle this preliminary issue will give an early indication of your bargaining style and of whether you tend to be forceful or intimidated. When you are negotiating over matters in the political arena, table shape and location may be a critical preliminary matter in setting a negotiation tone. During the Korean War, there were talks on where and whether to continue to talk. Even today, the demilitarized zone between the two Koreas features a table literally straddling the cease fire line that marks the post-truce border between South and North Korea, so that each side is able to remain on "home ground" while talking. The shape of the table was also an important preliminary issue in the Paris peace talks regarding the Vietnam War.

Why is the shape and location of the table so important? To illustrate how critical this issue may be, Henry Kissinger, Secretary of State during the Nixon Administration, was involved in resolving a deadlock that delayed the start of formal negotiations to settle the Vietnam war by four months. This initial dispute was about the shape of the negotiating table and how to designate the negotiating parties. Dr. Kissinger recognized the issue as a meaningful one, carrying important symbolic significance for our South Vietnamese allies. As the government of South Vietnam considered itself to be the legitimate government, they were not prepared to allow the negotiating table setup to appear to provide equal status to Hanoi's surrogate in the South, the National Liberation Front. Over a period of about ninety days, the South resisted the North's proposal for a table with four sides, arranged so that the North, the National Liberation Front, the South, and the United States were each accorded equal status. This dispute over the parties and the shape of the table reflected the North Vietnamese government's attempt to use negotiation preliminary issues to establish the National

Liberation Front as an alternative government for the South. The issue moved toward resolution when the Soviet Union offered a compromise solution on behalf of the North Vietnamese. An agreement then quickly emerged. The solution resolving the shape and parties issue was to utilize a circular table. No nameplates, no flags, and no markings were to be used. This arrangement served to create a mutually acceptable ambiguity. The Communist side was left free to describe the table as having four sides, while the United States and Vietnam were able to characterize the table and the negotiations as bilateral.

While in most negotiations it will be clear that there are two sides, this preliminary dispute over the identification of parties was critical and nearly derailed negotiations before they started. In negotiations to settle legal cases, such as civil rights sexual harassment claims, when a supervisor-defendant is sued in both a personal and a corporate role, plaintiff's counsel may have to engage in a three way negotiation, as the defendant-supervisor's and the defendant-employer's interests may differ, or may be approached differently. Commercial negotiations sometimes involve either multiple parties at the same table or simultaneous multiple negotiations with more than one potential partner. Obviously, these negotiations may become extremely complex and magnify the negotiation problems discussed here in the context of simpler two party negotiations. In some instances, an individual who is negotiating may move back and forth between more than one bargaining table.

Terrible Toys holds the patents on the Pretty Poison game. The game is a very hot seller in the marketplace and the major stores all want to buy as many of the games as possible. Terrible is negotiating a sales contract with three large potential buyers, Toys Are We, Aimpoint, and Stonemart. Terrible's chief spokesperson in each of the three negotiations is Grandon Master. Master moves back and forth between the three bargaining tables, using Terrible's hold on the supply of the faddish toy to drive the best possible bargain. Meanwhile, the three stores, aware that the multiple negotiations are in progress, are negotiating with each other about possible sales from the successful company to the others at, of course, a substantial markup. They discuss the possibility of pooling their bid for the games to eliminate Terrible's supply advantage and then sharing the supply obtained. A negotiation of this sort may become incredibly complex.

Should you bargain at a rectangular table? Rectangular shaped tables are inherently adversarial as they formalize a distribution of people into two sides. Round tables promote working together, but may provide quarters that are too close for taking notes and lull unwary negotiators into forgetting that the other side has its own aims. If more than two parties are negotiating together at the same time, some other variant such as a U shaped table may be needed. In many commercial negotiations between relative equals, rectangular tables will be most appropriate and may even be assumed without discussion. They are the norm in labor contract negotiations. However, in personal negotiations and in the type of informal office negotiations that go on all the time between co-workers, it is often best to get out from behind a desk or a dividing table and talk in side chairs or at a round table.

✐ TIP

If only two to four people are negotiating a commercial arrangement or a sales agreement, consider what impression you want to project. If informality and a sense of cooperation is desired, get out from behind a rectangular table or a desk and sit at a round table. This table should be small enough to promote friendly relations, yet large enough to permit you to look at your notes and take notes without having them observed by the other party.

Henry and Gerry are respectively the labor relations and organizational development directors for a large organization. Henry's office features a desk at which he sits when he meets with union officers. Gerry, who needs to build strong interpersonal relationships with people and who is normally dealing with non-adversarial matters, fosters cooperation by putting a round table in his office and coming out from behind his desk to meet with people at his round table. Henry, who often deals with confrontational people, wishes to keep a greater sense of formality, power, and distance, and offers no such option. When he meets informally with people, he uses a round table, but one that is located away from his office.

The type of table you may wish to use should be tied to the atmosphere you prefer. Determining where the parties will meet will tend to give you control over the shape of the table and the atmosphere. This also applies to many smaller negotiation and day to day relationship meetings in the work place.

Where should you negotiate? If you are involved in an internal negotiation within an organization, the answer is likely to be very clear if one of the participants has a much higher position in the hierarchy than the others. That individual may demand that the meetings be held on home turf. Rank and setting tend to intimidate and often serve to foster the ranking person's agenda. Large organizations frequently have conference rooms available which are more neutral meeting places than one of the participant's office. More typically, negotiations are between arm's length parties or different, but co-equal, segments of an organization.

In the National Football League, teams who have already made the playoffs strive to win additional regular season games to gain "home field advantage." In the movie, "The American President," Michael Douglas, playing the role of President, remarks that the White House is the single greatest home court advantage in the world. Playing on home turf not only provides comfort and familiarity, but it makes logistics for support services easier, and it tends to make the other side more uncomfortable and their work more difficult, which may lead to their making critical errors.

🖉 TIP

If you cannot lure the other party onto your home turf, always try to avoid negotiating on the other party's ground. If your bargaining power permits, insist on a neutral location such as a hotel meeting room, conference room at the public library or a government office, or some similar location which is off either party's premises. Try to select a location easily accessible and close to you and which is far away from, and difficult to access, for the other party. If you are representing management in a labor negotiation, avoid meeting at a union hall, even of a different union. You should try to win the battle of location by default. One way to do this is to suggest that you or your side handle the logistics of setting up a location, before the other side makes the same suggestion. If the other side cedes this to you (and inexperienced or lazy negotiators may well do so), quietly accept this advantage for your side and graciously facilitate the necessary arrangements.

John, a newly admitted attorney, representing an employee-plaintiff who has a potential sexual harassment claim, senses that settlement with the defendant-company may be possible. He asks Martha, the Company's human resources manager, for a meeting, but fails to suggest it be held at his office. Martha agrees to meet with him and finesses the location issue by offering him three possible meeting times, but all at her office. John accepts one of them. Arriving at the corporate offices of the defendant, Multimega Giant Enterprises, John is somewhat intimidated by the plush surroundings. Martha deliberately keeps John waiting while a group of people shuffle in and out of her office with papers. When they finally meet, in her corner office, she is in a leather high back executive chair behind a massive desk. While she is cordial, she makes clear that if the corporation thinks it is right, whatever resources the corporation needs to fight the case will be made available. John, a bit intimidated by his luxurious surroundings and the trappings of corporate power, agrees to a settlement well below what Martha was empowered to offer. A half hour after the meeting, the Vice President who really owns her corner office returns from a meeting and Martha moves back to her own considerably smaller one in a less opulent office complex. Had the meeting been held at John's office or at a neutral site, John might have negotiated a better deal for his client.

WHO PAYS FOR NEGOTIATION FACILITIES AND TIME?

"Bargain like a gypsy, but pay like a gentleman." [Hungarian Proverb] In personal and commercial negotiations, it would be extremely rare to find a case in which you are expected to pay the other side's representatives for their time. In many neutral ground negotiations, one side will offer to, or agree to, pay any charges for the meeting space (but not usually the other side's caucus rooms, if any). The cost and image of these facilities should be chosen to parallel the impression that you want to give.

The Galactic Widget Corporation is planning to build a new man-ufacturing facility in an area that badly needs more jobs. Officials of Galactic Widget are holding a series of meetings with county and local officials to discuss possible tax abatements should the company build within their respective jurisdictions. Spencer, the corporation's new government affairs manager, volunteers to pay for a meeting room at a hotel in the state's capital city. When city and county officials arrive at the meeting spot, the ultra-luxurious Swank Inn, and are seated in the plush seats in its executive con-ference room, they look around at the deep carpeting and beau-tiful appointments and become far less inclined to give the corpo-ration the large tax breaks it is seeking. "This corporation has too much money and they are just exploiting us," the county manag-er says to the local mayor. Spencer has made a huge mistake. He should have chosen a more modest location, one designed to con-vey the image of a cost conscious company worthy of public sup-port. In the end, the government officials needing jobs for their constituents may still give the demanded abatements, but the opulent atmosphere of the meeting site may lend itself to a feel-ing on their part that they have been used.

✐ TIP

Select a meeting location that is in keeping with the specific image which you wish to project. If you are claiming poverty, select a low cost modestly appointed location. If you are seek-ing to impress the other side with your organization's power and wealth, select an upscale location.

In labor-management negotiations, unions often demand that employers pay for the time of union representatives spent at the table and some businesses do pay for this time. Unions will certainly request that those employees who will be negotiating with the employer be excused from work to attend negotiations sessions or to prepare for these meetings. An additional issue is whether employer paid negotia-tion time should be counted for purposes of determining when over-time premiums apply. The law does not require this time to be consid-ered in overtime eligibility.

An employer is under no legal obligation to conduct collective bargaining negotiations on company time or even during normal working hours. Its only obligation is to meet at "reasonable times and places" to negotiate in good faith about wages, hours, and conditions of employment. Even when the employer agrees to meet during the normal working day, it is under no legal obligation to pay those employees sitting at the table as union representatives for their lost wages from being away from their jobs. Of course, the expiring labor contract itself may contain terms regarding release time and payment. Some unions pay their representatives themselves out of union funds and do not request that the employer pay for their negotiators' time.

What are the pros and cons of an employer releasing and paying union represented employees to sit at the bargaining table for the union? Employees who are released during regular hours are likely to be more attentive and better able to concentrate on negotiations. On the other hand, depending on the nature of the relationship and bargaining power, an employer may prefer that union bargaining team members negotiate after hours on their own time so they are tired, have less time for preparation, and are less desirous of spending too many hours at the table.

The question of the employer paying these employees for representing the union creates other problems. An employer may not want to subsidize those against whom the employer is negotiating and who do not always have the best institutional interests of the employer at heart. It may well believe, as some unions also do, that payment for negotiating time on behalf of the union is properly a union function, with payment to come from the union treasury. On the other hand, the issue is often contentious and some employers will simply pay the money to avoid the problem.

🖝 TRAP

Releasing and paying union representatives for negotiating time may elongate time spent at the table, particularly if the time commitment to be paid is open ended. Under most circumstances, extended time at the table is not necessary. On the other hand, when there are complex issues and union cooperation is essential, exceptions may well be made.

⚡ TIP

An employer agreeing to paying for union time at the table should cap the amount of time to be paid in line with the employer's objectives as to the amount of time deemed necessary for negotiations. The employer should also do so only on an ad hoc basis and not as a permanent contract provision. This may be done by stating that this year's payment "is on a non-precedent basis only."

⚡ TRICK

Union representatives and counsel should always ask the employer to both release desired employees for negotiating and to pay them, without a time cap. Given the irritant value of this demand, the relatively small amount of money involved, the desire to get started "on a good footing," and the fact that "so many employers do it," many employers will simply give in on the point. If possible, you should secure contract language that will cover release and payment of union negotiators employed by the company for the next and all subsequent negotiations.

NEGOTIATION LOGISTICS

"Logistics is the ball and chain of armoured warfare." [Guderian] Logistics refers to the provision of supplies and support services, without which an enterprise cannot be advanced. The selection of a base and considerations of supply lines are logistical concerns that are applicable to negotiations. The character of any negotiation should be taken into account when deciding when and where to negotiate. Special circumstances may cause logistical nightmares and these nightmares, in turn, may justify abandoning some of the conventional negotiation practices, such as negotiating at a neutral site.

Galactic Widget Company is in merger talks with Cosmic Widgets. Both corporations have appointed committees to meet and negotiate on various aspects of the merger, such as environmental concerns, pension and human resources matters, and technology. The environmental negotiating committees have agreed to meet at a "neutral site," halfway between their respective corporate headquarters in the States of East Carolina and West Dakota. Because of the use of a "neutral site," six corporate level managers fly to the neutral site for each meeting. Once there, they discover that they need literally thousands of documents which are stored back at their respective corporate headquarters. They consider shipping all that paper to the neutral hotel and securing sufficient space to store it all, plus bringing in support staff to handle the documents. At the end of the discussion, it is agreed that future meetings will alternate between the two corporate sites. In this instance, using a "neutral" site is a logistical nightmare.

In deciding how to proceed with a negotiation, there are a host of logistical factors to keep in mind. These factors may include travel considerations, the location of necessary documentation, adequate support staff, effective telecommunications, computer and technical support, security services, and all of the other resources needed for your negotiation.

XYZ Cellular and ABC Wireless Services mutually agreed to negotiate concerning a large sales contract. They retained several rooms at a neutral site hotel. Only after the negotiators arrived did they discover that the hotel was not equipped for in-room computer use and that it was located in a "dead spot" for cell phones, on which both sides preferred to rely for their communications. Delays caused by finding another site led to the breakdown of negotiations. The persons selecting the hotel are now hoping that a roaring economy means that they will not be left unemployed for too long. In short, they may well lose their jobs over what seemed like a relatively minor decision at the time, the hotel site.

SCHEDULING NEGOTIATIONS

"In spells and labors a certain time is always set, and I might be at sea when mine expires." [James Thurber] Time, power, and information are the three key factors in negotiating. Scheduling is an aspect of the time element. An advantage may be gained by controlling the schedule as schedulers may have a great deal of power. In professional football, which opponents a team is scheduled to play, when the week with no game to play is slotted, and the order in which difficult opponents are placed are all factors that bear on a team's ultimate success. Whenever possible, you will want to exercise as much dominance as possible in setting a negotiations schedule.

Scheduling negotiations requires a determination at the outset of how many meetings will be required overall and of the optimum time to be spent during each phase. Most negotiations have three phases: opening game, mid game, and end game. Experienced negotiators will have the experience background to make a reasonable estimate of how much time is likely to be required for the completion of a negotiation project. Budget too much time and the negotiations may bog down in details. Budget too little time and important issues may be left unresolved or left to the future through devices such as ambiguity or joint study committees. If there is no real time deadline, the optimum moment for resolution may slip away.

Vikki Chen-Rivera is a sports agent for a number of free agent major league baseball players. She is planning negotiations with the New Jersey Yankmets, which she intends to conclude before Spring training opens. Since she is relatively new to this business, she anticipates three meetings ought to be enough to settle her clients' contracts. She schedules these three meetings three days apart in the last week and a half before Spring training. By the time the second meeting begins, she realizes she needs more time between meetings and more meetings to allow her to move through a series of position changes, but the Yankmets refuse to schedule extra meetings. She has to race through her strategy and in the process shows unnecessary weakness, costing her clients a lot of money. She has erred on the side of insufficient meetings, a less desirable course than scheduling too many meetings.

Suppose the same facts are true, except that Ms. Chen-Rivera sets up twelve meetings. With so many meeting scheduled, her clients insist on attending them. They become overly involved in the picky details of their contracts. As a result of the constant wrangling in these talks, the Yankmets decide they would rather not deal with one of her clients and he ends up playing for Charley Brown's team instead. Ms. Chen-Rivera would usually be able to avoid the excess meetings with "schedule problems" or other excuses to cancel, but her clients' involvement makes this impossible.

☞ TIP

Plan fewer meetings at the outset of negotiations and increase the number of meetings during the middle and end phases, allowing more time between early meetings. Leave gaps in the schedule that can be filled with more meetings if they are required or considered beneficial by both sides. If too many meetings are planned, some may usually be cancelled, but unless adequate spacing is placed in the schedule, the parties may run out of time. Always have a firm commitment for the next meeting before getting into substantive discussions at the current meeting. Should things "blow up" and one party walk out, having already arranged another meeting date facilitates a graceful way to resume talks without a loss of face.

At this point, all the planning and preliminary work has been done. You are now ready to enter the "negotiation tennis court" and begin the actual process of face to face negotiating and of winning "game, set, and match." In the next chapter, we will look at a critical phase, opening negotiations. If you've followed the process to this point, you will appreciate how much work successful negotiations require before sitting down at the table with the other side for your first meeting. Successfully accomplishing the preliminary planning, completing simulation training, and committing the necessary resources will leave you feeling comfortable, prepared, and ready to play and win the negotiations game.

CHAPTER 11

THE OPENING GAME

"The beginning is the most important part of the work." [Plato] The time has come to start the negotiating game. You and your opponent are in the stadium. Our national anthem has been played. Now that you've completed any necessary planning; gotten approval for your mission, goals, objectives, and strategy; and resolved any negotiation preliminaries, at last you are ready to launch the face to face negotiating process.

Students in my bargaining simulation course at the New York State School of Industrial and Labor Relations at Cornell are expected to spend a disproportionate share of the available time on the opening phase. Why? The initial phase is a critical part of the overall negotiating process. In the early game, first impressions are made and the tone is set for the entire negotiation. Many of the "process values" that will come to govern the negotiation will be set at the initial few sessions. A good start is particularly important when the negotiations are the first between the sides. If you get off on the wrong foot on opening day, you may as well be trailing by twenty-eight points going into the last quarter of a National Football League game.

If, for some status related reason, you come to the negotiating table with institutional clout, you need to be sure that you retain the aura of that status. Few bargaining relationships are between individuals, peers, or organizations who arrive at the table with equally persuasive bargaining auras. Someone usually has high status.

Gigantic Motors is seeking to negotiate a contract with a supplier of high quality widgets. The number of widgets to be utilized is astronomical. The widget manufacturing industry is highly fragmented, with no company having more than a two percent share of the highly competitive market. World Wide Widgets is seeking to secure a contract with Gigantic Motors, under which World Wide Widget will supply only three percent of Gigantic Motors' needs, but which will double World Wide Widgets' gross sales. Given the disparity of size and resources, when the purchasing and sales agents of the two corporations sit down for their first negotiating session, there will be a tendency for Gigantic Motors' negotiators to take over the first meeting, to set the agenda, and to assume command. In doing this, they will be acting from the knowledge that they have, by far, the lion's share of bargaining power.

✐ TIP

Although you may have lower status or less bargaining power, do not simply concede control of the process by default. One method of getting around the tendency for the more powerful side to assume that it is in control is for you to immediately take the initiative by speaking at the outset of the meeting and making a comment that the agenda and ground rules must be mutually established.

In any form of negotiation, whether personal, commercial, or labor-management, there is a psychological tendency for people to respect the power and position of those high status individuals who may come to the bargaining table, such as the well reputed art dealer, a middle or upper level executive, or a plant manager. This is normal societal or work place deference and it is habitual human behavior. Corporals respect the power and authority of generals, while generals expect to take command. But, high status negotiators should not assume they will automatically receive this deference in every case or as a matter of course.

In labor-management negotiations, in which the law provides rank and file union negotiators with protected rights, there are countervailing incentives to deferential behavior. Rank and file union negotiators have several motives for being unusually aggressive. This unaccustomed behavior may be a bit shocking to their opponents, throwing them off stride. Aggressiveness may lead to success at intimidating the other side. An intimated opponent is more likely to allow concessions than a secure one. For people who generally are on the short end of day to day power relationships, aggressiveness during a period of negotiations may bring them a certain psychological pleasure, derived from forcing those who are normally are far more powerful to have to sit and listen.

It may be helpful for you to think of the early game in negotiations as analogous to the early stages of a chess match. In either contest, the process oriented objective is to start out well so that you may quickly gain control over the squares that command the center of the board. In military terms, if you remain passive during opening negotiations, you lose that most valuable commodity, the initiative. If you fall behind in the opening game, playing catch-up in the mid and end game will be an uphill battle. You will then be playing according to your opponent's preferred game plan, not your own. Inevitably, this will cost you advantage and impair your ability to achieve at least a portion of your objectives.

CONTROLLING THE AGENDA

"Never let the other fellow set the agenda." [James Baker] Why is it important to maintain control over the negotiation agenda? Power over the agenda tends to equate to control over the issues on which the bulk of the negotiating time will be consumed. When you control the agenda, you have an advantage that is equivalent to that enjoyed by a football team which establishes a high time of possession, keeping the other side's offense off the field. **Often, arriving at an agenda is the first real test of who will exercise table dominance. If the other side lets you dominate and control the agenda, you have stolen a march toward achieving your goals.**

The Board of Education of the Aaron Burr-Alexander Hamilton Unified School District is about to make a potentially controversial decision to raise school taxes—this process is a form of negotiating with the public. The ultimate size of the proposed increase has been previously and privately negotiated among the various school board members. The public meeting on the budget is set to begin at 8:00 P.M. At that hour, a large crowd is in the auditorium.

> *Despite pleas from the audience to move the tax discussion to an early hour, the Board uses its control of the agenda to keep a large number of boring and lengthy items at the head of the agenda. The School Board President makes sure the meeting drags on until 11:30 P.M., several times saying there is a need to move on, but making sure that discussion on minor items is prolonged, before the school tax item is reached. By then, as the Board planned, many tax increase opponents who have babysitters and jobs to go to the next day have left. Insider tax increase supporters, told how the agenda game will play out, skip the early part of the meeting and first show up at about 11:00 P.M. The next day, the Burr-Hamilton Gazette reports that sentiment for and against the budget, as expressed at last night's meeting, was largely in favor of the tax increase and that the Board voted accordingly.*

If you find yourself in a buyer-seller negotiation, it is often the buyer who has advantages in setting the agenda, provided, as is usually the case, the buyer is able to shop for the goods or services which are freely available elsewhere. It is usually the seller who is trying to adapt both the sales pitch and, if possible, the product, or its presentation, so that the buyer will be satisfied. In automobile negotiations, unless they are purchasing the rare automobiles that sell at a premium, most car buyers forget that the seller probably needs them more than they need to buy from that particular dealership.

Should you try to take complete control over the agenda and to hog all the time? This is an unwise strategy. Each party at a negotiation table expects to have its time and turn to place its proposals on the table and to have them discussed. As Ecclesiastes teaches, "To everything there is a season and a time to every purpose under heaven. . . a time to keep silence and a time to speak." If you take complete control of the agenda, assuming the other side allows it, expect a high probability of simmering discontent and an eventual outburst that may come at the worst possible time, in the middle or near the end of the negotiations.

🔥 T I P

If you are able to dominate the agenda, target for around two-thirds of the discussion time. If you take, or claim, more than about two-thirds to three-quarters of the time to discuss your issues, you greatly increase the probability that the other side will react negatively and cause a crisis.

ᘓ TIP

Begin discussions with the introduction of your team and focus first on ground rules. Ground rules should include who will speak for each side, who will make authoritative commitments, how the parties will contact each other, and a re-statement of the decisions made in the preliminary pre-negotiation phase. Always be sure to secure agreement on the schedule for the next meeting at the beginning of the current meeting, in case substantive discussions should result in a walkout or other problems should arise which might interfere with scheduling another meeting.

ᘓ TRICK

Start substantive discussions with an easy and uncontroversial issue as the first item on the agenda. Try to get a feel for the other side's negotiating style. If you select a controversial or difficult issue as the first one for discussion, unnecessary early discord may later complicate progress.

ᘓ TRAP

If the other side makes you the gift of an agenda, be wary. Examine the proposed agenda for balance of time, placement of issues (so that your issues don't get buried at the end of sessions or delayed until late in the negotiations), and be sure to think about what the other side has omitted from their proposed agenda. It is usually better to be ready with your own proposed agenda. **As a general negotiation rule, strive to get the other guy to negotiate from your agenda, your documents, and on your schedule.**

In summary, don't overlook the importance of controlling the agenda. The key to winning many a battle is to gain, then keep, the initiative. The party that controls the agenda enjoys the initiative. Great generals like Robert E. Lee, George S. Patton, and Erwin Rommel all practiced exploiting the initiative. Doing so afforded them great success. In tennis, holding the serve gives advantage. So, too, in the negotiations game. If you do find that you have been disadvantaged by an agreed upon agenda, remember that the agenda is not a substantive agreement. You may press for agenda changes, particularly if time and developments since the agenda agreement was reached now make it less applicable.

SETTING THE TONE—OPENING STATEMENTS AND POSITIONS

"One often contradicts an opinion when what is uncongenial is really the tone in which it was conveyed." [Friedrich Nietzsche] Your opening statement is the chance to set the tone for the negotiations or, at the least, the tone for your own side's approach to negotiations, while signaling your basic themes in a controlled, polished way. Even when your message contains unwelcome news for the other side, be sure your statement is delivered in polite tones, free of personal attacks. In individual negotiations, such as with an auto sales representative or with the buyer or seller of a house, there is no formal "opening statement," but what you initially tell the sales representative or other person about your goals and objectives will serve much the same purpose. For example, you might open by saying, "I'm only looking today," or, "Price is my main concern." To avoid awkwardness and overly informative opening statements, real estate agents often prefer to have a seller out of the house before it is shown to a prospective buyer. When you are a prospective buyer, it is generally good advice to remain non-committal and not to say anything enthusiastic about the house.

In large scale commercial and labor negotiations, or in complex negotiations between attorneys, an opening statement gives the initial clues or "signals" to the other side about not only where you plan to go, but also the way in which you intend to get there. If the other side's opening signals substantively or procedurally parallel your own, there is a much greater likelihood that negotiations will go smoothly.

Supersecurity Services and the International Union of Security Workers, Local 1, are opening negotiations for a successor labor agreement. In her opening speech, the spokesperson for Supersecurity sets the scene for the soon to be presented company proposals by stressing that the company is facing a raft of new competitors and is having to adapt rapidly to changing technolo-

gies. She ties this to a warning that the company will be seeking work rule changes to allow greater flexibility and speed of change. She points out that the Company is experiencing well above average health care insurance costs. Knowing that the history of negotiations between the parties has involved a lot of shouting and loud behavior at the table, she also states that the company insists that things will be different this year. "When it is your turn to speak, we will listen to you with respect and have no problem with your stating your positions strongly," she says, "but we will not tolerate personal abuse of any member of this team and when it is our turn to speak, we know that you will treat us with similar courtesy." Without getting specific about the health care program, she finishes with "Our expenses for health care are too high both absolutely and in relation to our competitors. We want to work out something with you to address this problem." This speech lets the other side know a bit about the general priorities and methods the employer is seeking to pursue.

Think of the opening statement as a kind of keynote address, similar to those given at the outset of the quadrennial presidential nominating conventions. Not everything mentioned in an opening speech will be attainable, nor should the speech put forth any details that will engender premature controversy. The opening statement should be brought to the meeting in written format, to avoid off the cuff errors, and should be delivered by the spokesperson using a form of delivery practiced beforehand and critiqued by members of the spokesperson's team.

Which side gives the first opening speech may be the subject of some debate. If you give your speech first, the other side may adapt its speech to yours "on the fly." As a result, you will not know what the other side's "pure or pristine" statement would have contained. On the other hand, going first sets a tone and perhaps a pattern, possibly for the entire negotiation. No hard and fast rule exists. Each situation should be evaluated beforehand and a decision made as to whether you want to be the first to open.

🔥 TIP

Set high but reasonable expectations for the other side.
Teachers and parents have known for years that if they set high, but achievable, expectations that make a child reach a bit, they will often be attained, but if they set low expectations

they will get only low level results. The same is true in negotiations, particularly when what is being addressed is the other side's conduct at the negotiating table. This is probable in labor negotiations and in the settlement of litigation, but less so in general commercial bargaining, which tends to be more amicable. Your setting expectations for the other side may even be done in the dreaded auto purchase mode. For example, a sales representative may be informed, "If you try to pressure me to buy immediately, I will walk out and you *will* lose this sale." If the salesperson is well trained and trying to adapt the sales pitch to the customer, this will register. If it doesn't, at the first sign, remind the sales representative of your message. If it happens a second time, leave.

☞ TIP

Listen very carefully to an opening statement if one is made, both for what is included and what is omitted. An opening statement cannot cover every point or issue, so what a side leaves out in relation to its own agenda is likely to be less important than its failure to address the other side's issues. When the opening statement addresses your side's issues (preemptively), listen for a tone of acceptance or rejection. If the other team is led by a professional negotiator, listen for subtle clues to the other side's position. Nuances of words are particularly important in "set piece" opening statements, as they are presumably very carefully drafted.

☞ TRAP

An opening statement must not be too inclusive. If the statement is very lengthy and provides a lot of detail on issues, it may give away information or signal a willingness to compromise too-early. For example an attorney or tax accountant at an audit should not signal that the client is ready to make concessions. A detailed statement also will be heard primarily for its adversarial points and will tend to poison the atmosphere. Keep the opening statement strategic on matters of substance, although as to behavior, ground rules, meeting arrangements, and procedures at the table, more detailed tactical considerations are appropriate. The purpose of an opening statement is to provide general themes, not to create specific points of resistance to detailed and controversial proposals.

EXCHANGING PROPOSALS

"Ants are so much like human beings as to be an embarrassment. They farm fungi, raise aphids as livestock, launch armies into war, use chemical sprays to alarm and confuse enemies, capture slaves, engage in child labor, exchange information ceaselessly." [Lewis Thomas] One of the first serious exchanges of information in a human negotiation comes when you reveal your initial proposals to the other side and obtain their proposals. Do you want the first or last word on proposals? With the ground rules set and opening speeches, if any, delivered, the parties should be ready to get to work. The next step may be an exchange of proposals (in the labor negotiations game the union's proposals are often labeled as demands), or of offers and counteroffers (as in a house or auto purchase). Since bargaining should not be retrogressive (adding new proposals or demands as negotiations progress), a side's initial proposals should be all inclusive, although counter offers and conditional offers issued later may provide a legally valid back door for adding new things. Keep in mind that proposals at the initial level need not be highly specific, nor must they be accompanied by specific language for carrying them out, if they are accepted.

> *Fresh Water Taffy Company and the Sweet Tooth Workers International Union are engaged in negotiations. A specific union demand reads, "Amend Article VI, Section 3, Holidays, by adding Michael Jordan's birthday." More general union demands read, "Reduce employee health care contribution premium," and "Substantial wage increase." On the management side, they have chosen to use only general proposals. One reads, "Revise and simplify the job classification structure." By being fuzzy, management has avoided creating the instant adversarial reaction that its real aim, "reduce the number of classifications from 23 to 5," would probably have engendered.*

Nothing inherently requires a simultaneous exchange of proposals. If you gain access to the other side's proposals before you turn over your own proposals to them, you may craft preemptive ones. These may be offered in trade either for a blunting of the other side's aims or for a continuance of the status quo. Because professional negotiators are generally aware of this advantage, they may ask for your side's proposals first, then take a break, or wait until the next session, to present their own, sometimes modified, proposals. Think of knowing the other side's proposals first as akin to receiving advance (but lawful) information as to a stock.

Fat Free Lard and Slim Now are negotiating a commercial arrangement, under which Fat Free will supply pure beef lard to the Slim Now Corporation. Fat Free is represented by an experienced negotiator, while Slim Now's chief spokesperson has never negotiated before. When Fat Free asks for Slim Now's proposals (without offering their own), Slim Now's negotiator at first balks. "I'd like your proposals first," he says. Fat Free's experienced spokesperson responds, "Look, let's not play kid's games about who goes first. Let us see what you are seeking." Slim Now's spokesperson immediately gives way. One of Slim Now's proposals is that Fat Free permit Slim Now to inspect Fat Free's premises, for health reasons, from time to time. Fat Free had not anticipated that proposal. Now armed with the knowledge of its existence, when Fat Free later brings in its own proposals, one of them is, "Fat Free to retain complete quality control responsibility for its product, with no inspections."

✒ TIP

Try to get the other side to give you their proposals first. An amateur opponent may well make this mistake. If this works, take a caucus and examine the other side's proposals. There may be areas where your side will gain by erecting preemptive proposals to counter the other side's interests, on subjects which you had not planned to negotiate. There is no advantage in providing your proposals to the other side first, so if you cannot get them to give you their written proposals first, insist on a simultaneous mutual exchange of documents.

PROBLEM SOLVING VERSUS POSITIONAL BARGAINING

"If the only tool you have is a hammer, you tend to see every problem as a nail." [Abraham Maslow] Positional bargaining is the conventional negotiating technique. A more modern means of bargaining is problem solving, sometimes referred to as interest bargaining, productivity bargaining, or mutual gains bargaining. In positional bargaining one side says, "We hold our position that the price of the widgets is to be $230 each," while the other side responds, "We modify our position that we will pay $180 per widget to $190 per widget." After a positional review, the sides break off and go back and evaluate what the other side did, to assess relative bargaining power, and to determine which positions they must change. In the example given, in the next round, the parties may move their positions so as to converge toward a final agreed price somewhere in the $200-$210 range.

The use of problem solving bargaining techniques has become more common in recent years. In problem solving, the parties may put aside specific proposals and normal horse trading and instead discuss each other's underlying problems and interests, seeking agreement in principle before worrying about proposing specific language to cover details.

Acres (the seller) and Malls (the buyer) are locked into a negotiation over the price of a large parcel that Malls wishes to develop as a shopping center. They are conducting traditional positional bargaining through their respective commercial realtors. That negotiation has reached an impasse on price. The parties and their realtors meet and agree to set aside positional bargaining and to examine the underlying needs of both parties. It emerges that Malls' position is grounded in the fact that the shopping center they wish to build will not reach full profitability for five years. Accordingly they cannot accept the debt load that moving toward Acres' position would entail. Acres is selling the tract because it is changing its core business away from real estate holdings. Acres offers to defer some of the selling price for five years in return for a number of shares of stock in Malls, a trade which fits in well with Acres' new commercial orientation. The deal is struck because the parties have found underlying mutual interests that might never have been revealed in traditional positional bargaining.

Peter Peach Chocolates and the Food Handlers Union are negotiating overtime arrangements. The present contract calls for a

complex system of identifying and notifying employees of volun-
tary overtime opportunities in order to provide an equitable distri-
bution of overtime, followed by a mandatory overtime draft. Peter
Peach wants to simplify the process which it finds costly and cum-
bersome, but the Food Handlers are resisting. Positional bargain-
ing is not working. Peter Peach suggests the parties put aside the
proposals and look at the underlying interests. The management
negotiating team suggests that the company's interest is simply in
"obtaining qualified and available people to do the needed work
in an administratively simple manner," and that they are open to
any system the union might propose that accomplishes that goal,
not necessarily the one the company has on the table. They sug-
gest that the employees' real interest is in money and in distribu-
tional equity and that overtime could be equalized among quali-
fied employees by distributing it by seniority, or by hours worked
on overtime, or by overtime opportunities (regardless of the num-
ber of hours per opportunity). The union caucuses and offers to
change the system to a simple one based on seniority, a system
that meets the company's needs, in return for certain other eco-
nomic concessions to be paid for out of part of the company's sav-
ings on administering the overtime program. A seniority based
system meets the union's needs to advance this typical union
agenda item. Instead of fighting over the words of the company
proposal or arguing about positions, the parties have looked at
each other's underlying needs. Both sides perceive they have won
something from the bargain.

Problem solving requires excellent listening skills and a measure of empathy for the other side's needs and interests. The objective is to identify areas each side does not care about very much to enable each side to make concessions to the other in these areas of indifference. Problem solving is not a panacea. Neither side is likely to concede any true core interest as a result of problem solving. If nothing else, problem solving is a more modern approach to conflict resolution, because it works for understanding between the sides as to each other's needs. It cannot turn an inherently adversarial process into a cooperative one.

✒ TIP

Problem solving should be introduced late in the opening game. It is most useful in mid game negotiations, when time still permits rational exploration of alternatives. Problem solving techniques sound easy, but they are difficult to learn. For a complex negotiation, mock problem solving exercises involving issues likely to be discussed with the other side should be conducted during the negotiation preparation phase, as part of negotiation simulation training. What is particularly important is to identify the core interests of each side on the issues, before using the technique. In the case of labor-management negotiations, keep in mind that the ultimate core interests to be considered will usually be those of the employees represented by the union, not necessarily the institutional interests of the union itself.

✐ TIP

When negotiations enter the end game phase, abandon problem solving. Usually, time pressures for completion make further problem solving inappropriate. By the time the end game phase of negotiations has been reached, the number of issues still open and active on the table should be decreased to a manageable number. Those where problem solving might have been helpful should already have been completely explored. In addition, in the end game stage progress is more likely to be made by the application of various forms of pressure than by argument and reasoning.

GIVING AND READING SIGNALS THROUGH WORDS AND BODY LANGUAGE

"Beware of the danger signals that flag problems: silence, secretiveness, or sudden outburst." [Sylvia Porter] Signals are a key aspect of negotiating. A signal is a clue you provide the other side, consciously or unconsciously, in words or through body language, of your intentions regarding either your own, or the other side's, position. You give the other side information through signals. To be an effective negotiator, you must be able to control both your own signals and to read the signals being given by the other side. Signals are not always obvious. They may be subtle and decoding them may require good listening and observation skills. *The single biggest mistake committed by most amateur negotiators is giving erroneous, confusing, or mixed signals.* Mixed signals, that is contradictory ones, confuse the other side and can lead to unwanted consequences. Nowhere is this more evident than in diplomatic negotiations and statements.

> *In January 1950, Secretary of State Dean Acheson made a widely quoted extemporaneous speech before the National Press Club. He declared, "America's line of defense runs along the Aleutians to Japan and then goes to the Ryukyu Islands . . .the defense perimeter runs from the Ryukus to the Phillippine Islands." He thus drew a line on a map in which Korea was demarcated as being outside the area we would defend, a clear signal to the North Koreans. On June 24, 1950, the Korean War broke out when North Korea invaded South Korea. "To the end of his life Acheson would vigorously deny that this had given the green light for aggression in South Korea by excluding it from the perimeter, but when he told the press club that the United States was waiting 'for the dust to settle' in China after declaring that America's line of resistance lay south of the Korean peninsula, the Communists could only conclude, as they did, that the United States was leaving Rhee [South Korea] to fend for himself." [William Manchester, American Caesar, Douglas MacArthur, 1880-1964, Little Brown and Company (1979)] It is possible that this faulty signal from Secretary of State Acheson was a primary cause of the Korean War.*

To be consistent, professional negotiators may employ a series of coded signals which are either evident to the other side from prior negotiations or which, in a first negotiation, become obvious over time. These formal signals are used to indicate the intensity of a stated position.

> *Upstart Technology and Legacy Wembly Technology Corporations are negotiating a merger. Legacy is longer established with a better known name but operates at a much lower profit margin than Upstart. Upstart, the somewhat smaller company, has a new highly innovative and profitable line of wembly technologies and a lot of cash. The parties are exchanging positions through their negotiators (some of whom are attorneys) concerning the nature of the acquisition or merger. Each side has a proposal which contains a merger method and name for the new organization. Legacy wants to describe the new company as "a merger of equals" and to name it "Legacy-Upstart Corporation." Upstart wants to describe the transaction as an acquisition by Upstart of*

Legacy and to rename the company "Upstart L Corporation." On the first review of Upstart's proposal on form and name, Legacy responds, "That won't happen." On the second pass, they state their position as, "That would be very difficult for us." On the third positional review, Legacy's negotiator states, "We could consider your name proposal, provided that the form was a merger, not an acquisition." Legacy is signaling a series of position changes in which it is weakening its position each time. Upstart's negotiators recognize the signal shift and note it. Understanding Legacy's need to save face and because their instructions allow some wiggle room, Upstart's negotiators have gradually also shifted their position through signals. Both parties are encouraged that the issue is closer to being worked out.

When you start a negotiation, your list of proposals or things you want probably will not, and usually must not, signal your specific priorities. If you place your proposals in significance order, the other side will soon figure this out and you will lose any chance to achieve the lower portion of your list. Signals are used to begin to gradually demonstrate your priorities and to respond to movement by the other side.

⌨ TIP

Have a pre-defined series of signals that you use. There is no magic formula for a list of signals but, whatever you decide to use, make sure the gradations are clear and that you use your signals consistently. For example, a set of signals and their meanings, translated here in the parentheses, might range as follows:

- We agree and accept your proposal as written (you've got it);
- We agree in principle (we accept your concept, but need language);
- We expect to work this out (this one should get resolved);
- We should discuss this (we are open to change);
- This will be difficult for us (not likely);
- No (adverse to the proposal, very unlikely);
- We have no interest at all (forget about it); or,
- We have less than no interest at all (this is a deal breaker).

Your set of signals might have different gradations. Care should be taken not to use those gradations nearest the top or bottom of your signals list, if your position on the item is a pure bluff. Movement from "we have less than no interest at all" to any other tier is a usage that weakens the credibility of that terminology on other proposals and in the future. Use it sparingly. Similarly, it will rarely be advisable to fully accept a proposal on first discussion, particularly if nothing is achieved in return for agreement.

Similarly, your reading of the other side's signals is very important. If you determine that you are receiving written or oral "mixed signals" from the other side, say so, by asking for clarification and pointing out the contradictions. In negotiations, as in military science, there is a "fog of war." Remember that information, power, and time, are the three key negotiation variables. The more information you have about the other side's position, the better you will be able to evaluate your own position. In this evaluation game, don't forget the possibility that you may be fed "disinformation" by the other side. They will want you to have only as clear a view of their plans and intent as they choose to reveal. You will want to know more than that.

Not all signals are formal, written, or oral. Some signals are given by body language. For this reason, if you are negotiating through a team, assign someone the responsibility to carefully watch the body language of the other side.

Latisha has recently become a chief spokesperson for the union at negotiations. She is running through her position list at a meeting of the union and management teams. The management team observer notes that for some proposals on which she is taking a strong position she makes eye contact with the company spokesperson. On others, she looks down, fidgets, and looks nervous. They test out the hypothesis that Latisha is unconsciously signaling when she is serious and when she is bluffing by watching her subsequent movement on issues and determine the hypothesis is accurate. Latisha would not make a good poker player, nor a good negotiator. Her body language is giving away her positions. Suppose now that the union team has assigned someone to watch their own side for body language symbols. They pick up Latisha's problem and alert her to it. She alters her behavior so that she now sometimes gives eye contact when she is bluffing and avoids it when she is serious. Now Latisha is engaging in disinformation and may win some of her bluffs.

✐ TIP

Observe not only the spokesperson for each side, but all the members of both teams. A team member's body language may give away something the team is trying to hide. For example, one team member may unconsciously smile a bit when a position isn't real or lift an eyebrow. Reading signals is in some ways similar to playing poker. If you can identify signs that the other side is bluffing, you will win more pots.

✐ TRICK

Make sure that your team members are trained not to give away information through inadvertent body language signals. One way to do this is to conduct pre-negotiation simulation training. Video tape the training process and look for any body language clues. Continue the observation process throughout negotiations.

Near the end of a long and difficult negotiation for the sale and purchase of a group of television stations, the parties are doing a position review. The seller notes that on the last critical issue between the parties, the purchase price, the buyer has changed position and is now offering enough money (although the buyer is unaware of this) so the deal can be closed on terms acceptable to the seller. The seller still hopes to get more than the minimum target price. The members of the seller's team, remembering their training, keep a poker face when the buyer puts in place the last term needed to complete a deal. They know that although they can have a deal now they may still get more. Had a single member broken out into a grin or mumbled "deal," it could have cost the seller a lot of money. Pre-negotiations simulation training has paid off.

ASKING AND RESPONDING TO QUESTIONS

"A prudent question is one-half of wisdom." [Francis Bacon] The process of negotiating requires giving and obtaining information, always in a controlled manner. Asking and responding to questions is the key way in which information is exchanged. Knowing whether, when, and how to ask questions is a critical skill. Questions may be answered fully, given a partial response, be diverted off course, be ignored, or may be answered with disinformation. We are all familiar with the way in which politicians handle and often evade questions.

> *You are the buyer in a sales negotiation. The seller has proposed a low price, but that price is conditioned on your purchasing a number of unwanted items (a tie-in). The tie-in is a deal breaker for you. Nevertheless, you ask a lot of questions about how the tie-in would work. Asking these questions encourages the seller to believe that a tie-in might be acceptable to you and that you are interested in making it work. Under these circumstances, you, the buyer, are sending a misleading signal by asking questions. Instead, you should state "we understand your proposal and we have no questions."*

When should you ask questions? When the other side presents a proposal that you are interested in, by all means try to find out as much as possible about their concept and how it would work in practice. Sometimes parties make proposals without thinking them through. Surprisingly often, you may find the other side doesn't understand its own proposal. Never accept a proposal you do not understand. If you are unclear, or the other side is evasive, but you might be interested in the proposal, ask questions until you know exactly what is in the proposal and how it will operate.

> *Carlos is the spokesperson for Ace Services, which is negotiating a successor labor agreement with the Service Specialists Union. Carlos and his management team have made a proposal to the union for changes in the job transfer system, to specify that an employee may only bid on a classification once every twenty-four months. The union team asks, "Would an employee have to stay in a current position, if the company could not fill a vacancy with another employee, and had to hire from the outside?" The company has not thought about this possibility. One management team member promptly answers, "Yes," while another simultaneously says, "No." This forces an embarrassed Carlos to call a caucus so the management team may discuss the issue. It is clear that the management team has not thought through its own proposal and doesn't know how it will actually work. The better*

response might be, "That's an interesting question. We'll get back to you on that."

When you might be interested in a proposal, there are many reasons for asking questions. Questions will help you to get a better picture of the merits, and flaws, of the other side's proposal; to elicit information about their commitment to various aspects of a proposal; to determine if their proposal is unworkable; to get them to modify their proposal; or, to provide you with a basis for a counterproposal. Also, showing some interest in selected proposals from the other side facilitates negotiations in general. If you have no interest in anything they say, they will likely display a similar attitude toward what you are proposing.

Once you have the other side's proposal list in hand, you can use the available time between meetings to decide whether to ask questions about their proposals and to frame those questions. Unless you are an unusually fast thinker when on your feet, have a question list ready before you begin discussion of an item. If you need to ask follow up questions, do so. If you want to regroup or frame new questions, remember that you have the right to call a caucus. Take the time to get your questions right.

An excellent question to ask is keyed around the phrase "have you considered [whatever]?" In asking a question this way, you are not implying that the other side is ignorant, just suggesting something they have not considered. Questions have different purposes:

- To get the other party talking, perhaps too freely;
- To elicit factual information;
- To obtain information on the other side's positions;
- To suggest modifications of the other side's positions;
- To show a proposal is flawed and should be withdrawn; or,
- To redirect the other side toward a different solution.

Paul Buyman is close to purchasing a house from John Sellman. Buyman tells Sellman, "Your house fits most of my needs, but I really want four bedrooms, not the three in this house, so I can use one as an office." Sellman replies, "Have you considered taking a chunk out of the large recreation room downstairs and making it into an office?" Buyman responds, "No, I haven't. That idea meets my objection, but I'm concerned with the cost of that kind of alteration." Sellman, who wants to reach a deal, then propos-

> *es, "Suppose I paid half for the remodeling. That should go a long way toward resolving your problem. We're in agreement, right?" Buyman who wants more information and who won't be pushed into a deal until he is ready, answers this question with a question. "Who would choose the contractor and materials?" Eventually, the two agree on an allowance for construction of the partition, with Buyman selecting the contractor.*

Sometimes it is a good idea to ask a question, although you already know the answer. Why? A question of this type is not designed to elicit information. Its purpose is to test the other side's credibility and their willingness to share accurate information with you. You need to have an idea as to what extent the other person is answering your questions truthfully. You also need to know whether the other person is being overly technical in responding to your questions. Does the other person demand definitions of every word in your questions or split hairs in answering your questions? An evasive person is often hiding something.

Responding to questions is also tricky. The ideal answer will give just the amount of information you are willing to share and will sound sincere, but it should avoid areas that you prefer to leave closed. If the question is one you really don't want to answer, consider the old politician's trick of answering some other question than the one asked, or reframing the question the way you wish it had been asked.

> *Edwards, an attorney negotiating a contract for a client who is concerned about the safety of a product the client will be buying, asks the seller's attorney, "Have you put these widgets through a fire safety test?" Burr, the attorney for the seller, responds to the question, "I'm glad you asked that question and I'll be happy to respond. We have an extensive test program. We test for all kinds of things. We pride ourselves on our quality control. I wish you could see our test labs, they are really quite extensive. Our test record is outstanding. Your client need have no concern over our product." Despite all the verbiage, note that the question about putting these particular widgets through a fire test has never been answered. The question that was answered was about testing in general. The subject of fire testing was avoided. When this happens, you must ask follow up questions.*

Even in adversarial bargaining, such as labor-management negotiations, the other side will sometimes ask a good question, which may be acknowledged as such with little or no damage to your fundamental interests. If it is possible to acknowledge the question as a good one, consider doing so. One of the mistakes amateur negotiators frequently make is to think they must never be complimentary to the other side.

If your proposal calls for an outcome to which the other side may vigorously object, don't pull your punches on what you want done, or you will be watering down your position in advance. **If your position seems unreasonable even to your own side, it may be because it is an initial proposal which is purposely overstated and designed to give you room to compromise later, or because your proposal is really flawed. In either case, maintain the position now, retreat later.**

Allover Enterprises is negotiating a successor labor agreement with the United Workers Union. Allover has a proposal on the table that would prohibit an employee from bidding downward to a lower paid classification under any circumstances. Allover's justification of its bidding proposal is that people need to stay on a given job long enough for the company to recoup its training cost investment and to preserve job stability. When discussion turns to the proposal, the union asks the question, "Suppose an employee who is getting older wants to bid downward to a lower paying, but easier job, for health reasons. Does your proposal mean this would never be allowed?" Allover plans to eventually modify the proposal to allow for hardship cases. Management's spokesperson replies to the question, "That's an excellent question. The proposal, as written, does not allow it." This response makes no apology for the proposal, yet it contains in the words "as written," an implicit signal that change may be possible. If Allover is about ready to make a move, the spokesperson might add, "We see what you are saying. We'll discuss it among ourselves when we go into caucus and get back to you." Then, when Allover makes the concession it had planned all along, the union may perceive that it was the union's question that brought on the change.

In some instances, the answer to a question should be a simple "Yes," or "No," with little or no explanation, or the question should simply be avoided. Calling a caucus before offering any response is one method of temporarily avoiding a question. Another is to say, "We heard your question. We will answer that later. Right now we'd like to move on to something else." You might try to avoid responding to a question:

- When you need more time to frame a careful answer;
- When you need to check with higher authority before answering;
- When you do not consider the time ripe for opening a discussion; or,
- When you need to resolve internal dissension regarding the response.

Some questions must not be answered. For example, if a prospective buyer of a business demands to see a secret proprietary formula before the sales contract is signed, it must not be disclosed without legal protection which, in the judgment of counsel, is sufficient to be fully protective. Some questions contain two or more parts and an adverse inference. Suppose you are asked, "Why haven't you stopped beating your spouse?" This question simply presumes you have been beating your spouse and asks for the reason you haven't stopped. Questions with inferences should only be answered with the preface that the inference is incorrect. The "why" part of the question is therefore meaningless. To cope with double part questions, ask the questioner to break the question down into two parts or to restate the question as two separate questions.

Finally, some requests for information are surrounded by legal obligations or protections. For a detailed discussion of the duty to provide information under the National Labor Relations Act, see Chapter 3. In short, in labor-management negotiations, an employer and a union must provide each other, on request, with quantified data relevant to the negotiation, but they are not obligated to give up internal estimates, disclose strategies or tactics, or to divulge conversations with their legal advisors. In commercial negotiations, copyright, patent, and trade secret laws provide a shield against certain forms of disclosure. In real estate transactions, state law may require various disclosures from seller to buyer. In automobile purchases, particularly of used cars, state law may also require certain disclosures, such as that the vehicle has previously been in a major accident.

PAUSING BEFORE ANSWERING QUESTIONS

"The notes I handle no better than many pianists. But the pauses between the notes—ah, that is where the art resides." [Artur Schnabel]

In negotiations, you need to know when a quick response is required and when a pause is proper. The other party to a negotiation may seek an immediate answer to its question and then demand you respond at once. Unless you are prepared and have thought through your response, avoid responding on the spot. The more complex the matter, the more critical it is to take the time to frame not only your substantive response but the tone in which it is delivered. Don't be moved by statements from the other negotiator that your failure to respond immediately will be deemed to be evasive. You are not responsible for the other side's improper perceptions.

During a commercial purchasing negotiation, the buyer asks the seller to detail exactly how it plans to meet the "just on time" needs of the seller and demands an immediate response. The seller says, "We'll get back to you on that after lunch." The buyer responds, "That's not good enough. We think you should be able to give us an immediate response on such an important question. Haven't you thought it through?" The spokesperson for the seller blunts this criticism with the comment, "It is an important question and we have thought about it extensively. We intend to give it a full response and before doing so are going to review our notes. In any event, its too close to lunch time now to get into that question and do it justice. As I said, we'll explore it with you in full a bit later." The negotiators move on to a minor issue that can be handled in the remaining pre-lunch session.

When should you seek an immediate response to your own questions? You may do this when you wish to determine how well prepared the other side is or if you want to catch them off guard, in the hope that they will make a mistake. In some cases, you may get your quick response and be rewarded with information about the other side's position that they may have held back if you had allowed them more time to think. In trying to rush, they may become confused and let something slip. In short, it is not a bad thing to put some time response pressure on the other side, but when the tactic is applied to your own side, you will want to be ready to fend it off. Experienced negotiators often press the other side for a quick response, but find subtle ways to delay their own response, without appearing to be unreasonable.

OBSERVING

"Observe all men, thyself most." [Benjamin Franklin] If both sides are negotiating through teams, the probability is that there are differences of interest among members of each team. Team members may have been chosen to represent different expert areas. For example, a management team may contain a maintenance manager, a production manager, a human resources and labor relations specialist, a finance person, and a general manager. A union team may contain a mechanic, a production operator, a technician, a local union officer, and an international union representative. In either case, each of these representatives may have both personal and business agendas to advance.

Whatever the differences between members of your own team in private, in speaking with the other side, always speak from the same page. No matter who is talking, a team should always speak to the issues with a single voice. Never unintentionally show a split. Unity is one of the most critical aspects of any team negotiation. In caucus, you may have lost your argument against the position being taken by your team. At the table, you must enthusiastically support the team position. Further, your team should create the impression that, if for any reason, the spokesperson changed, or team members were changed, your side's position would not change as a result. **The positions you take at the table are your organization's positions, not your personal ones, and should survive any change of negotiators.**

Upland Malls is negotiating with the City of Upland for a million dollar tax abatement, if it builds a mega-mall. Representatives of Upland are meeting with a delegation from City government. The Upland Malls finance manager is stressing how critical tax abatements are to the project and how many jobs the mega-mall will bring into the City. As the finance manager pauses for a drink of water, the construction manager, who argued in private that Upland Malls should go ahead even without abatements and who fears they will not be obtained, comments, "These abatements would really be helpful but we could build without them." An astute observer on the City side recognizes this as a split. Upland is now unlikely to get the abatements it seeks. The construction manager may have cost Upland Malls a million dollars, and should soon be looking for a new job.

Splits are not always revealed by direct words or overt behaviors. For example, if while a team is making a presentation to you four of its five members look interested and maintain eye contact with you, but one member, who does not normally behave that way, looks down and away, as if embarrassed, you may be observing a split. It is important to observe body language. The other side is likely to be observing your side in a similar fashion. For this reason, negotiation team members should remember that they are "always on stage" when the parties are together. Telephone negotiations deprive negotiators of the opportunity to observe body language and to look for visual clues. Some experts discount body language as being too difficult to read or possibly misleading. There is that risk, but when properly used, body language observation may be a useful tool.

Because tensions and splits between members and interests on the other side's team may reveal fault lines for the application of pressure on them or may reveal information about the other side's strengths and weaknesses, it is important to watch for such behaviors. As negotiators may be busy with making presentations, answering questions, and listening intently, it can be difficult for them to focus on the task of spotting the other side's weaknesses, or identifying their own.

⚑ TIP

Assign each member of your negotiating team the responsibility of watching one member of the opposing team for any signs of splits or conflicts. With each team member concentrating on one person on the opposite side, important clues are less likely to be overlooked. Also, assign each person on your team the responsibility for watching one other member of your own team. The purpose of this is just to become aware of any splits or tensions that may have slipped out and been observed by the other side.

⚑ TIP

If you show a split on your side, make sure that it is deliberate. This technique may be used when it is important for the other side to have someone on your side they view as more sympathetic to their needs. See the discussion on "good cop, bad cop," below.

If you do see a split on the other side and conclude that it is genuine, consider how it may be exploited. For example, if in a labor negotiation there is an "international agenda" being pursued by the international representative and local union representatives show signs of not being very interested in it, the possibility exists of driving a wedge between the local and international unions. The wedge may be useful in heading off a strike over the international's goals. A caveat is in order. Exploiting a split carries certain dangers, particularly if what you are doing is too obvious. You may alienate both sides of a split. So, if you are going to exploit a split, generally it will be wise to do so in a low key way and after carefully considering to what extent to make the attempt.

SILENCE AND HOW TO USE IT TO YOUR ADVANTAGE

"A sage thing is timely silence, and better than any speech." [Plutarch] Good negotiators understand general human psychology. When there is a silence in a meeting, most people feel an overpowering need to rush in and fill the "dead air." This is a temptation you must learn to avoid. Filling a silence is an invitation to saying too much or giving away too much information.

Robin Round is the spokesperson for Omni Industries, which is negotiating a contract with Flora, Inc., for the landscaping of its large corporate headquarters campus. Looking at Flora's proposal, Robin remarks, seemingly with no real interest, "As your plan is proposed, I see you have not included any form of in-ground sprinkler system." Flora's spokesperson, Paula Plant, replies, "That is correct." Robin says nothing but remains silent, waiting to see if Plant will add anything else. After a pause, Plant adds, "Putting that in would have added ten percent to the overall price." Robin's silence has won a gratuitous statement as to the maximum cost of adding a sprinkler system, something Omni wants to know. Now, Omni may begin the process of trying to bargain down the ten percent extra cost for the sprinkler system. Omni has also not given away to Plant the existence, or strength, of its interest in a sprinkler system. What Plant should have done was either waited out the silence or suggested moving on to another topic.

It is not easy for an entire team to remain silent. Negotiating teams should practice this tactic during negotiations simulation training. Similarly, your negotiators should get into the habit of inviting the other side to keep talking, by creating silent pauses.

"GOOD COP, BAD COP" TACTICS

"Every sweet hath its sour; every evil its good." [Ralph Waldo Emerson] The "good cop, bad cop" routine is a frequently used technique which often proves quite effective, even with people who should know better. The classic use, of course, is by two police detectives, one of whom savagely grills a suspect while the other plays the role of a friendly, gentle, questioner. Another use of this ploy occurs when an automobile sales representative "wants to help," but tells you, "The deal must be approved by my tough minded sales manager, who won't want to let me do that."

In team negotiations, one or more players on each side may be assigned to the "good cop" or "bad cop" role. It may also be a very effective technique for the good and bad players to reverse roles in order to make a point. When the sympathetic and gentle player turns harsh and demanding (by design, not accident), it will command attention that the same behavior from the usually angry "bad cop" will not. For this to be effective, it must be used quite sparingly and unexpectedly, similar to the "trick play" a National Football League coach may save for a critical moment.

In a labor-management negotiation, Avram is a member of the management team. Avram is ordinarily very intellectual and soft spoken. Throughout the course of the negotiation, Avram's main contribution has been to calm things down. Avram is clearly viewed by the union team as a "good guy." Negotiations have become stuck on a critical issue and it is management's conclusion that the union is just not taking seriously the company's determination on the point. In a caucus, the team decides that when they go back to the table Avram should give a very tough speech about how management must win its point. The team puts together an angry, emotional, speech for Avram. It is difficult for him, because it is out of character. When table discussion resume, Avram gives the speech of his life, the union is thorough-

ly shocked, and realizes the company is very serious. Progress begins to be made.

⚜ TRAP

It may be a trap to assume that a good cop, bad cop routine is anything more than a negotiating device. When a good cop becomes a bad one, or the other way around, always consider the possibility that the reversal was staged. One of the difficult parts of negotiation is sorting information from disinformation. Never assume that what you are observing is genuine and not pure theater. Good negotiators often use theatrical techniques.

⚜ TIP

Try to assign members of the negotiating team to good or bad cop roles which tend to fit naturally with their real personalities. It will be difficult for a quiet, cooperative, person to play a bad cop role, but it will be effective if it is only done occasionally. Similarly, it will be difficult for a hard, aggressive, individual to come across as a peacemaker. Remember that in many negotiations both sides already know something about each other, so out of character roles are hard to sustain or credit.

USE OF "SIDEBARS" AND "OFF THE RECORD" DISCUSSIONS

"Curiosity is lying in wait for every secret." [Ralph Waldo Emerson] Sometimes called a "back door approach," a sidebar is a private, behind the scenes, meeting between the principals in a negotiation. Sidebars will be relatively rare in commercial negotiations, but they are far more common in labor-management bargaining. In fact, in union collective bargaining, despite an elaborate show of negotiating at a table with teams, it is sometimes the case that the essential outlines of the final deal, or even a complete deal, have been worked out and agreed to by the principals, before the face to face team negotiations ever begin. In such cases, table discussions amount to little more than a sham, designed to cast some measure of participation and legitimacy on a deal already cut by the employer's agents and the union's leaders.

Sidebar meetings may be held with, or without, the knowledge of either, or both, sides' negotiating teams. This is a question of style and of an organization's willingness to trust all the members of its team with all the information. In a sidebar, each side may probe the other's intentions and try to get a fix on the "settlement window" that will resolve the negotiations. How much information is to be shared is a very critical decision and should be made on a case by case basis.

Because there is significant danger of giving away too much information at a sidebar meeting, only experienced bargainers should consider using this technique. Inexperienced negotiators are likely to give up far more information than they will be able to extract. Further, sidebars conducted over drinks run the additional risk that too much alcohol may induce too much talking, particularly if one side's representative is better able to handle significant liquor intake.

World Wide Wembly Corporation is about to enter a labor negotiation for a plant in a newly acquired division. The employees are represented by the MegaWorkers union. World Wide Wembly bought the plant only because it was tied-in to a package deal. The plant is losing money and the old fashioned labor agreement needs to be completely replaced in order to gain the productivity necessary to keep the plant operating. After discussion with the management team, Zoltan Zee, chief management spokesperson, is authorized to set up a sidebar with Alpha Adams, the union's business agent. The two meet in a restaurant, where they explore each other's negotiation themes. At the end of the meeting, there is agreement in principle between them that management must get its productivity changes and that in going along the union's interest is in saving 250 memberships in the union. The spokespersons also agree that the employer will not attack the union's standing under the union shop (mandatory union dues) and checkoff (available automatic payroll deduction of dues by the employer) clauses. While they discuss wages in general, neither side trusts the other to be specific, but both agree that the settlement will be somewhere around the "area trend." This type of sidebar does not resolve all issues and negotiations which are still real, but it does limit the scope of outcomes. While both sides inform their negotiating committees of the sidebar, neither side informs either the union represented employees or other members of management.

What about "off the record" discussions? The problem here is that few such discussions can really be protected from possible disclosure. In labor-management negotiations, an agreement between the parties that a meeting is confidential, even an agreement in writing, will not shield the "off the record" discussions at that meeting from legal processes. So, these parties must assume that "off the record" does not necessarily mean totally privileged. In commercial negotiations, the same risk of legal discovery of the "off the record" data also exists, although the parties may be more successful in using agreements to shield information, at least in civil actions by one against the other. Any agreements to hold off the record discussions and to make them unavailable for legal discovery, even when a shield is permitted by law, should be drawn up by counsel. No such agreement will protect against disclosure of conversations in criminal investigations.

VERIFYING EXPECTATIONS OF THE OTHER SIDE AGAINST REALITY

"Trust, but verify." [Ronald Reagan] One of the keys to a successful negotiation is that both sides have realistic expectations and goals. The other side's real goals cannot be determined from simply reading its list of proposals or demands. Some of these—in fact many of them—are secondary objectives, mere smokescreens, or "wish list items." Asking prices and wage demands are particularly irrelevant. A seller will be afraid to set an asking price that is too low for fear of having that price accepted outright. There is less danger in asking an unrealistically high price, while signaling that there is room for negotiation. However, this is not true in real estate negotiations. If an asking price is set too high, out of fear of offending the seller, many potential buyers will walk away rather than submit a much lower, although realistic, offer. In union-management negotiations, a union's initial wage demand figure is particularly irrelevant. They must ask for far more than they hope to get. Such requests are often "pie in the sky." Naturally, a union representative will not want to prejudice the chances of getting an above average settlement by initially asking for too low a figure.

In a labor market and industry in which recent contract settlement hourly wage increases have run about three percent in the first year and two percent in each of the next two years, the World Wide Workers Union enters negotiations with a demand for a ten percent wage increase in the first year and for six percent increas-

es in both the second and third years. If the union is serious about these demands and really expects to settle at that level, a labor dispute is close to certain. The union may have set such a high initial demand level to be sure they have asked for at least as much as they will ultimately be able to obtain. Management's negotiators need to probe to find out the rationale for the union's demand and to start laying a foundation for lowering excess expectations.

An attorney and her client are conferring about a planned lawsuit. They must decide on the amount of money damages to demand. Demanding too little will automatically limit their potential recovery. Demanding too much may cause a prevailing plaintiff to receive a reduced attorney's fee in cases in which the court is allowed to shift legal fees, if damages are ultimately fixed in an amount much lower than was demanded. The attorney and client may find themselves actually negotiating with each other the level of the demand for damages.

☞ TIP

When setting a money objective, be sure to research what is reasonable. Then, if you are the requesting party, be certain to ask for more than that, but either cap your demands at the outer limit of what might be achievable or refuse to provide a number. Remember that when you ask for the moon, the other side will likely treat your demand as a non-serious one and consider it to be an open ended, non-specific, claim.

☞ TRAP

Don't let yourself be conned into a "split the difference" routine, when the other side's proposal is unrealistic. Halfway between "low reasonable" and "unreasonably high" may still be too high. In commercial negotiations, when both sides have choices, asking and offering prices on each side will more likely track reality, compared to labor-management negotiations, where the parties have a long term relationship from which they cannot withdraw. In the labor-management context, both sides know that the union's initial demand is rarely a serious one. A way to test the reasonableness of the other

257

side's number is to ask how it was derived. Even an unreasonably high number should have some arguable, logical, basis. If there is none, the number is a throwaway.

CAUCUSES

"No grand idea was ever born in a conference, but a lot of foolish ideas have died there." [F. Scott Fitzgerald] A caucus is simply a break that is taken by one side or by mutual agreement during a negotiation so that the parties may separate and meet privately amongst themselves. The caucus is one of the most useful tools available to a negotiator and a lot of foolish ideas and potential mistakes do indeed die there. **You have the absolute right to call your own caucuses. You do not need permission from the other side to do so. Take as many caucuses as you need, of whatever length is required.** A caucus may be a very short one of a minute or two's duration, or a long one. Courtesy dictates giving the other side an estimate of how long you might need, but this time frame should not be considered binding. If more time is required, call or notify the other side that you are not ready at the end of your estimated time.

When do you call a caucus? When in doubt, caucus. Do so, if:

- You aren't prepared to answer a question and the other side will not agree to put it aside while other matters are discussed;
- You become confused about your own proposals;
- Someone on your side seems about to make a mistake;
- There is a perceived need for internal discussion before acting;
- The time is not ripe to move ahead with discussions; or,
- Time is needed to let tempers cool.

One of the most frequent mistakes made by amateur negotiators is to spend too much continuous time at the table. Long, unbroken, talks magnify the chances of making an error either with your own proposals or in responding to the other side's proposals. Participants in collective bargaining simulations often tend to make this mistake. They are often surprised to learn how much negotiation time is spent apart from the other side.

✦ TIP

Establish an internal procedure on your side of the table as to who may call a caucus and as to how it will be done. Don't let all members of the team openly call for a caucus, lest someone do so at a time when something important is about to come to closure. Yet, any member of the team should be able to alert the spokesperson to the need for a caucus, as when one member of a team senses that an error is about to be made, or when an unlivable commitment is about to be offered. One method for calling a caucus is for any member of the team to pass a note to the spokesperson that says, "Caucus now?" The spokesperson must then decide whether to pause. Unless certain that it is better to continue at the table without a break, the spokesperson is best served by calling the caucus, even if it is only for a few moments outside the negotiating room.

✦ TRICK

Management representatives in labor-management negotiations should keep in mind that with management's usually larger logistical resources, hierarchical structure, and time to plan and work together during the normal working day, management is usually able to respond far faster than labor. Labor caucuses tend to be longer, particularly in unions which practice internal democracy. One way in which management may keep pressure on a union is that after a long union caucus and a brief table discussion, management may caucus very briefly and use its rapid response speed to present the union with new materials. This will force the union to caucus again. The purpose of this ploy is to "keep the ball in the union's court" as much as possible.

✦ TRAP

Never get caught inside the negotiating room after your side has called a caucus. Always leave as a group, crisply, and without lingering. If one team member stays behind, that individual may be pumped for information or may make a mistake. Always be sure when leaving the room for a caucus, even a very short one, that sensitive papers and documents are taken with you.

WALK OUTS

"I leave before being left. I decide." [Brigitte Bardot] Walking out of a negotiation is a drastic step which should not be undertaken lightly, yet it may be appropriate, or even necessary, under the right circumstances. Perhaps the classic example of a walk out coming back to haunt the party walking out rather than continuing to negotiate was the Soviet walk out from the United Nations Security Council at the outbreak of the Korean War. The absence of the Soviets from the table allowed the United Nations to wage the Korean War, without the possibility of a Soviet veto.

The term "walk out" is used here to cover those situations in which a party leaves the table or exits negotiations, not for a temporary caucus, but rather to put an end to negotiations for the day, or for the duration. Barring exceptional circumstances, a walk out should be a deliberately planned act, not an emotional response. Only the spokesperson should initiate a walk out. When the spokesperson does initiate one, all members of the team should go with the spokesperson, crisply and as a unit, with no member hanging back. When the walk out is pre-planned, confidential materials should be ready to be taken from the room. When a walk out is spontaneous, the only delay should be to ensure that all sensitive materials are collected and removed.

When would a team engage in a pre-planned walk out? A walk out is appropriate when:

- You have alternatives, as in many commercial negotiations;
- It is clear that a settlement window cannot be achieved;
- A dramatic step is necessary to demonstrate your displeasure;
- You want to send a strong message; or,
- You are confident you can resume negotiations, if desired.

Walk outs which are only for the day should not be undertaken unless the next meeting time has already been scheduled or it may be difficult to resume negotiations. Such a temporary walk out might be announced, "We're finished for the day. We will continue, as scheduled, on [next meeting date]."

Acahti Mining Corporation and the Mining Employees Union are negotiating a successor labor agreement. Acahti has placed a very large wage offer on the table which is not a final offer, but is still quite substantial. The Mining Employees Union responds to the offer by wadding it up and literally throwing it at the Corporation's spokesperson, yelling, "This is a piece of garbage. No self respecting union could accept such a cheap offer." Acahti expects the union to demand more, but finds the tone and extent of the union's response to be unacceptable, as the amount offered is already close to the area trend for settlements. The Acahti team has discussed how to handle such union reactions during negotiations planning and has rehearsed walk outs in negotiation simulation training. They have also decided that in order to avoid abusive union behavior, they must send a strong message whenever it occurs. Having prearranged for the next session at the outset of the current meeting, Acahti's spokesperson decides it is appropriate to walk out of this session. She makes a speech stating, "The Corporation has placed a generous offer on the table worth over ten million dollars over the life of the contact and your reaction is to literally throw it back at us. That offer is highly competitive. I strongly advise you to go back and rethink your position. Today's session is over. We'll see you at the next scheduled session." With that, the spokesperson picks up her books and materials and she and her team walk briskly from the room.

Planned walk outs may also be appropriate in negotiations for automobiles, for houses, and for collectibles, such as rugs. If you are willing to let the opportunity to buy be lost if nothing happens as you walk out, you might be rewarded by the seller calling you back to offer concessions. In cultures in which bargaining is traditional in the market place, you may be expected to walk out at least once. You may even be permitted to walk out and be called later by telephone to try to revive negotiations. However, if you walk out and are not called back, it would be a real sign of weakness to go back.

One circumstance in which a unplanned walk out is appropriate is when members of your negotiating team are being subjected to personal attacks. Students often assume that personal attacks do not occur today. However, they do, particularly in labor-management bargaining, especially when the technique has worked in prior negotiations. Methods for handling those attacks are discussed in the next section. However, when those methods fail, an on the spot walk out from the rest of the session may be in order. Keep in mind that in walking out of a session, you may be losing time on your planned time line for negotiation completion. This is a strong reason for making sure there are some blanks in the schedule, so that additional meeting dates may be added when they are necessary.

Who should initiate a walk out? In team negotiations, only the spokesperson should be able to initiate a walk out. Other team members who think one is advisable should instead call for a caucus, so the further line of action may be discussed.

In commercial negotiations, walk outs may be of either the single session variety or permanent. Ending negotiations which cannot be successful should ordinarily not be done by an abrupt walk out, but rather on an amicable basis. You may need to negotiate with the other side at a later date, on another matter. Walking out abruptly is appropriate in these circumstances only when the other side is entirely unreasonable and an agreement with them is no longer needed or attainable.

TIP

When you walk out with an intention to resume at the next session, always make clear that your leaving is not a simple caucus and covers the entire day. There should be nothing ambiguous about a walk out. The other side will be unnecessarily angered if they think you are caucusing, they wait, and you don't return.

TRAP

Don't overuse walk outs. This is particularly important to remember in situations such as those commercial negotiations which carry time deadlines and labor contract negotiations when there is the looming possibility of a labor dispute. A walk out is a dramatic step. With overuse, it loses its drama and begins to indicate a lack of good faith. A walk out should never be the result of childish pique. Before using your feet for a walk out, be sure your brain has been engaged to make a conscious decision to take that step.

INTIMIDATION, PERSONAL ATTACKS, HOW TO RESPOND

"He's a businessman. I'll make him an offer he can't refuse." [Mario Puzo] Intimidation is a frequently used negotiating technique, far more common in labor-management negotiations than in commercial or personal ones. In labor negotiations, you are locked into a continuing relationship and cannot deal with intimidation by walking away. Historically, some unions have been noted for the use of intimidating techniques. Employers used some these techniques in the 1930s, but that conduct is rare among them today, and has also become far more unusual among unions. Intimidation may take the form of direct personal threats, aggressive behavior, similar to Nikita Khrushchev's table pounding in the 1950s, implications of violence or sabotage, threats of striking by a union, or of locking out by an employer.

If intimidation works, it will be used. Indeed, once intimidation is established as a successful negotiation technique to be used against you, it will become a perennial facet of your negotiations. Once it works, it becomes an expected negotiating tactic. To stop intimidation, you should make clear that you are not, and will not be, intimidated, that such tactics are counterproductive, and that you will resist them. After a long history of successful intimidation, it will be necessary for you to frequently reiterate your determination to stop it. Your credibility may require a demonstration.

Walter Mittey Enterprises is negotiating a successor labor agreement with the Biscuit Workers Union. When the company was under its original Mittey ownership, the union found that table pounding and threats of strikes usually brought concessions. Mittey Enterprises was recently acquired by Warbucks & Associates. At this year's negotiations, the Warbucks' spokesperson, in her opening speech, sets an expectation of mutual courtesy and calm discussion at the table, acknowledging that past negotiations have not run that way. She states, "Warbucks will not condone violence or sabotage and will prosecute vigorously anyone engaging in them. There will be no amnesties negotiated for violators. Warbucks doesn't want a strike but we are not afraid of one." The Biscuit Workers wait two sessions, then test the company team by yelling and screaming across the table to see what will happen. The Company first caucuses, then resumes talks. When the behavior is repeated, the company team walks out for the day. Later, when the union threatens a strike the company responds, "We hope you won't do that, but if you do, we'll be ready. We know a strike can happen. That's part of the process sometimes, but it's not good for either side." When an incident of sabotage occurs, the company terminates the offend-

ing employee. It soon becomes plain that intimidation tactics will no longer work and the union abandons them.

Not all use of unequal bargaining power or tactical advantage is to be considered as intimidation. In commercial or personal negotiations, you may have considerably more bargaining power than the other side. When you swing your weight around, you are not using intimidation within the meaning of this section, although the other party may indeed feel it has little or no choice but to accept your proffered terms. Gary Trudeau covered this well in his Doonesbury cartoons, in reference to technology acquisitions, with a series of strips parallel to the example below.

A small technology start up, BigCode Software, has developed a new software application which has the potential of threatening the predominant market share of MegaGiant. Representatives of MegaGiant approach BigCode about selling the company to MegaGiant. Negotiations about acquisition begin. MegaGiant lays a number of terms on the table which will make stock holders in BigCode reasonably rich, but which will result in the total takeover of their business. BigCode's negotiators are unable to get any substantial changes in the offered terms and tell MegaGiant they are not interested. MegaGiant hints that if BigCode doesn't sell out to them, MegaGiant will create and give away, without charge, its own version of BigCode's "killer application." BigCode gives in and sells out. Certainly, BigCode has been intimidated, but the intimidation here is economic and for bargaining advantage, not personal. If instead BigCode continues its resistance, as a similar company did in the Doonesbury comic strip, MegaGiant may follow through and effectively put BigCode out of business. Provided it doesn't rise to an antitrust violation, this is lawful intimidation.

What about personal attacks? Personal attacks, as used here, means going after individuals to isolate or neutralize them. This route might be taken when one side really dislikes someone on the other side or fears that they may be too effective in either achieving results or in blocking desired results. **It is vital not to allow personal attacks to be conducted against yourself or members of your bargaining team. No spokesperson who permits such attacks is likely to be an effec-**

tive negotiator. You should understand that isolated and limited snipes don't require a heavy reaction.

How do you stop personal attacks? The following steps usually work:

- Set expectations that courtesy and civility will be maintained;
- Never let your own side engage in personal attacks;
- React quickly to a personal attack, at an appropriate level;
- Demand courtesy and civility, then try to continue;
- If the attack continues, warn the other side again;
- If the attack still continues, take a caucus for tempers to cool;
- If the attack still continues, walk out for the day; and,
- If attacks resume, repeat the pattern.

If you allow personal attacks on yourself or your team members, you will have a very long and unhappy negotiating experience. In pre-negotiation simulation training, participants spend time learning how to use the counteracting techniques listed above. Some people are incapable of handling these situations, These individuals should not be named negotiation spokespersons, nor are they good candidates for negotiation team membership. The bottom line is that if you permit yourself, or your side, to be intimidated or to suffer personal attacks, you will already have lost half the battle at the negotiating table. The odds are very high that you will also yield substantive gains to the other side and that you will set a long lasting pattern of negative behavior for future negotiations.

✐ TIP

Voice control can be an effective method of regaining control of the table. A loud, firm, statement, cutting through bickering or personal attacks, does tend to get attention, particularly when it comes from someone who has hierarchical rank and high status. At the risk of stereotyping (there are, of course, exceptions), voice control is one area in which many women who serve as spokespersons are often physiologically at a disadvantage. A deep, loud, commanding, voice is definitely an asset at the table for a spokesperson. Those without it need to find other ways to work around the problem. One method is to substitute cold, icy, silence for the dominance projected through a commanding voice. "Going cold" may be viewed as much a sign of anger as a verbal outburst. In some cases, this may actually be more effective, as it is a fairly unusual technique.

TRIAL BALLOONS

"There are three principal means of acquiring knowledge. . . observation. . ., reflection, and experimentation. Observation collects facts; reflection combines them; experimentation verifies the result of that combination." [Denis Diderot] A trial balloon is a form of experimentation, sometimes termed "sending out a scout." A trial balloon floats an idea or possibility in a vague general sort of way in order to draw and evaluate a reaction. Its purpose is to determine how much resistance might occur if a proposal, offer, or counteroffer were made. A trial balloon does not have to be made directly at the negotiations table, but may be slipped to the other party by indirect means. One method of launching a trial balloon is by letting out a rumor and listening for the reaction.

Antarctica Widgets and Thule Wemblies are in a commercial negotiation to determine whether Thule will become sole source supplier to Antarctica for all of its wembly needs over the next five years. Antarctica has expressed a concern that Thule has only one manufacturing plant and that, as the plant is unionized, a strike at the plant could take down Antarctica's critical wembly production, should it accept Thule as a sole source supplier. Thule's negotiators would like to know if Antarctica would contract with them if they had a non-union second plant, but top management has not authorized them to discuss this possibility. Thule's negotiation team decides to float a trial balloon on this issue. One of the team members calls a friend who knows a local reporter and asks the friend to hint to that reporter that Thule is considering building a second wembly plant in West Carolina. The next day's newspaper speculates on whether Thule may be moving away or building a second plant. At negotiations that day, Antarctica's team reports seeing the newspaper and suggests that if the newspaper report of a second plant is accurate, it might go a long way toward alleviating Antarctica's problem in relying on Thule as a sole source. Thule's negotiators remain non-committal, but they report Antarctica's comment to their top management. Given that the Antarctica contract would be a huge one for Thule, its executives begin considering whether securing the contract would warrant an expansion.

NEGOTIATION AUTHORITY

"SCEPTER, n. A king's staff of office, the sign and symbol of his authority. It was originally a mace with which the sovereign admonished his jester and vetoed ministerial measures by breaking the bones of their proponents." [Ambrose Bierce] In negotiations, authority generally carries the power of commitment with it. Most negotiators are representing the interests of others and derive their authority from these others. Obviously, when you are negotiating in your own interest, you may make no claim that you lack sufficient *authority* to make a deal, although you may desire to consult others or to talk matters over with your spouse. Prospective automobile or home buyers have very little they may do to ostensibly limit their own authority in negotiations. On the seller side of an automobile deal, the sales representative will frequently hide behind the claim, "I can't cut that price any further on my own. I'll have to get the approval of my sales manager."

In commercial negotiations, there is no law that requires an organization to provide any set level of authority for its negotiators. When you are an individual negotiating with a corporation, or when two corporations are negotiating, at the outset of negotiations you should inquire into the other side's authority to enter into binding arrangements. Counsel should be consulted for advice on what must be done by the other side, under applicable state law, to legally empower its negotiators to sign binding commitments on behalf of the organization. Corporate bargainers may be preliminary bargainers, that is any deal they might reach may be made subject to express approval by their hierarchical superiors.

Labor-management negotiations in the private sector is different from commercial negotiations. Employers are legally required to send to the table individuals with sufficient authority to commit the employer. On the other hand, unions, as democratic rather than hierarchical organizations, often enter into tentative agreements only, expressly subject to ratification by the union represented body of employees. You are probably familiar with newspaper accounts of tentative labor agreements that have been rejected by the rank and file. In public sector labor relations, the actions of a board or agency's negotiators may be subject to ratification by the employing governmental body.

What level of personnel should serve as negotiators? If the level of negotiators is too low, they will usually lack credibility and sufficient authority to act as representatives. If their level is too high, the negotiations may take on an unwarranted aura of artificially exaggerated importance. This top level exposure may lead the other side to seek more extensive gains than it would otherwise. Further, using high level negotiators eliminates the possibility of referring some things back to higher authority, deleting what can be a convenient delaying technique. If you bring in someone with higher status for the first time in the middle of a negotiation, you may be sending a signal that you are more interested in settling than previously indicated. Or, you may be displaying a lack of confidence in your current negotiators and undercutting their authority.

L-Mart Corporation is seeking to buy a large acreage site for the future home of its Kramerston store and is negotiating with GetMore Commercial Realtors concerning a land sale. L-Mart and GetMore are each using a three person negotiating team. The L-Mart team is led by the Corporate Manager of Acquisitions, while the GetMore team is led by its Commercial Sales Manager. Negotiations have become stalled over price related issues. The GetMore team has reviewed its position and is concerned with the possibility of losing the sale. However, at the latest negotiation session, L-Mart added a fourth person to its team. L-Mart's Senior Vice President for Store Locations, an individual who seldom appears at any negotiation, took over as chief spokesperson. GetMore noticed this substitution and correctly concluded that L-Mart needed to close the deal or they would not have sent a Vice President. GetMore held its price and was rewarded when L-Mart's agreed to pay it.

In negotiating to buy a car, you should be aware that the "insufficient authority" ploy is sometimes utilized to try to remake a deal to extract more money from you. As a prospective buyer, you may be told that the deal you have just negotiated is not final until it is approved by the "sales manager." After the sales representative disappears for five to ten minutes, leaving you to commune with your beautiful new car while the representative supposedly confers with the sales manager, the representative returns and informs you, "I'm sorry. The sales manager would really like to close the deal, but I made a mistake and we must get another one hundred dollars." Even if the signature of the sales manager is a formality, you may be shepherded into the sales manager's office to be given a long, almost captive audience, sales pitch, urging you to buy rust proofing, extended warranties, or other profit enhancing add-ons. As to those extended warranties, if the quality of the product the sales representative has just been touting is so low that you absolutely need an extended warranty, what does that say about the product? Now that you've virtually bought a car, you may be reluctant to walk out. Sellers' negotiators know this and often get the "extra nickel" on the sale.

Should your team spokesperson be an attorney? Attorneys tend to raise caution flags on the other side. If you use an attorney, the other side may also feel compelled to use an attorney. "The first thing we do, let's kill all the lawyers" [Shakespeare] is a sentiment still common among the general public. When a negotiation is complex, or when there are real legal issues or concerns, consider using an attorney as your team spokesperson. If this is considered unwise, at least consider having an attorney in your "back room," or available by telephone, to give immediate advice. Sometimes the best course is to designate someone to be your spokesperson who is an attorney, but who is also a person from within your organization who performs other functions, for example, a Director of Labor Relations, who is also an attorney, but who does not report to the General Counsel.

A word about attorneys and real estate negotiations. Simple real estate negotiations and agreements can often be handled by an experienced real estate agent, but your own attorney (not the bank's or the seller's attorney trying to represent more than one interest) is there to represent your interests, not those of the bank, the realtor, or the other party. Attorneys specialize. Although an attorney may be an expert in labor relations, human resources, or civil rights law, that attorney may have had little training or experience practicing real estate law and usually should retain a real estate lawyer when buying or selling a home or commercial real estate. Sadly, there is no "professional courtesy" among attorneys.

Unless you are getting free legal services from a close relative, there is no viable economic justification for using an attorney in your automobile related negotiation. In commercial negotiations, the other side may be sufficiently sophisticated not to be put off by your attorney-spokesperson. In labor-management negotiations, an attorney, operating as such, can turn into a barrier to settlement. Of course, when you are negotiating to settle a matter in litigation, an attorney should almost always be utilized. Regardless of whether you use an attorney to negotiate on your behalf, attorneys should be regarded as a resource in negotiations, as many negotiations are tightly woven into far reaching legal contexts. If you do use an attorney, don't be penny wise and pound foolish on the question of legal fees. You will tend to get what you pay for. Don't select a generalist, but rather an attorney who has the appropriate specialty and experience for your type of negotiation.

NEGOTIATION SECURITY

"The aim of the wise is not to secure pleasure, but to avoid pain." [Aristotle] Observing proper security techniques during negotiations is no pleasure, but security errors may lead to serious pain. Particularly for those negotiations in which large sums of money may be at stake, security should be a prime concern. Even in small scale negotiations, you should at least make an effort to be certain that your confidential instructions, authorizations, plans, and future offers are secured and are not left where they may be viewed by the other side. **If the other side obtains a copy of your plan and your negotiation limits, you will lose any chance to obtain a better settlement than your minimum.** During the Civil War (or the War Between the States), a security lapse led to General Robert E. Lee's orders for his entire Confederate army being wrapped around a cigar and left behind where they were found by federal forces. The result was the drawn battle of Antietam and the near destruction of Lee's army.

♪ TIP

If you must take confidential documents into the negotiating room, be sure that you, if you are negotiating alone, or some member of your team always checks the negotiating room for confidential materials before leaving, even if you are stepping outside for a one minute caucus by the door.

♪ TIP

In large scale negotiations, when there is a great deal of money at issue, consider having a security sweep of the negotiation room done, particularly if you hold any caucuses or private discussions in the meeting room. You may need to hire a professional service to do this. If your side is renting space in a hotel for the duration of negotiations for a caucus room, or for sleeping rooms for your negotiators, ask the hotel to change the locks, with no staff and only the hotel manager retaining a key. Admit the staff for cleaning and other purposes only when you are present. Have your telephone lines swept and try to avoid telephones that go through the hotel switchboard.

If all this security seems excessive, remember that when millions of dollars may be at stake, it is not wise to take chances to save small amounts of time or money.

The Big and Huge Corporations are conducting negotiations about a possible merger. The two companies are competitors and until a deal is reached need to keep certain financial and other data from each other. The most important documents bear on the price per share that Huge will pay for Big's stock. Huge's negotiators carry briefing books into the negotiating room with them which contain a complete set of confidential documents, including those relating to their bottom line share buying price. During negotiations, a question comes up on which Huge's chief spokesperson wants to consult the other members of the negotiating team. The Huge team takes just two minutes outside the door of the negotiating room. One of the team members leaves a briefing book open to the page which contains, in large type, the ultimate stock buying price. Without meaning to snoop, a member of the Big team, who is going across the room to get coffee from an urn, observes the page and absorbs the numbers. She quickly retreats and when the Huge team returns everything is in the place where it had been left. Big now has precious intelligence information, acquired without an active ethics violation, on which to base its final position on stock buy price. However, Big will need to consider the possibility that Huge did not leave that material on the table by mistake, but rather left disinformation to be found. Further, Big will have to decide whether to tell Huge what it now knows or whether to hide, and use, the information.

⚖ TIP

Never take confidential documents into the negotiating room unless absolutely necessary. When essential, they should be carried only by the spokesperson or those team members with a need for the documents, such as for use in making a presentation. When different members of the team have secure documents, each copy should contain a number (e.g. copy 1 of 7, on each page), so that if papers are copied, the source of the security lapse may be identifiable.

☞ TIP

Be alert for the other side's security errors. While no reputable negotiator will engage in negotiation espionage, if the other side wishes to be accommodating and to leave behind useful information, it is not unethical to acquire it.

☞ TIP

Never discuss confidential or secure information in hotel lobbies, men's or ladies' rooms, or in restaurants, particularly in small towns. The person near you may have some connection with the other side. Be paranoid about this. The larger the stakes, the greater the need to watch what you say and where you say it. Commercial, labor, and settlement negotiations may carry very high price tags that should not be compromised by discussion in inappropriate places.

☞ TIP

Try to avoid hotel copy services, unless you can watch what is being done with your confidential documents. Be sure you get back all your originals and take any "bad copies." If you have a caucus room, consider bringing a personal cross-cut shredder with you. Remember, ordinary cell phone conversations are carried on the air and can be monitored by sophisticated techniques. At the end of a negotiation session, take down any charts or materials put up for presentations and police the room to be sure no confidential information is left for the other side or even to be read by the staff of the organization renting you the space. You probably won't want your latest proposal in the local newspaper. Erase blackboards and shred flip chart pages as soon as possible.

NOTE TAKING

"The twelve jurors were all writing very busily on their slates. 'What are they all doing?' Alice whispered to the Gryphon. 'They can't have anything to put down yet, before the trial's begun.'" [Lewis Carroll]

Once negotiations begin, it is quite important to keep a record (although this step may be skipped in a negotiation simulation game). Notes may be the near verbatim record of a negotiation taken by a professional stenographer or secretary, your scribbling on documents, or your summary of what happened at the table on a given day. What is the purpose of taking notes during negotiations? These records provide you with a defensive shield to fend off the other side's claims or an offensive sword to pursue your own claims, in the event of later disputes. At the same time, notes are a mixed blessing that may sometimes be used against you when their disclosure is compelled by law.

Notes may be used to refresh your recollection if post-negotiation disputes arise about what was said at the table or about the intended meaning of language in the final agreement. In labor contract and commercial negotiations, notes may be introduced into a later arbitration procedure over the interpretation and application of your negotiated agreement. However, be aware that if you testify from notes, or if you read them in preparation for testifying, the notes may be subject to subpoena by the other side. This can be a problem if some portions of the notes don't support the point you are making.

Parties do sometimes take joint notes. This creates a problem in that the note taker may lean toward one side or the other and both sides will have access to the work product. You may spend precious time arguing over the correct wording of the notes.

🖋 TIP

Consider refusing any request for joint notes, particularly if you have greater resources for note taking. Having your own notes also means that you will be able to edit them before they are finalized.

You may think that you can eliminate the tedious task of note taking by recording an audio or video tape of your negotiation. If both sides are aware that a recording is being made and consent, you are free to adopt these methods. However, the result will be a truly verbatim record. Having every word taped may inhibit free and frank discussion. Accordingly, experienced negotiators often reject the idea of taping. In labor-management negotiations, the taking of *fully* verbatim notes (by shorthand) without the other side's consent, or over their objection, may be an unfair labor practice. However, an accomplished stenographer can take "near verbatim" notes, provided the minutes do not comport to be all inclusive. Finding someone with the superb stenographic skills to keep up with the pace of those speaking and who catches all the important points may be very difficult and expensive. If no one with these stenographic skills is available, consider assigning note taking to the junior or lowest ranking member of a negotiating team. Be sensitive. Note taking is not a job that should automatically be assigned to a female team member.

Negotiation minutes can be very useful to give you background and history when a key negotiation player has left the organization before an issue comes up in litigation or arbitration. Also, for professional negotiators who move frequently from table to table, keeping good notes is a way to remember in detail what may have happened a long time ago.

☞ TIP

When presenting complex proposals, consider handing out written examples of how your proposal would operate. For example, a health insurance plan might be accompanied by several examples of how the deductible and stop loss (out-of-pocket limitation) provisions are intended to work. A copy of these handouts should be preserved in your negotiation minutes.

☞ TIP

The date and time that a proposal is handed across a negotiating table or is received should be recorded in the notes and also in the spokesperson's personal negotiation book. To avoid confusion among various drafts of a proposal, each proposal should contain a revision number on each page. For serial offers, such as a series of economic offers, using color coded paper is an excellent method to prevent handing over the wrong document, such as a final offer when you intend to distribute a first offer. For example, you might arbitrarily decide that documents you prepare to be shared by both sides will be copied on white paper, your own confidential documents will be copied on yellow paper, and documents to be handed to the other side will be copied on blue paper.

PRESS BLACKOUTS OR OPEN COMMUNICATIONS

"I won't say that the papers misquote me, but I sometimes wonder where Christianity would be today if some of those reporters had been Matthew, Mark, Luke and John." [Barry Goldwater] A question that frequently arises in large scale negotiations, whether commercial or labor relations related, is how much to tell the press and, through the media, the world at large about what is happening. Why not communicate openly? What you have to say may not be reported accurately. It may be distorted or twisted, or important nuances may be ignored or changed. In negotiations, you may need to take initial positions which are extreme and which are designed to allow you room to make concessions as you move toward the center. However, if the interested public hears about a proposal, particularly an initial one, they may treat it as though it was your final stand. This may generate considerable negative public reaction. The result is that it is rarely in the interest of either party to disclose negotiation details to those without a need to know. At the same time, you may wish to keep necessary support groups informed in general terms of the outstanding issues and progress that is being made.

You may gain a significant advantage if you are able to completely control the flow of information to your constituents. For example, if you are negotiating on behalf of a labor union, you are likely to prefer having a monopoly on communications with represented employees. Note that management communications with rank and file union represented employees are subject to legal limitations, including a requirement to share the communications first with the union. When management is considering direct communications, they should always consult with their labor relations counsel. Both sides may agree on some form of general limitation of communications about what is happening at the table. As negotiations develop, the need or desire to communicate may change.

☞ TIP

Don't sign any "news blackout" agreements. If you are willing to agree to a temporary blackout, always reserve the right to communicate with, or without, the other side's permission. This may be done by saying, "We have no *current* intent to negotiate through the press, but we reserve the right to do so if we should come to feel that it is necessary. Accordingly, we will not sign, or agree to, an absolute commitment as to a press blackout that is to be binding on our side."

✒ TRICK

In labor-management negotiations which involve highly paid employees in relation to most of the labor market, when you are seeking to put public relations pressure on the other side, consider publishing an annual earnings comparison between your top highly paid skilled workers (including annual overtime) and lower paid, but well regarded, occupations in your area's general labor market. For example, you might compare the wages of your top industrial maintenance mechanics or plumbers with the entry level annual pay of police officers or teachers. It is hard for highly paid workers to win sympathy for a labor dispute from those who do demanding work at lower pay.

Other devices that may be utilized to establish communications pressures include:

+ Communications to your own side, whether or not labeled confidential (they will inevitably leak);
+ Establishing a toll free dial in "hot line," whether or not the number is listed; or,
+ Planting rumors.

LYING WITH STATISTICS; AVERAGES; AND SPLITTING THE DIFFERENCE

"There are three kinds of lies: lies, damn lies, and statistics." [Benjamin Disraeli] Most negotiations involve at least some exposure to statistics and a certain level of numeracy. **Always approach statistical material with a good degree of doubt and always verify the source of the data.** Be sure you understand the definitions of all of the terms and of all of the bases that are used to arrive at the numbers.

Statistics issued against the compiler's own interest carry a much greater presumption of validity than studies showing results favorable to the interest group commissioning them. Statements against interest are an exception to the hearsay limitations of the rules of evidence used in the courts. A study that shows that smoking is healthy and is conducted by the anti-smoking society is far more credible than a similar survey conducted by the tobacco industry, because the results of the first survey are adverse to the surveyor's interests.

For example, you may bring to the negotiating table a survey of prices or wages. Most surveys are flawed in one way or another. Either side may construct a survey that proves almost anything it wants to prove. If a survey makes comparisons, make certain that they are comparisons of apples with apples, not of apples with oranges.

The parties in a merger negotiation are discussing how many jobs would be made redundant by the merger and what savings could be accomplished by eliminating overlapping personnel in the proposed merged organization. In doing this, they compare salaries paid for equivalent jobs across the United States, to determine what economies of scale may be achieved. Examining Company A's salary table, Company B's negotiator notes a wide variance in salaries for equivalent jobs at Company A's various locations. He asks, "Is this due to some form of regional pay allowance?" The response is, "No, some of these figures include cost of living allowances, others do not." Company B's salary data are all exclusive of cost of living, which is shown in a footnote. The two tables cannot be compared even handedly, unless they all include, or all exclude, cost of living allowances. Another variant found in the tables is that Company B, in showing salary histories for the last three years, has adjusted for inflation, while Company A has not done so. One table is in current dollars while the other is in constant dollars.

When surveying other organizations, your selection of the organizations for inclusion, or exclusion, from your study is a major factor and may heavily skew the outcome. In real estate negotiations, appraisal of a property is often done by looking at comparables. What is declared comparable may be very significant. But, in selecting what should be considered "comparable," professional appraisers may differ. Before appraisals are accepted for comparison purposes, they should be reviewed to see if there has been any "gerrymandering" in the selection of comparables.

☞ TIP

When preparing charts to show statistics that support your position, try to select benchmarks and time frames that support your position over those that do not. For example, if you are trying to show that your prices are lower than your competitors' prices, you might compare your "street price" against the competitors' "list prices." Even if such variables are acknowledged in footnotes, the visual impact will emphasize your point. However, negotiators should try to avoid transparent and obviously self serving distortions, which may hurt your credibility.

Evolving Ltd. has a proposal on the negotiating table to move its employees from a defined benefit contribution pension plan (so many dollars per month, per year of service, guaranteed at retirement) to a defined contribution plan (a named percent of salary contributed each month, with no guarantee of what the pension will be worth at the time of retirement). To emphasize the advantages of a defined contribution plan, the employer has prepared a table that shows how the account balance would grow in the defined contribution plan for an employee now age 25, if taken to retirement at 65. The table uses a conservative annual rate of investment growth and shows that at retirement the employee is projected to have an account balance of over one million (then current) dollars. This is accompanied by colored charts showing the projected growth of the fund over time. The employer also has a similar chart showing what inflation over the long term will do to the price of a combo hamburger meal at a local fast food outlet. It does not share this chart with the employees. To do so might well demonstrate that by the time the 25 year old employee reaches age 65, forty years from now, the purchasing power of a one million dollar account will be severely diminished.

Another pitfall lies in the use of averages. Averages are fine if, as to the item in issue, the situation of a party is actually average. That the average buyer of an automobile pays $21,500 for it, including an average amount of optional equipment, is not relevant for the buyer who is buying only the stripped down basic model. The average may be also be skewed. Suppose a small plant has fifteen employees. Thirteen of them each make $20,000 per year, the assistant plant manager makes $60,000 per year, and the plant manager makes $90,000 per year. The average (mean) salary in that plant is $27,300. The two high paid employees pull up an arithmetic or mean average. The median average (half above and half below) is still $20,000. Averages may be interesting, but negotiators should understand that they are only a tool. If they are unfavorable, they should be brushed aside.

"Let's split the difference and settle," is a frequently used line. Splitting the difference makes sense only if the high and low numbers to be split are both reasonable and the middle position is within your settlement window. However, if you split the difference routinely or aren't careful about how you regard the other side's position when it offers to split, you will encourage the other side to set its position too high before they suggest a split. **Never split the difference for its own sake or consider the mid-point of a disputed range to be pre-sumptively reasonable.**

John LowSay is negotiating to buy a car from HighSay motors. LowSay hopes to get the car for $23,500, at most is willing to pay $24,500, and has an offer of $23,500 on the table. The dealer's target for a sale runs from a minimum of $23,500 to a higher profit target of $24,500. HighSay moves its asking price down from $26,500 to $25,500. When LowSay still resists, although the sales representative knows he may, if necessary, accept the offer on the table, the sales representative frowns and announces he has done his best, but will see if he is able to get the "sales manager" to "split the difference," if that will close the deal. LowSay tells the sales representative to go ahead and try. After a few minutes in an empty office with a cup of coffee, the sales representative returns and announces, "He didn't want to do it and I had to twist his arm, but if you buy right now, the sales manager has authorized me to be reasonable, split the difference, and offer you the car at a rock bottom $24,500. I'll write it up." LowSay hesitates a moment, but it seems unreasonable to ask HighSay to split the difference yet again, or to hold out for a better price, so he nods his head and the deal is made. Although within his target, LowSay has spent an unnecessary $1,000 by "splitting the difference" on the car.

What is seductive about the concept of splitting the difference is its aura of reasonableness. This is designed to make you feel guilty if you don't go along or if you hold out for more. Unless an offer to split the difference brings you to your best (not your minimum) objective, be very careful about accepting it.

If, at this point, the opening phase of negotiations seems very complex to you, remember that not all of the points above are relevant to all negotiations. For those who want to be professional negotiators handling complex matters, the more you know about them, the more they become second nature, the more likely you are to win game, set, and match in the negotiations game. Good negotiations in complex situations require lots of work. Doing some homework and watching the fundamentals can also save individuals money when dealing with large ticket items such as a home or car; items we buy and sell only a few times in a lifetime. With the opening phase now concluding, in the next chapter, we will take a look at the middle portion of negotiations. In the next phase, time will become a more critical factor, but not quite as pressing as in the final end game stage.

CHAPTER 12

THE MID-NEGOTIATION PROCESS

"Depend upon it, sir, when a man knows he is to be hanged in a fortnight, it concentrates his mind wonderfully." [Dr. Samuel Johnson] Time, along with power and information, are the three key elements in any negotiation. Time pressure is one of the most effective factors in getting both sides to concentrate on resolving open negotiation issues. But, the mid-negotiation process takes place before time pressure becomes truly critical. Indeed, in some negotiations, such as public sector sessions between school boards and teachers, or in some commercial bargaining, real time pressure never develops. It is as though you are playing games and sets in tennis, but there is no prescribed number of sets that must be won for victory in the match. You simply go on playing until someone is too tired to continue. These situations usually produce glacially slow progress. If the opening phase of the negotiations game involves sparring for advantage, and the end game phase is marked by frenetic movement against a time deadline, the mid game suggests different techniques, such as measured movement, logical discussion, and the use of problem solving.

Turning points are not always evident. Hindsight makes it clear that the Battle of Midway was the turning point in the Pacific in World War II, but few people at the time awoke after Midway and said, "Well, that's it, the turning point." It is difficult to define exactly when the opening phase ends and when mid game phase begins. It may be equally difficult to determine when the mid game phase gives way to end game play. As a type of benchmark, the mid game phase begins approximately after ground rules have been set, opening speeches made, proposals exchanged, and first positions taken. It ends when time pressures force rapid movement or when all the easy issues have been resolved.

Newcomers to the negotiating process often become discouraged during the middle phase or experience wide swings of mood between optimism and pessimism concerning ultimate success. In the absence of an immediate deadline, it may seem that little progress is being made and that the negotiation process is crawling. The tendency to fall into this form of frustration is particularly acute for people with engineering and scientific backgrounds. For these quantitatively oriented individuals, the answers to many questions in their regular work world are black or white, not shades of gray.

The middle phase is an important part of any negotiating match. It is during this phase that each side struggles to identify the other side's critical positions and to explore solutions to both easy and seemingly intractable problems. The middle phase is also used to set up end game squeeze plays. For a sense of perspective, keep in mind that the lack of an immediate time deadline for resolution of any negotiation tends to magnify unimportant and minor issues. What seems important to you in the middle phase may pale to insignificance in the end game, when major economic or legal consequences may follow if issues are not resolved promptly.

This chapter focuses on the middle phase of the negotiating game. It suggests a number of methods that you may use during this phase to keep bargaining on track and to facilitate progress. It is critically important to manage the clock in such a way that end game negotiations may be resolved in time to accomplish your, or your organization's, goals. It is during the middle phase that much of the early planning you did, assuming you followed the prescriptions of the prior chapters, will yield significant dividends.

PROBLEM SOLVING DISCUSSION TECHNIQUES

"A problem adequately stated is a problem well on its way to being solved." [Richard Buckminster Fuller] The traditional means of negotiating involves volleys back and forth in which positions are changed. In this conventional method, these changes of position are the result of the applications of power through relative pressure and need not be the product of any real discussion of underlying interests. Although the outcome of a traditional positional negotiation may end up as satisfactory to both sides on the surface, the germs of potential conflict resulting from a lack of understanding remain. Since the parties never discussed the underlying interests or purposes of whatever it is they have agreed upon, they will have made no effort to find solutions that meet deeper needs than satisfying the power, information, and time pressure realities.

One of the problems of positional bargaining is that, in keeping with basic human nature, each side will begin to dig its heels in, sometimes over substantive matters, but also over detail or specific language. As the King of Siam proclaims in the show, "The King and I," people are very quick to fight to prove that what they do not know is so. Problem solving is a technique designed to break the log jam of positional bargaining and to prevent becoming bogged down over minor details.

What are some of the techniques for problem solving discussions? If you wish to involve the other side in problem solving, you must first get the other side to agree to work in that mode. This may prove to be quite difficult. If they are used to positional bargaining, they may naturally prefer to stay with what is familiar to them, or they may be afraid, sometimes validly, that they will lose advantage in problem solving discussions. In commercial negotiations, both parties are probably reasonably well equipped to engage in problem solving. In personal negotiations, such as those for real estate, antiques, or automobiles, problem solving may be useful in determining each side's hidden interests. In labor-management negotiations, it is usually to management's advantage, more than the union's, to use problem solving. This is true because it is usually management that is more adept at problem solving techniques, based on its experience in running facilities and making substantive decisions, at analyzing problems, and proposing solutions, within a hierarchical decision making structure that is capable of moving quickly. Also, many labor negotiations are guided by international union representatives who may see problem solving, which involves other members of their negotiating teams in active participation, as threatening to their leadership roles and control of the process.

In essence, problem solving involves putting aside the traditional positional exchanges in favor of discussing the underlying purposes and needs of each side. If you are the side presenting a proposal via problem solving discussion, you should first "apply empathy" and attempt to determine for yourself what you believe are the underlying needs of the other side. You should also be prepared to set forth your own intentions in clear terms and to fully identify what you perceive as your own vital interests. Try to find a way to address both your and the other side's needs in your proposed solution. Then, try to force a shift in your talks away from positions to problems and solutions.

Rock Musicians and Football Players Trust Company is in negotiations with the Human Tellers Union. The parties are in the middle phase of negotiations. The Trust Company has a number of proposals on the table, grounded in technological change, which it believes are necessary for company survival and growth. Negotiations started with positional bargaining and rapidly became locked into discussions of the specific words of both union and company proposals. The company broke the incipient hardening of positions by setting aside its positional posture and opening a problem solving discussion. Although the union was at first reluctant to participate, the rank and file members of the union committee became interested in the whys and wherefores of the company proposals, as revealed in the problem solving discussion. At the same time, the company showed its flexibility by offering to consider alternative solutions, provided these solutions addressed the underlying problem of meeting competition. This discussion revealed that the union's primary interest was in obtaining the necessary education and the chance to follow the jobs as they became more skilled. By concentrating on the needs of both the employees and the business, the company shifted the discussion away from the nit picking details of language and position. After a time, some progress was made.

✐ TIP

In problem solving mode, listening skills are very important. Problem solving is a less structured method than positional bargaining. Table discussion is likely to be far more fluid and less controlled. Listening carefully will give you a better window into what the other side really perceives as its needs and may also reveal a good deal of information about its true positions. Despite the fact that negotiations are ultimately adversarial, it is always possible, and it frequently occurs, that the other side comes up with an idea during problem solving that will meet your side's real needs in a different form and the idea is worthy of consideration. Great care should be taken to answer questions and to provide positive feedback to the other side when its role in discussions is productive and positive.

What do you need to do to carry out an effective problem solving discussion? If you are the person leading the discussion and are presenting one of your own proposals:

- Be sure you are well briefed on the substantive subject;
- Know the ins and outs of how your proposal will work;
- Have a thorough understanding of all the underlying issues; and,
- Refuse to be drawn into discussions of detail or specific language.

Problem solving discussions are discussions of general concepts and general solutions, not of specifics. The best answer to the demand for specifics is, "It is pointless to discuss specifics until we have reached a mutually acceptable agreement in principle. Without an agreement on what we want to do, we can't write language on how to do it. After we have agreement, we will work to resolve detailed language." When responding in a problem solving discussion, it should be made clear that exploring ideas does not mean that mere discussion is to be equated with agreement or a commitment to a course of action.

✍ TIP

If you are the person leading the problem solving discussion, stand at the front of the room in the center between the sides, while the others remain seated. Standing tends to give you an aura of authority. You may want to use typical training equipment such as charts, easels, slides, boards, and handouts. You should try to involve as many people as possible from the other side in your discussion. The thrust of your effort should be to channel the problem solving discussion down lines you have thought out in advance, while accepting deviations that may prove to be useful, either from the perspective of obtaining information or eliciting viable alternate solutions.

✍ TRAP

It is a trap for you as the problem solving discussion leader, or for other members of your team, to answer questions for which you do not have accurate or confirmed information. It is better to admit that you do not have the information currently available than to provide inaccurate information. You may want to promise to get back to the other side with the information. Once you make a promise to supply data, as with other promises made in negotiations, you must keep it.

When should you abandon problem solving? If the other side continues to be resistant to the process over time, problem solving may not be useable. Problem solving should also be abandoned when the time line constraints require a return to positional bargaining. If problem solving does result in an agreement in principle, working out the detailed language may well be done with a reversion to positional bargaining. A party planning to use problem solving techniques should try to set up a negotiations schedule that will allow sufficient time to use the technique. Positional bargaining is far faster.

Why do problem solving at all? Apart from its ability to break log jams, problem solving offers a means to devise solutions that both sides will consider they helped to design and which they are then more likely to work to make successful. The perception of "win-win" negotiations is enhanced when problem solving works. **Although mutually derived solutions have more "legitimacy" for those impacted by them, no matter how collaboratively the two sides worked in problem solving, despite having been able to reach a shared solution on a specific problem when their interests happened to overlap, each side was still seeking primarily to serve its own interest. Sugar coating or none, the negotiation process ultimately remained inherently adversarial.**

In theory, problem solving techniques sound easy. In application, they may be quite difficult to utilize. Good preparation and simulated problem solving discussion training is a key to the method's success. When properly used, problem solving techniques are an excellent alternative to positional bargaining in the middle phase.

CREATIVE WAYS TO GET THINGS MOVING

"Creativity requires the courage to let go of certainties." [Erich Fromm] No matter how smoothly a negotiation is progressing, there will be times when things either bog down or some kind of impediment to progress at the table will arise. When this occurs, there are a number of useful techniques for you to use to get things moving again. Some of these techniques include:

+ Abandon positional bargaining and switch to problem solving mode;
+ Change the subject to something less controversial;
+ Call a recess, or adjourn for the day;
+ Apply new pressure (external to the table) to the other side;
+ Try humor;
+ Give a heavy speech, or do something unusual; or,
+ Bring in a mediator or third party neutral.

As noted above, if you use positional bargaining, you may cause a "dug in" position. To get around this obstacle, consider switching to a problem solving mode. You may suggest to the other side that both of you put away your papers and positions and talk about issues and interests. The objective in doing this is to get away from inhibiting details and to work back to concepts. In this context, problem solving is utilized not necessarily as a means of achieving substantive ends, but rather as a tactical means to get things moving again.

You may want to change the subject to temporarily defuse a difficult situation which is holding up progress at the table. While this technique may get you past the momentary problem, the underlying issue will still be there and will have to be addressed at a later time. On the other hand, by the time you return to the subject, tempers may well have cooled or its importance diminished under the pressure of time.

Isaac Walltone is negotiating with Charles Bass to purchase a hunting and fishing lodge. The two individuals are having a heated discussion about what, if any, personal property around the lodge will go with the sale. Bass senses that if the discussions continue on point, the entire deal may be lost. He switches the subject to another less controversial point, concerning an easement that he wishes to retain. He knows that Walltone has no significant problem over the easement. Bass knows the issue of defining the included personal property in the lodge sale will come up again. He hopes that Walltone will be in a better mood at the time and that Walltone will be accompanied by his wife, who seems to have a calming influence on him. Barring that, Bass has decided to defer the question until all other issues are resolved. He believes that once both sides are that close to an overall agreement, the personal property issue will diminish in significance.

Calling a recess or adjourning for the day is also a temporary palliative designed to let tempers cool and to allow the resumption of talks later without any obvious loss of face for the other side. A short recess is usually relatively risk free, but adjourning for the day may be a problem, particularly if there are not enough negotiation sessions or time left. Too many cancellations of sessions, like the frivolous use of a time out in the National Football League, may have serious results in the end game phase. A short tactical recess may sometimes be enhanced by a shift to another subject upon returning.

Sometimes, you will need to give the other side a push to get them moving again, particularly if your side is trying to obtain their agreement to a proposal that they find unpalatable (perhaps for political or personal reasons). At heart, negotiation is about the relative application of power. An external demonstration, away from the table, may be just what is required to get the other side to accept your position and to move on.

Negotiations between American Androids and Electrotech Supplies had been progressing nicely, but they are now stalled. Electrotech is reluctant to accept the price point that American Androids currently has on the table. Electrotech's negotiation plan does allow it to accept the price proposed by American Androids, but the chief spokesperson for Electrotech has staked some of her prestige on bringing in a contract for somewhat less than is authorized. To overcome this reluctance and to remind her that American Androids is in a power bargaining position, American Android's spokesperson adjourns the talks for the day and contacts Technocrats, Inc., inviting them to submit a bid. In the process, she makes sure that word of this will leak to Electrotech. The added pressure causes Electrotech to back off its position immediately at the start of the next negotiating session.

⚡ TRAP

Your application of external pressure has the potential to backfire. Use external pressure with care and when you are reasonably certain it will be successful. If the other side has the ability to walk away from the negotiation and use of external pressure is a "deal breaker," your negotiation may well end. In the labor-management situation, where the parties are wedded to a continuing relationship by law, this concern does not apply and you may apply external pressure more readily.

One of the most effective tools to break up a serious disagreement is humor, preferably of the self deprecating kind. The fact is that people engaged in important negotiations often get so wrapped up in the process that they become unduly serious. In this context, humor should not be used without thought. The spokesperson or the bargaining team should decide that humor is appropriate and that a release of tensions may permit things to move ahead. Sometimes the best advice is to "lighten up a bit."

Occasionally, a "shocking speech," or unusual behavior, may serve to get a stalled negotiation back on track. A speech of this sort may be one that is out of character or which displays strong (but planned) emotion. You will want to assign this type of speech to an individual who is normally quiet at the table and for whom it represents an out of character occurrence. The purpose of this speech is to bring home the seriousness of the point, to cause the other side to begin moving on the open issues.

Finally, you may use a mediator or neutral third party to deliver a message that it is undesirable for you to deliver yourself at the table. This may be done either directly through a third party who you make aware of your strategy ("tell them we are serious"), or by using behavior calculated to cause the mediator or third party neutral to sense your seriousness and to deliver your message, without specifically being asked to do so. A third party may also be used to attempt to facilitate a way to resume progress.

EXAMPLES AND EXPLANATIONS TO AVOID FUTURE DISPUTES

"Facts which at first seem improbable will, even on scant explanation, drop the cloak which has hidden them and stand forth in naked and simple beauty." [Galileo] Examples and explanations help avoid ambiguity. Gray areas you create at the bargaining table may lead to later disputes as to what was agreed upon, either in principle or in detailed language. Sometimes ambiguity is necessary to allow both sides to seemingly resolve a problem. In reality, ambiguity simply serves to leave the issue indeterminate and deferred to another day. But, when you use ambiguity to avoid or defer an issue, this should be the result of a conscious decision, not by accident or omission. How is it possible to avoid ambiguous provisions? Giving specific examples and explanations, sometimes in writing, may serve this purpose.

SuperSafes is in negotiations with the Union of Safe Manufacturing Workers (USMW) for a successor labor agreement. The company has proposed a number of revisions in the health care plan, involving changes in deductibles, out-of-pocket limits, and imposing a requirement for a second surgical opinion before elective surgery may be performed. The USMW is unhappy with the company proposals, but is considering accepting them, in return for improvements in wages and pensions. However, they are not quite sure how the new health care revisions will work. During the discussion of its health care revisions, SuperSafes hands the following example across the table to the union:

Maria Juarez, an employee covered by the revised plan, needs elective surgery. She is required to get a second surgical opinion. If she fails to do so, she will be liable for 35% of the fees and expenses connected with the surgery, instead of the usual 20%, regardless of whether her out-of-pocket limit has been met. If she obtains the second surgical opinion, even if that opinion disfavors surgery, she may go ahead with the surgery, without any decrease in the amount payable by the plan. Ms. Juarez obtains the second opinion, which favors surgery, and she decides to go ahead. She has had no prior medical expenses in the calendar year. The surgery cost ten thousand dollars, all of which is allowed by the carrier as a reasonable and customary medical expense. Ms. Juarez must pay the first two hundred dollars from her own pocket (the deductible), without reimbursement from the plan. She will then pay twenty percent (20%) of the remaining bill until she reaches the out-of-pocket limit of five hundred dollars. In this specific case, Ms. Juarez pays from her pocket two hundred dollars, which is the deductible, plus 20% of the next fifteen hundred dollars (which is three hundred dollars, after which she has expended five hundred dollars in total and reached the out-of-pocket limit. Once her out of pocket limit is reached the plan pays one hundred percent (100%) of additional covered reasonable and customary medical costs for the balance of the calendar year. The entire remaining balance of nine thousand five hundred dollars for Ms. Juarez's surgery is paid by the carrier.

The example provides a concrete representation of how the revisions to the plan will operate. The company also hands out several additional examples with different variants. It then places copies of the examples in the negotiation minutes. If there is a later dispute about how the plan is supposed to work, the examples may be cited in a court or in an arbitration.

☞ TIP

Always check that the example you provide factually reflects the way you intend the plan to operate. If you provide an example across the table which differs from your intent, or if you make a mistake in what is covered, your side may later be forced to accept the interpretation provided in your own example. There is some danger in using examples. Once you have locked an example into your negotiation history, that interpretation will become authoritative, whether or not it works for you later. An example which is poorly thought out and which hurts your own side is worse than no example at all. **Make sure that the example you use reflects your current position on the table, not necessarily the one which you may end up signing.**

TENTATIVE AGREEMENTS AND NARROWING ISSUES

"Look for your choices, pick the best one, then go with it." [Pat Riley] In negotiations, once you make a choice, your options generally become more limited. But, you'll also want to feel secure that the choice you made won't slip away from you. Think of a negotiation as a giant jigsaw puzzle. The final terms of a negotiated agreement come together one piece at a time. When a piece is placed, you want it out of the way so that working with the remaining pieces becomes simpler and you don't have to struggle to place them again. If your negotiating opponent could repeatedly pick up your partially completed puzzle and drop the pieces on the floor, a complete agreement would be difficult to ever achieve. Obtaining signed "tentative agreement" documents locks the pieces of negotiation issues into a resolved category. This allows your attention and effort to be concentrated on the remaining outstanding issues. As each issue is put to bed, the parties experience closure on the issue and progress toward an overall settlement, an important psychological effect.

Tentative agreements on specific issues may be made subject to reaching an overall package and, in the case of labor-management negotiations, subject to a final ratification by the represented employees, if this is required under union bylaws. The role of tentative agreements should have been clearly established in the ground rule stage. At that time, the person, or persons, authorized to sign or initial tentative agreements for each side should have been identified. Copies of all tentatively signed, or initialed, agreements should be retained by each side in a master negotiation book and in each spokesperson's own records.

You use tentative agreements as a device in furtherance of the general rule of negotiations that issues should be narrowed as negotiations progress. Going backward in bargaining by revisiting positions that have already been closed is termed "retrogressive bargaining." It is an indicia of bad faith. In fact, in private sector labor-management negotiations and under most state public sector bargaining laws, retrogressive bargaining is an unfair labor practice. While in commercial negotiations there is no legal penalty for retrogression, it is an activity that is likely to undermine or destroy, a negotiation. There are ways around the retrogression rules. Revisiting proposals already tentatively agreed upon in the context of a larger counterproposal, accompanied by new concessions in other areas, is not technically retrogression.

The rules and practices surrounding tentative agreements and the narrowing of issues have been designed throughout the modern history of negotiations to allow the parties to move toward a complete settlement in an orderly manner. If all issues remained open throughout negotiations, it would be very difficult for the parties to know where they stood or to conclude a complete agreement.

Raisa Romanov is in a real estate negotiation. She is trying to sell a tract of commercial land to Vikki Sibelius. The proposed purchase contract covering the transaction has forty-two paragraphs. The parties begin by noting which provisions of the proposed agreement are fully accepted by each side. These are then initialed as tentatively agreed upon, the parties noting that there will be no contractual agreement until all terms are resolved. Twenty paragraphs are boilerplate language and accepted by both sides, as written. As discussions of the other clauses yield changes and then agreement on another twenty clauses, they are also initialed as tentative agreements. The parties finally reduce the number of open issue to two critical ones. At that point, they know which issues require concentrated attention and compromise.

✍ TIP

Set a time limit on the validity of your tentative agreements. For example, you might state that your tentative agreements are only good until a certain date, after which they are automatically withdrawn, unless you agree in writing to extend them. One reason for doing this is it reopens all options for your side and puts everything back on the table should negotiations ultimately deadlock, without engaging in legally retrogressive bargaining. Always try to preserve as much of your freedom of action as is possible, consistent with negotiation credibility and applicable law. **Similarly, any offer of a complete agreement, should contain a date after which it is either automatically withdrawn, or after which you reserve the right to withdraw it unilaterally, should it not be accepted.**

AGREEMENTS IN PRINCIPLE AND FINAL LANGUAGE

"God is in the details." [Mies van der Rohe] The phrase the "devil is in the details" is also frequently used. Detailed language is necessary to create legally binding negotiation agreements. What then is an agreement in principle? It is an understanding about how a problem or issue will be resolved in overall terms, but without the detail of specific language. Sometimes you may place a complete package on an issue on the table, including both a concept and specific language to carry it out. The problem with being overly specific at the outset is that people tend to concentrate on items of detail which they view as personally threatening. This concentration on what is often minor aspects of an overall system can greatly impede the success of your negotiation.

Agreement in principle is part and parcel of problem solving, a technique discussed at the outset of this chapter. In problem solving, the parties work toward identifying their essential interests, looking for overlap, and creating a solution acceptable to both sides that embodies a method of resolving a problem. When you have reached that point, there is "agreement in principle." Attaining this plateau does not necessarily mean that achieving final agreement is inevitable. It is often a long way from agreement in principle to specific words to flesh out the final agreement. This is so because, while you have reached agreement in principle, you may have vastly different ideas about exactly how that agreement should be carried out. You may also be jockeying for a position during language negotiations that gives your side a tactical advantage. Techniques for language writing were discussed in chapter seven.

Errata Books and Utah.com have been in commercial negotiations over the placement on Utah's web site of a number of books published by Errata. They have reached agreement in principle that, among other things, Errata will discount books placed in Utah's on line catalog by "a commercially reasonable amount which is to be in line with industry practice between a publisher and a large distributor." This term is one among a number of similar items, such as the time limit on returning unsold books and an allowance for damaged items. As the parties now work to formalize their agreement in principle, it develops that Errata and Utah are very far apart on the size of a "commercially reasonable amount" and the duration of the time limit for the return of unsold books. However, the agreement in principle has served its purpose of laying out the general tenor of the bargain. Now, the parties are left to work out the details. These details may be very important and, if unresolved, may yet result in failure of the negotiations to produce an overall agreement.

✒ TIP

Work out as many agreements in principle as possible before moving on to the details of any of them. Then, select the least controversial for your first attempts to finalize language. Try to insure that you have as much understanding as possible of where the other side believes the agreement in principle will take them. Make an effort to control the timing of when the details of agreements in principle will be considered, keeping in mind which agreements are likely to work out quickly. Encourage a psychology of progress and trust on the easy items. This will facilitate later resolution of problems which are difficult and controversial.

LETTERS OF UNDERSTANDING IN LABOR NEGOTIATIONS

"Don't write so that you can be understood, write so that you can't be misunderstood." [William Howard Taft] Letters of understanding are a technique to avoid future conflict. Until well into the twentieth century, governments often negotiated secret protocols to treaties. You may be willing to agree to an item but for political or face saving reasons, or to keep your concession temporary, may be unwilling to place your commitment in the final negotiated agreement. Letters of understanding are frequently used in labor-management negotiations, but may also be used in commercial transactions to amplify a negotiated contract. A union may prefer that the employees it represents not have easy access to specific provisions granting unpopular concessions. A company may not wish to place a concession in a formal agreement, because once it is there, it will prove more difficult to delete the clause. Removing a term from the contract will have to be negotiated with the other side, while a letter of understanding may contain its own built-in separate expiration. A company may also want to offer a program on an experimental basis, using a letter to take the program outside normal bargaining, reserving the right to unilaterally cancel or to amend the program. In such instances and others, both sides may agree upon, or the receiving side may accept, a letter of understanding. Letters are sometimes termed "side agreements."

Nuclear Houseboats Corporation (NHC) is in negotiations with the Houseboat Workers Union (HWU) for a successor labor agreement. The number of female employees in the bargaining unit has grown substantially in the last several years. Many of these employees are pressing the union to negotiate some form of company paid child care. The company is willing to experiment with a program, but it wants to retain the flexibility to abandon or modify the program, if its experience or cost factors warrant. It wants the right to do so without negotiating changes with the union (which requires a waiver to avoid violating federal private sector labor law). The union is very reluctant to have the contract contain any language which would grant the company a unilateral right to make changes. The company is also reluctant to place the experimental child care program inside the labor agreement, because the agreement contains a broad based grievance clause ending in final and binding arbitration that covers all disputes arising from within the four walls of the contract itself. The parties resolve the issue by agreeing that the company will issue a letter of understanding, expressly outside the labor agreement. This allows the union to claim a victory with the employees for bringing in a child care program, while addressing the employer's concerns about flexibility to experiment. The specific letter of understanding reads:

"No later than three (3) calendar months after the effective date of our next labor agreement, NHC will initiate an experimental child care program for employees represented by HWC. This program will provide a subsidy to employees of twenty percent (20%) of the cost of child care at such government licensed day care centers or with such family day care providers as NHC may, in its sole discretion, approve. It is understood that this program shall be deemed experimental and may be abolished or modified, from time to time, unilaterally by the company, at its sole discretion, regardless of cause, without negotiating with the union. The company agrees it will give thirty (30) calendar days advance written notice to the union of any abolition or changes. This letter of understanding is not to be part of the labor agreement. Therefore, it is not subject to any contractual dispute resolution provisions including resort to the grievance and arbitration procedure. Notwithstanding this, it is understood that disputes over this experimental program are covered by the union's "no strike" pledge. This letter of understanding will automatically expire should the child care program be abolished or upon expiration of our next labor agreement, whichever comes sooner, unless this understanding is extended by the company in a writing expressly to that effect and which is signed by its vice president of human resources."

NHC takes the position that without the use of this letter of understanding which allows it to retain complete control, it will not agree to a new child care benefit. The company is very concerned about both the cost and potential liability issues of a child care program. It is, however, willing to experiment with a program and to allow the union to take credit for something new, provided that total control remains with the company. Letters of understanding may be very useful under such circumstances.

TIP

Employers should avoid writing letters of understanding without specific expiration events or dates. One problem with open ended commitments is that they may outlive their usefulness. Without an expiration provision, dated materials may be eliminated only by mutual consent, for which concessions must usually be made. Another problem with long lasting letters of understanding is that the people who negotiated them, knew their intent, and who could testify about their origin in court or in arbitration, may leave the organization. Conversely, if you accept letters of understanding which give you a benefit, try to avoid clauses creating automatic expiration. Gains that you want continued, but which have expired, must be renegotiated.

TRICK

It may be to your advantage to place letters of understanding explicitly outside the main negotiated agreement. By doing so, typical dispute resolution machinery may not apply to the application and enforcement of the letter. It is not always legally clear whether a letter is intended to be part of the main agreement or to be a separate and independent agreement, so this should be clarified with express language. Further, in the case of labor-management contracts, because matters not subject to the grievance and arbitration procedure may arguably also be outside the quid pro quo "no strike pledge" in the labor agreement, application of the no strike pledge to the letter should be made clear, whenever the letter is not subject to grievance arbitration. The waiver by a union of its right to negotiate or arbitrate is not favored by the labor law, hence the need for express language. For unions, there is a need to reject such clauses when possible, unless what is being obtained is extremely valuable.

"LOWBALL" AND "TROJAN HORSE" OFFERS, CAVEAT EMPTOR

"There's a sucker born every minute." [P. T. Barnum] Usually an offer to a seller that is too high, or to a buyer that is too low, is too good to be true. Any offer that is far from what market forces indicate is reasonable should act as a danger signal. Such an offer may represent a "Trojan horse," made in an attempt to conceal important facts.

The All American Labor Council is in negotiations with Unethical Industries for a successor labor agreement. Area labor trends indicate that most wage increase settlements in comparable negotiations have been in the range of two to four percent per year. To protect itself against asking for too low an increase, the union has proposed that the employees it represents receive wage increases of eight per cent per year. To the union's surprise, Unethical Industries proposes a two percent first year increase and increases of ten percent per year in the second and third years of a three year agreement. In addition, they accept most of the other union demands, although shifting many of them to the second or third years of the new contract term. News of the company's offer is leaked to the rank and file employees, many of whom are quite pleased. The union happily accepts the company's offer. Six months after entering into the new agreement, Unethical Industries announces that the plant is being completely closed and torn down. Subsequently, the union learns that the plant closure and its timing were decided upon before the negotiations began, thus explaining why the high offer was back end loaded. The company needed labor peace until the closure. This is a "Trojan horse" offer.

As opposed to the high Trojan horse offer, seemingly lowball offers are more common in commercial negotiations and particularly in negotiations between auto sales representatives and car buyers. Unlike labor negotiations, these bargaining situations involve parties who do not necessarily need to continue dealing with each other on a long term basis. Usually when an offer is artificially low in relation to market forces, there is some "catch" not explained at the time, or there are mandated high costs and charges waiting in the wings. Greed is one reason why people get sucked into gleefully accepting artificially low offers.

Dinosaur Designs is holding talks with Fleecem Systems. Dinosaur is seeking new computer-aided design software essential to run its business. In response to Dinosaur Design's emphasis on low costs, Fleecem offers Dinosaur a stripped down version of its computer aided design software at a bargain basement price. For the low price, Fleecem demands that Dinosaur make a commitment to use their software exclusively for the next three years. Dinosaur's engineers, under tremendous financial pressure from top management, and anxious to obtain new software rather than work with their old and obsolete systems, make no objection to Fleecem's proposal, which is accepted. Two months later, the new computer aided design system is installed. Under the exclusive use terms of the contract, Fleecem insists that Dinosaur's old system be uninstalled. Unfortunately for Dinosaur, Fleecem's new system is very slow and clumsy and needs numerous technical fixes. Fleecem is happy to supply upgrades and fixes, but the price for these services is astronomical, while the three year contract commitment bars Dinosaur from using the better software available from Fleecem's competitors.

Reo Cord is negotiating with Cheap Motors for a new car. The sales representative offers a low price on the new car. Based on comparison shopping, Cord sees the price as a terrific deal. In addition, the representative offers an unusually high trade-in value on Cord's old car. Cord signs a purchase contract. The back of the form contract contains seventeen paragraphs of fine print, which Cord does not read. When the time comes to take possession of his new car, Cord finds that there are a number of extras for which he is being charged under the fine print such as rust protection and an extended warranty, finance charges are higher than he was quoted and computed in a disadvantageous manner, a mandatory pre-paid dealer maintenance program has been added and charged, and, the trade-in value has been revised because of "problems and defects in the car." All of these changes are supported by language in the fine print authorizing the dealer to impose and charge for them. If Cord tries to get out of the contract, Cheap Motors threatens a lawsuit and to impair Cord's credit record. He takes the car at what turns out to be a relatively high price.

In construction contracts, a low price may be offered for building, but with extremely high costs and surcharges imposed for change orders and a very broad definition of what necessitates a change order. These builders know that there is far more money to be made out of change orders than out of basic construction and that given any laxity in planning, change orders are virtually inevitable.

Lowball and "Trojan horse" tactics are not confined to sellers. Buyers may use the same tactics. For example, a buyer may hold out to a seller the prospect of future large purchase orders it well knows it is not going to be issuing. One clue to such behavior is when the buyer refuses to put any of its promises in writing. Another clue is their insisting on contract language that provides that the buyer "may" do certain things, while insisting that clauses related to the seller be written in "shall" or "will" form. The "may" language gives a party an option, a valuable right, while the "shall" or "will" language obligates a party, an obligation from which it may be impossible to obtain release, except at a very high price.

✍ TIP

Make sure that any additional services that you may wish to purchase or sell are spelled out, along with their prices. Don't sign agreements that contain "blank checks," such as "the seller shall have the right to change its prices from time to time and buyer shall pay the prices prescribed."

TIME MANAGEMENT

"Time is for dragonflies and angels. The former live too little and the latter live too long." [James Thurber] Since time, power, and information are the three key negotiation factors, time management involves the control of one of these key elements. The trick in time management, particularly in the middle phase of negotiations, is to be neither dragonfly nor angel, but to get the timing of the negotiations process just right. Sufficient progress must be made so that when the end phase of negotiations is reached (in negotiations with real deadlines or significant time targets), issues have been narrowed down, problem solving has been completed, and you are ready to move rapidly. If too many open issues are left on the table at the end of the middle phase, a timely conclusion to negotiations will be very difficult to achieve. On the other hand, clearing too many issues away too soon will not give sufficient room for concession and movement in the end game phase.

Clock management sounds easy. It is actually extremely difficult in practice. Consider the problem of a National Football League coach who must decide whether to take time out or take time off the clock as a game nears its end. Inexperienced negotiators are far more likely to have clock management problems than seasoned professionals. Good clock management requires that you make a reasonable estimate of how long it will take for both sides' presentations, of the time required to resolve problems with agreements in principle, and of how long it will take to reach acceptable detailed language. In negotiation simulation training exercises, both college students and business people tend to forget the clock at times. **Time management failure can derail an entire negotiation. Time, power, and information are the most important factors in negotiating.**

✐ TIP

When you are negotiating for an organization rather than personally and no one on your team has significant negotiation experience against which to benchmark clock management, bring in a consultant with negotiation experience to help keep your side on track. It is virtually impossible for an inexperienced negotiator, barring exceptional good luck, to manage the clock properly.

✐ TIP

In your caucus room or negotiation "war room," always keep a chart that shows the number of days or hours left in the negotiation. This will help build a sense of time perspective. Be aware of where you are on the time line for completion.

In the middle phase of a negotiation between Big Box Stores and Omni-Seller, there are three major outstanding issues (and a number of minor ones) on the table. The major issues are price, product specifications, and lead time on orders. Progress bogs down as both sides engage in a series of rancorous discussions about price. Session after session is spent on this problem which is finally resolved only days before Big Box Stores must finalize its purchase orders to meet requirements for the upcoming selling season. Only at this point does the inexperienced Big Box negotiating team wake up to the ticking of the clock (which Omni-Seller's more experienced negotiators have deliberately been running). Big Box's negotiators now find they must rush through discussions on specifications and lead time. They are unable to give methodical consideration to Omni-Seller's proposals. As a result, Big Box's negotiators make several costly errors by accepting unfavorable contract language. The ticking of the clock may be your enemy or your friend, depending on the circumstances, but do not allow it to run without being aware of its effects.

✒ TRICK

When you find that time is running out too quickly and there are too many issues left on the table to be dealt with in the remaining time frame by the full negotiating teams of each side, consider using sub-teams to work on various issues. This will allow the spokespersons to delegate out work. However, there is a danger that mistakes will be made in sub-teams, so you may want to place a reservation on their work limiting them to recommendations to their full negotiating teams. Use of sub-teams necessarily dilutes the error protection that arises out of the use of a full team of negotiators.

SEVERABILITY CLAUSES

"Off with their heads." [Lewis Carroll] Suppose you have negotiated a complete agreement and then one provision of it is found to be illegal, or the law changes to make the provision illegal. Could you lose your entire negotiated arrangement? If your contract says nothing about such an event, the law usually assumes that you intend to discard the entire pact. You need to think about this risk and to deal with it by negotiating a "severability clause" into your agreement. A severability clause might read, "If one part of this agreement is found to be, or becomes, illegal or void, the rest of this agreement is to continue in full force and effect." These clauses are usually easy to negotiate. Neither side is likely to want to risk losing the fruits of a negotiation because one provision of the deal is no longer permitted. But, you need to think about having this type of clause while you are negotiating.

Tinkers Gaming Software and the Chance Workers Union are negotiating a successor labor agreement. Assume that there is currently soaring inflation. Both sides are concerned the government may intervene and mandate price and wage controls which would impact both contractual wages and Tinkers' freedom to raise its prices to cover its increasing costs. Notwithstanding the wage increase provisions of the agreement, government wage controls making increases beyond a certain level unlawful may prevent these sections of the agreement from fully operating. However, should this occur, the parties do not want to be forced into new negotiations by voiding the rest of their agreement. They also want to be able to resume enforcement of any blocked clauses when controls are lifted. They include a severability clause in their agreement.

✒ TIP

Since the future is never fully predictable, include a severability clause in any agreement, unless there is a provision so central to the arrangements being made that should it be voided by illegality, you would actually prefer to cancel the agreement and negotiate a new one, with all the risks that entails.

STUDY COMMITTEES

"A committee is an animal with four back legs." [John LeCarre] Study committees are a device, a kind of negotiation sleight of hand, used to save face when removing certain intractable issues from the table. Sometimes an issue arises over which neither you nor the other side want to break off commercial or personal negotiations or to engage in a labor dispute in labor-management negotiations, but the issue is so politically charged that it cannot be resolved without an unacceptable loss of face. Suppose you are faced with such an issue which has been placed on the table because political needs required that it be surfaced. It may be that neither you nor the other side really want to have anything to do with the issue. The simple solution is to refer the matter to a jointly appointed "study committee." Occasionally, a study committee's report and results may be intended to be useful and seriously considered. The vast majority of study committees are established as mere intentional dead ends. Whichever side needs political cover, or both sides, report back to their constituents that the issue will remain "under study" (for a period not ending until after the new negotiated agreement is reached). A study committee is thus often a sham solution, but a useful one.

The City Council of Absolute Bluff is debating the issue of development of a large mall in close proximity to the entrance to one of the area's most scenic parks. The next general election is just two months away. The developer is pressing for quick action. At the same time, anti-development community activists are pressing for the Council to pass a moratorium on any further commercial development. Council members on both sides of the issue want to turn down the heat until after the election. In behind the scenes negotiations, they agree on a solution. At the next Council meeting, the Council votes to establish a "Development Study Committee," with a report due in three months. When the partisans of either side of the issue press their views while the Committee is working, the Council members repeatedly state publicly, "That matter is under study by a committee. We think it best to await their report."

⚡ TRAP

Never establish a study committee on an issue which is a primary or secondary objective for your side. Doing so will virtually insure that you will not achieve that objective. Reserve the use of study committees for political footballs which could impede an overall settlement and which, apart from their political consequences, do not need to be resolved in the context of negotiating some form of broad agreement. You should rarely expect any useable results from a study committee and, accordingly, don't waste a lot of time or expertise on its work.

COUNTER OFFERS AND CONDITIONAL OFFERS

"The first, 'the retort courteous;' the second, 'the quip modest;' the third, 'the reply churlish;' the fourth, 'the reproof valiant;' the fifth, 'the countercheck quarrelsome;' the sixth, 'the lie with circumstance;' the seventh, 'the lie direct.'" [William Shakespeare] A counter proposal is a response to a proposal from the other side, modifying it to make it acceptable to you. A conditional offer is a proposal or counter proposal, with strings attached. The same item may be both a counter proposal and a conditional one.

During the middle phase of negotiations, you will likely be exploring interests; seeking solutions which are consistent with your objectives in order to obtain agreement in principle; and, exchanging a series of proposals and offering position changes on language in order to implement your agreements. Whether you are in problem solving discussions or positional bargaining, you will, in essence, be making counter offers and conditional offers at numerous points along the way. Some of these conditional and counter offers may be part of complex packages. In all but the very simplest of negotiations, counter and conditional offers are essential.

A publisher and an author are negotiating the terms under which the publisher will print and market the author's book. The parties have reached agreement on all of the issues with the exception of royalties generally and particularly the impact on royalties as a result of returned copies by booksellers. The publisher offers the author royalties of ten percent of net sales, after allowances for bad debts. The publisher also wants the author's royalty account to be charged for books which are returned, on which royalties were previously paid. The author, whose position has been royalties should be twenty percent of net sales, now counters with an offer to accept seventeen percent (a counter offer), provided that the publisher assumes the risk of book returns without impacting royalties previously paid on those sales (a conditional offer). After considerable discussion on the rationale and reasonableness of each position in relation to both sides' interests, they work out a compromise settlement which allows their negotiation to end in an agreement. The counter and conditional offer is part and parcel of positional bargaining, but in this example is accompanied by further efforts at problem solving and mutual interest exploration. The intent of both these sides is to reach an agreement that recognizes the needs of each party. Nevertheless, each side is still trying to extract at least some advantage over the other, but neither is willing to go to the full extreme that insisting on its unilateral position would entail. Provided that both sides are able to bring the proposed settlement within their bottom line objectives, agreement is possible and is likely to be reached.

In pure positional bargaining, you may offer to withdraw a proposal in return for the other side's withdrawal of one of its own proposals. If the position sought to be closed out is not a primary or strong secondary objective for the other side, this offer to trade proposals (conditional mutual withdrawal) may work. Another reason for carrying out this type of trade is to reduce the number of issues on the table. This is particularly useful when you are approaching the end game and need to focus on a few, important issues. Think of this type of trade like a mutually acceptable exchange of pieces in chess.

TIP

When you offer to trade one of your proposals for one or more of the other side's proposals, you show weakness as to the proposal you are offering to trade away. Once you have signaled that type of weakness, your chances of securing the objective represented by the proposal you offered to trade is severely diminished.

TIP

Don't be afraid to propose receiving multiple proposal withdrawals by the other side in return for withdrawing only one or a few of your own proposals. Not all proposals have equal weight. If you make a conditional offer which contains something of great value to the other side, it is perfectly proper for your side to ask the other side to abandon a number of low import proposals in return.

CREATIVE AMBIGUITY—ADVANTAGES AND PERILS

"If I take refuge in ambiguity, I assure you it's quite conscious." [Kingman Brewster, Jr.] Ambiguity is sometimes essential. Mid game talks, whether problem solving or positional, may reveal that getting too specific on detailed language will cause your negotiations to stall and break down. When this happens, you have two choices. You may still try to get as much detail into the final agreement as possible, taking the risk that your negotiation will fail. This option is advisable when the underlying issue is highly important to your side or when the risk of negotiation failure is not significant. If, however, some agreement on the point is better than none at all, or if the risk factors in pressing for clarification are high, consider deliberately accepting ambiguous language.

Many commercial and individual negotiated agreements today contain alternative dispute resolution provisions, such as arbitration. Virtually every labor-management contract has such a clause. The chances of your prevailing are problematic should ambiguous language end up being interpreted by a court or an arbitrator. But, if you cannot clearly win your point at the table, you will usually be better off leaving the matter to the potential alternatives of litigation or arbitration, having to accept clearly negative language, or being forced to terminate the negotiation. As Charlie Brown once pointed out, winning may not be everything, but losing isn't anything.

Booker Clef is an agent for a number of song writers and bands. Clef is reasonably well known, but does not represent the top talent needed to solidify his reputation. The Stoned Rockers is a band that is on its way to the top, but has not yet arrived. It has not had much luck with agents. Clef and The Stoned Rockers are talking with each other about an agency contract. Clef would like to set his fee at ten percent of gross earnings per booking. The Stoned Rockers would like to set the agent's fee at ten percent of net earnings per booking, after taxes and expenses. After a number of meetings, each party is certain that it wants to work with the other, but neither Clef nor the band want to risk losing the arrangement because of a dispute over how the agent's fee will be calculated. Accordingly, they independently decide to engage in some creative ambiguity. The final contract says that, "Band shall pay Agent ten percent in commissions." An arbitration clause is added. These parties may try to reach agreement on fees later or, if this fails, will take their chances with an arbitrator as to the precise fee calculation method to be used.

An advantage of creative ambiguity is that it may allow you to get by an issue that, if defined, would irretrievably block settlement. A disadvantage is that current ambiguity is an invitation to a future dispute in which both sides are at risk that the outcome will be unacceptable or may intolerably strain their relationship.

☞ TRAP

An agreement with too many ambiguous provisions which were deliberately left that way to avoid problems during a negotiation may be a ticking time bomb. While you may shrug off one or two such disputes, a series of painful litigations during the term of an agreement may utterly poison your long term relationship. Ration ambiguity. Don't use it as an excuse to avoid resolving problems during negotiations.

COMPLEXITY, EXPERTISE, AND OVERWHELMING WITH NUMBERS

"We can lick gravity, but sometimes the paperwork is overwhelming." [Wernher von Braun] Consider this provision from an employer's pension plan, as negotiated with a labor union: "Upon the termination or partial termination (as may be determined by the Secretary of the Treasury or the Secretary of Labor) of the Plan, the rights of all affected beneficiaries to benefits accrued to the date of such termination or partial termination shall become non-forfeitable, provided, however, no affected Participant shall have any recourse towards satisfaction of such non-forfeitable rights to an Account Resolution, other than the assets of the Fund." Whether your negotiation is commercial, personal, or between labor and management, today's legal environment suggests that your agreement may well be packed with negotiable, complex, legal language. Certainly, your attorneys (particularly if you are negotiating for an institution) may help with this problem, but if you are negotiating an agreement, you need to understand what you are negotiating. This will be a particularly serious problem if you are negotiating in a field covered by extensive federal or state laws and regulations, such as employee benefits, antitrust, or environmental issues. In individual negotiations for a house or car, or in commercial negotiations, when one side is far more sophisticated than the other, encounters with complex areas may be traumatic for the less sophisticated side.

You may overwhelm the other side with information or numbers or be overwhelmed by them yourself. Sometimes, huge volumes of numbers are used as a bargaining ploy which is designed to confuse. Often, data overload is unavoidable in light of the complexity of the subject matter under discussion. For example, it is impossible to intelligently negotiate a pension plan without expert guidance. If you are working with people on the other side of the table in a problem solving mode, it is essential to allow sufficient time to educate them on the complexities being addressed and why you have included certain things in your proposals. There may even be occasions when faced with complexity and having sufficient trust, one side may simply be willing to let the other side handle the complexity, relying on the other side's good faith and sense of justice. Of course, there is risk in trusting overly far.

It is possible to overwhelm the other side's negotiators by supplying them with more information than they really want to have or they are able to handle. Few people will want to wade through reams of loosely organized data. If you are engaged in problem solving discussions, avoid overwhelming the other side with too much information. Using experts may help you in dealing with "information overload."

Dora Dollar is chairing Evergreen Enterprise's human resource and environmental due diligence sub-committee for a proposed acquisition of Dioxin Producers, Inc. Dioxin proposes that Evergreen acquire its PCB Works with an "environmentally as is" clause. Dollar consults Evergreen's environmental and legal compliance experts and outside counsel who suggest to her that if Evergreen accepts Dioxin's proposal as written, Evergreen could be assuming both millions of dollars of potential future liability for cleanup and personal injury and be risking future unfavorable publicity. Dollar spends a number of hours with her experts so that she can intelligently explore the environmental issues with Dioxin and try to find an environmental clause that will protect her organization or hold damages down to a level that will make the acquisition economically and politically acceptable.

✒ TIP

Be sure to leave sufficient time in your negotiation schedule to cope with complex issues. When problem solving under circumstances where your side knows more about the issues than the other side, be prepared to teach them what they will need to know (but don't unnecessarily flag potentially troublesome issues). When you have an expert on staff, consider bringing that person to the table, but only when, in your judgment, the expert has sufficient training to work safely within your negotiating style.

✒ TRAP

While being helpful in explaining complex systems, be very careful not to accidentally expose confidential information that must not be shared. Open and frank discussion does not mean revealing certain internal financial information or making suggestions that would unnecessarily open a can of worms.

BLUFFING—DANGERS AND OPPORTUNITIES

"You can fool some of the people all the time, and all of the people some of the time, but you cannot fool all of the people all the time." [Abraham Lincoln] We all bluff at one time or another. Bluffing may be a useful tool, but it is not without risk. Your bluff may be called, with serious consequences. In negotiations, a primary form of bluff is to walk out (and wait to be called back) or to threaten to break off bargaining. Another bluff is to assert that your position on something is strong, when it is weak. Knowing when you may successfully bluff and when to call someone else's bluff is an important negotiation skill. Bluffing activities may occur at any time during negotiations.

Nash Studebaker is negotiating to buy a car from Snake Oil Motors. Studebaker has asked innumerable questions and spent hours talking to Bill Linton, the sales representative. Linton, who has invested much time and effort in Studebaker, is wondering if there is ever going to be a sale. At the third meeting, Studebaker says that if the dealership won't drop its price by another hundred dollars, he will buy elsewhere. In fact, Studebaker knows from meetings at other dealerships that he cannot do much better than the offer on the table. Linton says, "I can't do it." Studebaker replies, "I'll be leaving then," and starts for the door. Having invested six hours in wooing Studebaker's business, Linton calls him back and offers a fifty dollar reduction in price, which Studebaker takes. Had he not been called back, Studebaker would have walked out, waited two days, then called Linton to take the last offer. Studebaker's walking out was a bluff, one which was partially successful.

✒ TIP

Never bluff that you will break off negotiations when you really need to reach resolution with the other side. The risk of such a course of action is not supportable. You may bluff on issues that are important, but not critical. A bluff is best when supported by evidence (whether real or imagined) that makes your position plausible. For example, a threat to make a deal with another supplier will be more credible if the other side is made aware that you have actually made at least some preliminary contact with that supplier.

⚡ TRAP

Bluffing is largely inconsistent with problem solving or interest bargaining and is more in tune with traditional positional bargaining. A negotiator who develops a reputation as a constant bluffer is not likely to be believed when it is critical to have the other side accept a position as accurate. Don't bluff too often.

RECOVERING FROM MISTAKES

"It isn't making mistakes that's critical; it's correcting them and getting on with the principal task." [Donald Rumsfeld] No one is perfect, including professional negotiators. At one time or another, we have all made mistakes during the course of negotiations. Some mistakes may be minor but others will be substantive. Is it possible to recover from mistakes? The answer is sometimes yes, sometimes no. Keep in mind that a negotiator's stock in trade is established credibility. Violate your promises or fail to keep your commitments and you are likely to be an unsuccessful negotiator. The most important thing about mistakes is never to repeat the same mistake twice.

When it proves difficult to convince the other side to let you off the hook about a major mistake, there are two alternatives. First, you and your organization may honor your promise or commitment, even though doing so may be painful. The reward for absorbing this cost is that you maintain credibility. Second, you may announce that you misspoke and that you must withdraw your statement. This may be your only course if your organization is unwilling to pay the price entailed in honoring your promise or commitment. Withdrawal is only possible with tentative agreements. Once you have reached a complete agreement which resolves offer and acceptance, you have a legally binding contract.

The Geometrical Figures Union is negotiating a successor labor agreement with Tesseract Corporation. One of the major issues is a cost of living clause. The union has proposed that workers receive a one cent per hour increase for each 0.2 percent change in a selected consumer price index. The company has agreed in principle to granting this cost of living escalator clause, but at the rate of one cent for each 0.4 percent change in the controlling index. In fact, the economic authorization in the company team's white paper negotiation plan permits no further movement from the 0.4 percent level. Paula Polygon, the company's chief spokesperson is asked if the company would "split the difference" and accept a one cent increase for each 0.3 percent change in the index. Paula, who has a very bad headache, without thinking blurts out, "Yes, agreed." Another member of her team, Tina Triangle, calls for an immediate caucus. Polygon has only limited choices. She may convince her top management to authorize the extra expenditure to validate her table commitment or she may go back to the table and simply admit, "I made a mistake. We cannot go to 0.4 percent." As Paula points out in the caucus, if she retracts, the other side is unlikely to believe that she does not have, or cannot get, the extra 0.1 percent authorization. In the end, the company's top management goes along with the extra authorization, trimming away an equal amount of money from another item on which the company has not yet made a commitment. Whatever happens, there are few satisfactory options for a negotiator who errs.

TIP

You may be able to correct a mistake through a private meeting with the other side's chief negotiator. When the other side graciously allows you to withdraw a mistake without challenge, you owe your counterpart a similar favor. Be prepared to pay that price. Cooperation in this type of situation is more likely among negotiators who carefully preserve the line between personal relationships and substantive positions. Having a friendly personal relationship with a negotiating "adversary" is easier when you remember that the other negotiator represents the positions of the other side, not necessarily personal views. In personal negotiations, this separation is not possible.

✐ TIP

The best way to handle mistakes is not to make them. Reduction in mistakes is one of the reasons why many negotiations are done through teams. Team members are more likely to catch and correct each other's mistakes before they are revealed to the opposition. The danger of mistakes is also why only one person on each side should be able to make formally binding commitments.

EVALUATING THE OTHER SIDE'S PROBLEMS AND INTENTIONS

"Knowledge is power." [Francis Bacon] In World War II, the turning point of the Pacific war against Japan came with the Battle of Midway. Midway was won by a less powerful United States fleet because our cryptanalysts had cracked the Japanese ciphers, allowing the American fleet commander to pierce the fog of war and place the fleet in just the right place at the right time. The more you know about the other side's problems and intentions during a negotiation, the better you will be able to judge how far you must go in satisfying their needs in positional bargaining, or in gratifying their interests when you are in a problem solving mode. Of one thing you may be sure. The other side will have problems of its own. They may include internal political problems, fear of your side, or an inability to articulate their own needs.

Once you have determined what the other side's problems and intentions are, you will be in a much better position to counteract them or to gain from whatever concessions you are able to make. It is not the quantity of power available that matters, but the ability to effectively apply it. Today, a few "smart bombs" allow far more effective military air campaigns that thousands of tons of imprecise World War II carpet bombs.

Wilma Packard is talking with NoGo Motors about purchasing a new car. Packard knows from reading the local business newspapers and from friends in the banking industry that NoGo is having trouble with its "floor plan" financing (the bank loans which enable a dealer to hold and control an inventory of capital consuming automobiles). From research, Packard has fairly accurately determined the cost to the dealer of the car in which Packard is interested. After taking up a lot of a sales representative's time, Packard offers to buy a car at little more than dealer cost. She knows that under ordinary circumstances the dealer would refuse her offer. When the dealer initially declines the offer to see what Packard will do, she begins leaving, commenting as she goes, "You really need to clear some of those cars from your floor plan. I can help you do that. My offer gives you a small profit and it does clear one more car out of your bloated inventory." Two hours later, the sales representative calls Packard to say they will make the deal. Packard's knowledge of the dealer's problems has brought her maximal success in her negotiation.

Superb Gizmos is negotiating a successor labor agreement with the Gizmo Workers International Union. The union is represented at the table by an international representative and a five member local union negotiating team. The employer is aware that the international representative is new and struggling to establish some dominance in relation to the local union president, who has questioned her ability to achieve success. Determining that the international representative is more reasonable in relation to employer needs than the local president, the employer determines to give the international representative a status boost. To make uniform, for easier administration, diverse benefits programs under which all other employees have coverage for abortions and vasectomies, the employer has already determined that it wishes to add abortions and vasectomies to the employees' health care plan. The union has failed to ask for this benefit. The employer spokesperson arranges a private side meeting with the international union representative. At that meeting, she says, "I have available an improvement in the health care package to cover abortions and vasectomies which we want to throw in, but you guys didn't ask for it. Why don't you expand on your health care proposal, explain that it is intended to cover these items, and then demand them from us forcefully. We will put up a big struggle at the table, but will reluctantly let you win the point. I don't want to embarrass you at the table by talking about your not asking for the benefit." When the international representative wins the point at the table, her status is boosted. She also owes the employer spokesperson a counter favor at some point. Knowing about the internal struggle within the union has enabled the employer to enhance the status of the more settlement prone individual.

✐ TIP

You should ethically obtain as much information as possible about personalities within the other side's organization and about the stresses and strains on that organization. Also you should look for any indications that the other side may be under time pressure or has the greater need to settle. Factor the other side's needs into movements and concessions that you make.

GIVING AWAY ICE IN THE WINTERTIME

"But here in the struggle for fame and pelf / I want to be able to like myself. / I don't want to look at myself and know / That I'm bluster and bluff and empty show." [Edgar A. Guest] Consider the following empty "concessions" from someone with whom you are negotiating: "We agree that we may, at our sole discretion, give you a check for one million dollars within one year," or, "We agree that we will pay all those employees who are not legally exempt time and one half for hours actually worked over forty (40) in a work week, so long as the law requires such payment." Don't rush out to spend the one million dollars. The "concession" is discretionary and merely repeats something that the other side would always be free to do if it wished, namely write you a check. But, this "concession" places the other side under absolutely no enforceable obligation to write you a check. So, the clause is totally hollow. Similarly, the second "concession" to pay time and one half under the circumstances required by law is also "ice in the wintertime." The party making the "concession" is merely agreeing to do what it has to do in any event and has even protected itself against a change in the law.

Surprisingly, "ice in the wintertime" concessions may sometimes have an impact or provide a politically face saving method for knocking a problem off the negotiating table. Also, the party making the "concession" may feel some sense of moral and ethical obligation. "Ice in the wintertime" proposals are frequently used in the mid-game.

Hungry for Ice Cream, Inc. is negotiating a contract with Dan & Harry's Premium Ice Cream Company, under which the ice cream distributor will purchase large quantities of Dan & Harry's ice cream for wholesale vending to a number of supermarket chains.

Hungry for Ice Cream is insisting on the right to inspect Dan &
Harry's production lines to determine wholesomeness. The
founders of Dan & Harry's are upset about the inspection provision
and instruct their negotiating team to seek some easing of the
requirement. Hungry for Ice Cream's team decides to do something
to appease Dan & Harry, but only something which fundamental-
ly preserves inspection rights. They place on the table a revised pro-
posal that reads, "Hungry for Ice Cream may at random times of
its choosing from time to time inspect the ice cream production
facilities of Dan & Harry. However, if after two inspections no prob-
lems are found, Hungry for Ice Cream will consider waiving further
inspections for the duration of the agreement." Note that no waiv-
er is actually required, only consideration. Dan & Harry accept the
clause because they want to make the sale and, as people often
do, they convince themselves that two clean inspections will be no
problem and that on reflection, Hungry for Ice Cream will waive
further checks. It is, of course, possible that they will ultimately do
so, but Dan & Harry should not count on it.

⚟ TIP

You may want to offer "ice in the wintertime" concessions
when the other side has a political problem to solve and when
you may be able to end their resistance to your proposal by
giving them something, no matter how meaningless. Be careful. Such meaningless concessions if made on a matter that is
truly and deeply of interest to the other side may be regarded
as a gratuitous insult.

⚟ TRAP

You should always examine the other side's proposals, counter
proposals, and conditional offers for "weasel words," such as
"may," "will consider," and "at its sole discretion." Think about
whether a concession is couched in meaningful terms or if it is
merely excess verbiage, written at length, signifying nothing.

NEGOTIATING AGAINST YOURSELF

"We have met the enemy and he is us." [Pogo Possum]
Negotiating against yourself is one of the most common errors

made by non-professional negotiators. It is difficult enough negotiating with both your own side internally and with the party on the other side of the negotiating table, without negotiating against, and making concessions to, yourself. Negotiating against yourself may be defined as reducing the import of your own proposals by diluting them on your own motion, before hearing any objections from the other side. This weakening may be done out of fear that your proposals sound harsh, unreasonable, or may draw a serious negative reaction. Initial proposals frequently are intended to be harsh, unreasonable, or to provoke reaction, because you must allow yourself room to retreat from them. This allows you to show how reasonable you are and how willing you may be to listen to the other side's positions and interests and to move accordingly. **Wait for the other side's objections before modifying any of your overstated proposals.**

Aerospace Devices is in a negotiation for a successor contract with the Space Products Union. Aerospace Devices wants substantial changes in the bidding system under which employees move between work classifications when there are vacant positions. The employer's problem is that employees may bid as frequently as they wish. The expiring labor contract was negotiated years ago when Aerospace Devices was known as the Always Leaky Washer Company and the tasks assigned to employees were very simple. Today, most classifications require sophisticated training. The company is seeking to keep employees on their positions long enough to recover its expensive training investment before the employees move on to other positions. Accordingly, it has proposed that employees who successfully bid be placed in a "bid restriction period" of sixty months before being allowed to bid again, unless waived by the Company on a case by case basis. Company negotiators know that a sixty month period is far longer than necessary. They have a primary objective of attaining a twenty-four month bid limitation period and a secondary objective of achieving a thirty-six month limitation period. In internal discussions, some members of the company bargaining team lobby to lower the initial proposal to thirty-six months to "be more reasonable." They seek to avoid having to defend the long limitation period and to avoid the anticipated adverse reaction. However, they are negotiating against themselves. If the sixty month period is in the initial proposal, the union will almost certainly react negatively. The company may then seek the basis of their objection and in response modify its proposal. It will have room to compromise toward its secondary objective. Further, once the proposed limitation period is reduced through self action, any intermediate period which the union might have accepted has automatically been forfeited.

✒ TIP

Don't be afraid to make initial or "going in" proposals that might seem harsh or difficult to defend. Initial proposals should allow room to compromise toward your real objectives. Try not to apologize for your proposals. Instead, listen carefully to the other side when they make reasoned objections and when you concede ground to them, link the concession to their comments. Only rarely should you retreat on a proposal or position without either getting something in return or demanding "in kind" concessions from the other side before making further concessions of your own.

CONCESSION TIMING

"Life is about timing." [Carl Lewis] In the nature of mid-negotiations discussions, whether positional or problem solving in nature, you will usually be trading concessions. But, what is the right time for you to make a concession? Who should make concessions first? Is a concession a sign of weakness? The timing of concessions is a tactical question of great import.

It does not necessarily show weakness to move first on an issue, once it has been discussed at least once. Depending on how much room you have built into your proposal, the first move may be either generous or very limited. The purpose of a first move is to act both as a process facilitator, demonstrating reasonableness, and to show a desire to settle. You may be sending out a scout to determine how the other side will react to movement. The timing of concessions also takes place within the overall timing constraints of a negotiation. When there is a time limit to finish the negotiation, you must make things progress so that it is feasible to complete your negotiation within the allotted time. You should also try to make concessions initially on those proposals which are tertiary or smokescreen objectives or which you believe are low priority items for the other side.

When you make a major concession, it is normal to expect the other side to respond in a measured way. If your major concession nets little or no movement, consider carefully whether you should make any further concessions until the other side responds effectively to your gesture. Retreating continuously without getting something in return will evoke a natural human reaction. The other side will sit back and let you make more and more concessions. In essence, you will be bargaining against yourself.

DOES THE OTHER SIDE REALLY WANT AN AGREEMENT

"No man likes to have his intelligence or good faith questioned, especially if he has doubts about it himself." [Henry Brooks Adams] During mid-game negotiations, it may be become apparent to you that the other side does not really want to reach an agreement in good faith. Why would someone enter a negotiation without intending to reach a resolution? One reason could be because the other side is negotiating with you only as a ploy to put pressure on the other side in a different commercial or personal negotiation. In a labor-management context, an employer might want to set the stage for a decertification election (National Labor Relations Board conducted election in which the employees might vote the union out), or might seek to provoke a strike so it could hire replacements. Similarly, a labor union may have political objectives related to its national agenda which they may insist upon, although they know the employer will not accept their proposals.

How do you know the other side is reluctant to actually enter an agreement? Watch for stalling tactics and for demands which the other side knows have no chance of success. A stalling negotiator can usually block any settlement by placing on the table some form of demand which constitutes a fundamental assault on the other side as an institution and which they will never be able to accept.

The Brad and Tack Workers Union (BTWU) is negotiating for a successor labor agreement with Titanium Nails Manufacturing. Assume current labor markets are very tight, unemployment is low, the BTWU has a large strike fund, and BTWU is certain that with Titanium Nail's low wage rates, the company would have trouble attracting replacement workers who would be willing to cross a picket line. BTWU, with newly elected militant leaders, has determined to cause a strike to gain massive concessions from Titanium

Nails. Despite the existence of strong management's rights and no strike clauses which have been in prior agreements for decades, BTWU places on the table demands that these clauses be deleted from the labor agreement. BTWU makes certain that it offers up a number of concessions on unimportant issues to avoid any successful charge of surface bargaining or of failing to bargain in good faith. However, BTWU's leaders know that the company will never agree to a contract that impinges so heavily on management's basic rights. These proposals will only be withdrawn after Titanium Nails makes massive concessions to the union.

🏷 TRAP

Never assume that merely because some progress is being made on minor issues, the other side really intends to reach a full agreement. Even the initialing of a number of tentative agreements does not mean that there is a sincere desire to reach an overall accord. The best measure of the other side's underlying intent may be found in the totality of their conduct. In the vast majority of negotiations, people and organizations do not go through the negotiation process without a good faith intent to reach an agreement.

With the conclusion of the mid game, the time element of negotiations often moves to the fore. You may need to move quickly and be prepared to be decisive on open issues. Problem solving will usually be set aside in favor of positional bargaining. Bargaining power will tend to determine the outcome and clock management will be a key element. In the next chapter, we turn our attention to the fast moving end game.

CHAPTER 13

THE END GAME AND CLOCK MANAGEMENT

CLOCK MANAGEMENT IN TIME DEFINED NEGOTIATIONS

"There is a tide in the affairs of men which taken at the flood leads on to fortune; omitted, all the voyages of their life is bound in shallows and in miseries." [Shakespeare] Assuming you've won several games and sets, it's time to reach closure in your match. By now, you may have become comfortable with the techniques for the opening and mid game phases of negotiating. In *time critical negotiations,* your end game will be as different from these earlier phases as the two minute drill is to the rest of each half in professional football. As the clock ticks toward a deadline that carries significant economic or other consequences for both sides, the pace of your negotiation will accelerate and leisurely problem solving will give way to far faster positional bargaining. Minor issues are abandoned by both sides. Consultation and deliberation yield to forced decision making.

In time critical negotiations, the end game process may take on the character of a ballet. You must take each step at the right time, in the right order, and at the right speed. If you materially err, you may never reach a complete agreement or it may be attained only by making too many concessions. In the earlier and more leisurely phases, you had time for reflection, for participative interchange between members of your negotiating team, and the chance to correct mistakes. In the end game, speed, accuracy, and command of detail become critically important. If you have the expertise to manage the clock and the other side lacks this skill, you may actually find it necessary to help them to plan timing parameters so that a timely settlement may be reached.

Under what circumstances are you likely to find yourself in a time critical negotiation? In commercial negotiations, you may be faced with a time line that requires that a purchase or sale contract be completed in time to satisfy a customer's needs or to meet a required lead time. In real estate negotiations, your mortgage commitment may have a defined end, your realtor's contract may be subject to expiration, or there may be an occupancy issue. In auto negotiations, the rapid approach of a new model year may change many of the parameters that influence relative bargaining power.

Private sector labor negotiations, excluding those in railways and airlines, are almost always time critical. On expiration of a labor contract, provided proper notice has been given to the mediation services, you become legally free to resort to economic self-help through a strike or lockout. While both sides may mutually agree to extend an extant labor agreement or the union may offer, and the employer may permit, work to proceed without a contract, any absence of a defined time deadline will slow negotiations and subject both sides to the further risk of economic instability.

Collective bargaining in the United States is bottomed on the principle that both sides have a need to settle to avoid risking economic consequences. A looming time deadline is an extremely powerful force for the resolution of open issues. In the opening and middle phases of a negotiation, the absence of immediate time pressure allows you to take the time to dispute minor matters involving smokescreen objectives and to set the stage for end game bargaining. In time critical end game negotiations, you will pull issues that once seemed to be worth considerable time and effort from the table to concentrate on achieving your primary and selected secondary objectives. It is in this often frenetic time critical process that the investment you made in negotiations planning will more than pay for itself. If you have a clear idea of your bottom line and your vital interests were identified well before the negotiation began, you will be in a position to move quickly and to avoid the panic driven errors that come from making judgments "on the fly." If you prepared end game materials during the quieter earlier stages of negotiation, you will also have an advantage.

Many commercial and personal negotiations are also time critical and many of the comments related to labor negotiations also relate to general bargaining, except that the end sanction may be that one side walks away and leaves the other with the need to seek a new negotiating partner with whom negotiations will have to start at square one. There may also be major consequences from the loss of a potential contract for production, supplies, sales, cars, or houses. In those negotiations which are not time critical, the end game will more closely resemble a prolonged middle game. Unless some external factor injects a form of time pressure, these negotiations may go on for a very long time. This is one of the factors that separates private sector negotiations from the vast majority of public sector ones, where negotiations go on well past contract expiration.

⚓ TIP

When you reach a time critical end game, place a large clock in the negotiating room and another in your caucus area. Remember you are in a two minute drill. **Watch the clock. Move quickly. Don't waste time on side issues.** Assign someone to remind the team that the clock is running. Always consider where you are in the settlement process and be aware of how much time is left in relation to the number of steps still ahead. If you plan to make a series of concessions and time is running short, be prepared to truncate the process and move more rapidly by using larger increments per move and making fewer moves.

⚓ TIP

If your negotiation is not time critical, consider trying to reach a mutual agreement to establish an "artificial deadline" for the completion of negotiations. To make an artificial deadline work the same way as a real one, both sides must agree on sanctions for running over that, although not necessarily identical or mirror image, impose proportional mutual pain. We all know people who set their clocks fast to try to fool themselves into being punctual. But, as they are aware their clocks are artificially fast, they often ignore the cushion and arrive late. If there are no sanctions, it is unlikely anyone will treat an artificial deadline as a real "drop dead" date.

There are graphic examples of what happens to a negotiation in the absence of time pressure. Consider how little actual legislation emerges from Congress until a session is about to adjourn or an election is about to be held and the legislators seriously negotiate with each other. Another example of a type of negotiation which lacks any time penalty is a labor negotiation between a school board and a union. Because most education contracts are ultimately made retroactive, pay lost from an academic year may be made up. Strikes by public employees are usually unlawful and there are no penalties for foot dragging in concluding negotiations, so it is a rarity for any public school teacher contract to be settled at or before expiration of the current agreement. It has become the norm in public sector bargaining for the two sides to continue negotiating for a year or two beyond expiration. At that point, both sides will reach a retroactive two or three year contract and immediately begin their next negotiation. It is hard to conceive of a system that is less conducive to settlement than one with no time pressure.

⚡ TRICK

When time is short and matters are pressing, a spokesperson may have to assume full authority to act without consulting other members of the team. This authority should be used sparingly, with caution, and the mantle should only be assumed by experienced negotiators. The reason for caution is that quick decisions by one person may contain expensive errors. Still, there are times when someone must decide.

⚡ TRICK

When time pressure mounts during end game negotiations, work must often be divided among members of a bargaining team to permit all necessary matters to be addressed within the available time. It is common for a five member negotiating team to have all members working on separate activities during the end game. Spokespersons should reserve adequate time in their own schedules to coordinate these activities.

MONEY—WHEN TO TALK IT

"A nickel isn't worth a dime today." [Yogi Berra] Most negotiations ultimately boil down to a question of money. Few things stir people's passions as much as the distribution of money. Talking about money too early in a negotiation increases the chances that the negotiation will fail. Consider that if you are trying to negotiate the price for the construction of a custom home with a builder, it will be futile to get into price until you've at least decided what kind of house you want to build, how many square feet it will have, and have established most of its specifications. Until you know all, or at least almost all, the parameters of a proposed agreement, it will be very difficult to properly evaluate its overall economic cost.

John Lackland and Jane Acres are negotiating a purchase contract for a private home. They have yet to define exactly what will be included in, and excluded from, the sale. Acres, the seller, intends to reserve the appliances in the house, including a number of those that are customarily included in realty contracts. Lackland, the buyer, wants Acres to do certain remedial work on the house prior to closing and intends to have certain personal property, normally excluded in a house sale, such as drapes, expensive pottery, and interior plants, included within the realty contract. If Acres and Lackland attempt to negotiate a final transaction price without first agreeing on what is to be included and excluded from the transfer, they will likely end up with a major misunderstanding of their seeming agreement. In the end, they may fail to close the deal or they may close under protest and find themselves in court.

Amerind Arrows is negotiating with Babe Ruth Sporting Goods Stores to provide the Ruth Stores with a nationwide supply of archery arrows. Although no specifications or quantity levels for the arrows have yet been negotiated, the Ruth Stores demands that a price be quoted. Arrows responds that prices vary widely depending on the quantity of arrows ordered and their specifications, which must be negotiated first.

Boom Chemicals and the Substance Workers Union are negotiating a successor labor agreement. There are a number of provisions on the table relating to the bidding process under which employees may initiate moves between classifications. Each time an employee moves to a new classification, Boom provides weeks of classroom training and then months of on the job training. The average employee takes six months to become fully proficient in a new classification. To recover its training investment, Boom is proposing that employees be limited to one successful bid each thirty-six months. The current agreement contains no limit on bid-

ding. Boom's economic offer to the Substance Workers union depends, in part, on the significant productivity savings from limiting bidding. Accordingly, it will be difficult for Boom to make an economic offer without first securing agreement on the proposed bidding limitation and the resolution of other proposals which relate to work rules and productivity. Boom therefore declines to discuss detailed economics or to make an economic offer until the open productivity related language items are resolved. Boom has been advised by counsel that in private sector labor negotiations an employer may not unilaterally set a precondition for discussing economic issues. However, pending language resolution, Boom may legally restrict its discussion of economic items to a general discussion, without putting specific numbers or a specific economic offer on the table. Since such general discussions are usually futile as a practical matter, this effectively delays economic negotiations. In commercial negotiations, there is no equivalent legal constraint and you may withhold discussion of price and other key economic matters until you have a general contractual framework.

TIP

If you are a management or commercial negotiator, try to clear as many non-economic items from the table as possible before making an offer containing specific prices or wages. For political or other reasons, the other side may sometimes have to leave certain non-economic items on the table until the very end of negotiations, but this does not necessarily mean they are serious about them.

TRICK

In labor-management negotiations, *if you have far more bargaining power than the other side* and they insist on leaving many non-economic issues open well into the end game, consider placing an express condition in any economic offer you place on the table that to obtain the offer they must withdraw some, or all, of their open non-economic issues. Do not attempt this ploy without strong bargaining power. If you are in a weak position, once you show any money it will be assumed that it may be attained unconditionally. As long as you are offering new money, you have the legal right to make a conditional offer. Be explicit that your offer is conditional on the other side making the necessary concessions and that the money consideration on the table is only made available because acceptance of the condition is presumed. State the condition in writing on your offer document. Once people with low bargaining power have seen the money that compliance with your condition will bring, they will be more likely to retreat on non-economic issues. You may say something to the effect that, "Our economic offer is expressly conditional on your withdrawing your remaining open non-economic proposals, numbers [identify them]. The offer includes compensation for this. Understand that our offer would necessarily have to be reduced, but for the condition." You must also decide whether, if push comes to shove, you will modify or retreat from your condition. However, if you make a conditional offer and modify or reduce the condition, you signal great weakness when you don't reduce the offer proportionally. Conditional offers are a very useful tool. You will seldom complete any negotiation without resorting to them, although they will generally be less sweeping that the one discussed above.

WHEN DO YOU GIVE A FIGURE AND WHEN DO YOU AVOID DOING SO?

"Figures won't lie, but liars will figure." [Charles Grosvenor] Why avoid giving the other side an economic figure prematurely? In any type of negotiation, it is usually desirable to delay economic negotiations until the end game. Without specific figures, agreements in principle will be far easier to obtain regardless of whether you are in positional or problem solving bargaining. If you are the first to name a number, you risk placing yourself at a disadvantage. Why? You may cite a number that is outside an acceptable range, thereby indirectly conceding an economic reward that you might have obtained. Until you have as much information as you can reasonably gather about the other side's real interests and needs, offering up a number is like taking a shot in the dark. There is a significant probability of missing your target and killing yourself with the ricochet.

Juana Jobchanger is seeking a two level promotional jump with a potential new employer. She has survived three rounds of inter-

views and Tom Catburt, the employer's human resources manager, is extending Jobchanger a job offer. Catburt tells Jobchanger, "We are pleased to offer you the position, provided we can agree on a salary. We hope you will join our firm. Now, I see you are making $40,000 per year in your current job. What salary figure are you expecting from us?" Jobchanger should avoid giving Catburt a number in answer to this question. If, for example, she suggests a salary of $44,000, and Catburt was about to offer her $46,000, Catburt is likely to happily scale that number back to $44,000, on the theory that there is no point in paying Jobchanger more than she requested. If Jobchanger suggests she wants $60,000, Catburt, who has only $46,000 available, may decide that Jobchanger's expectations are not reasonable, break off the salary negotiation, and offer the job to a second choice applicant who will accept $46,000, or less. Jobchanger's problem is that Catburt has far more information about competitive salaries and available resources than Jobchanger. Catburt enjoys these salary negotiations because he knows the salary range in use by the employer, the minimum, mid-point, and maximum of the range, and has extensive wage survey figures from other employers in the area and in the industry. He knows that Jobchanger cannot compete with his knowledge when she provides a figure. How then should Jobchanger answer the question? Answer she must. Professional recruiters may respond well to the reply, "I know you will make me an equitable offer. The figure you choose will tell me quite a bit about how your organization values my potential input and values the function I will be joining. If the offer is acceptable, I will be pleased to join you." This places the burden of going first on the more knowledgeable person.

The salary figure dilemma is a classic example of the importance of information in negotiating, a kind of "the lady or the tiger" problem. Offering up a salary figure in the end game of a job change negotiation is the most frequent error made by many applicants who are, after all, negotiating their entry salary with an organization. If you ask for too little, it may be years before you attain the salary level you could have had if you had given a better answer as to your desired salary. If you ask for too much, you may lose the job.

An automobile purchaser is in a partly analogous position. Sales representatives will often ask, "What will it take to get you to buy this car today?" Unless you have a great deal of information, it is usually dangerous for you to give the sales representative a figure at which you will buy, until you are in end game discussions. Sales representatives may also use a technique known as spotting. They offer you an incentive, such as a low financing rate, and while you are waiting for approval of the loan (which will not be forthcoming at the low quoted rate), give you the keys and have you take the car. The principle is that after you've driven it and shown it to your friends, you will be embarrassed to take it back and so will accept ultimately paying a higher price for your auto loan.

✒ TIP

Avoid the temptation to respond to the question about what figure you need to buy, sell, or close a deal. Seek to make the other side give you a number first. The more knowledgeable person is the one who is more likely to put out the first figure because that person will be more secure about the validity of a figure. If that is you, and you have more information than the other side, you do not need to be as concerned about offering up a number.

USING MEDIATORS, ARBITRATORS, AND OTHER THIRD PARTY NEUTRALS

"Neutrality is at times a graver sin than belligerence." [Louis Brandeis] Mediation is an alternative dispute resolution process in which an individual serving as a neutral third party, who is given no authoritative decision making power, is brought into a negotiation to assist both sides in reaching their own mutually acceptable resolution. By contrast, in arbitration, the neutral third party is given the power to make a binding decision. Mediation has ancient roots. Suppose you were an ancient Sumerian with a complaint. History tells us that before you could go to court, you would first have to submit your claim to a "mashkim," who had the duty to try to settle the case.

Mediation is the most widely used form of alternate dispute resolution among the 1,000 largest U.S. corporations. However, it is far more widely used to settle disputes arising under existing contracts, commercial and labor, than in the process of arriving at agreements themselves. In private sector labor negotiations under the National Labor Relations Act (which does not cover railroads and airlines), federal and state mediation services must be notified in advance of a contract negotiation, but no one is under any legal obligation to actually utilize the services of a mediator.

A mediator's function may include:

- Defining the issues;
- Clarifying both sides' interests;
- Providing a channel of communication;
- Focusing the negotiations on productive areas of discussion;
- Proposing options for the resolution of the dispute;
- Assisting all concerned in documenting an agreement;
- Clarifying alternatives to agreement; and,
- Coordinating between and educating both sides.

Mediation may be categorized as either facilitative or evaluative, or it may be a hybrid. In facilitative or "pure" mediation, the mediator seeks to bring both sides together, but avoids giving advice or predicting an outcome. In the evaluative model, the mediator analyzes and weighs both sides' positions and offers an opinion on how the matter might be resolved. Which type is best is a judgment call. Mediators may be very useful in getting stalled negotiations moving because they bring fresh and neutral perspectives to the table. They are used in commercial negotiations, labor negotiations, and in the resolution of legal disputes. In some courts, mediation may be required prior to trial.

Mediation will only work when both sides are open and receptive to working with a mediator. In private sector negotiations of any kind (except under the Railway Labor Act), neither side has the right to impose mediation on the other. Why doesn't everyone use a mediator? The answer may lie in the view that face to face negotiations are often more effective than communicating through a third party. Certainly, face to face negotiations are usually faster than those which require filtering communications through an intermediary. Direct communications may be clearer and less distorted. A mediator must also be "brought up to speed," on everyone's positions. Finally, there is the question of how far you should trust a mediator with truly sensitive confidential information. That said, there are definitely circumstances under which both sides will find the use of a mediator to be very helpful in getting around deadlocks.

Buildit, a large box commercial real estate developer, and the City of Anywhere, have been negotiating over Buildit's plan to bring one of the nation's largest malls to Anywhere. The new mall would represent many new jobs for the community and a large new tax ratable. However, Buildit wants significant tax concessions from the City for locating the mall within its boundaries. Negotiations are at a deadlock because the City is demanding that Buildit, at its own expense, install a large number of road and landscaping improvements. Buildit is willing to do the work, but wants a lengthy property tax exemption in return. Negotiations are about ready to broken off, because the City is adamant about not granting a full tax exemption. Members of the public suggest a mediator be obtained. The mediator enters the picture and suggests an alternate solution. Buildit will pay some real property taxes, but they will be capped at a low level for fifteen years (saving face for the City), and the City will accept having Buildit install the majority, but not all, of the improvements (saving face for Buildit). The parties are now able to reach agreement.

✍ TIP

Use a mediator in situations in which positions have hardened and when face to face communications are proving difficult. Avoid bringing in a mediator too late in the process. In the normally fast paced end game, briefing mediators slows the negotiating process, so restore direct face to face communications as soon as practical.

✍ TIP

Sometimes a mediator may be useful in conveying the seriousness of your position when the other side is resistant to recognizing your needs. During a lengthy negotiation, some "speeches" become almost routine and lose their impact. If you are able to impress a mediator with the strength of your message, the mediator may provide a channel to communicate your message in a different and more credible way.

Should mediators or outside parties be allowed in to assist both sides in the end game of a negotiation? Some parties find it helpful to use mediators to suggest solutions to negotiating problems and to convey messages to the other side without face to face bargaining, at least some of the time. Mediators differ from arbitrators in that they may only suggest solutions or try to bring the sides together, but they have no power to impose any settlement terms. A member of the clergy or a government official might serve as a third party neutral.

In commercial and personal negotiations, the use of a mediator is entirely at the discretion of the parties. For attorneys, exposure to a mediator prior to trial may be mandated as part of "court annexed" alternative dispute resolution requirements. In labor-management negotiations, the parties are required by law to notify the Federal Mediation and Conciliation Service (FMCS) and the state mediation service (if there is one in the applicable state) of the intent to negotiate, or renegotiate, a labor agreement. Failure to do so carries serious consequences. The defaulting party is barred from economic self help, such as a strike or a lockout, even if the current agreement has expired, until at least sixty days' notice has been given. However, nothing in the National Labor Relations Act requires you to make actual use of the services of a mediator. You, the other party, or both of you, may reject any participation in your negotiation by the assigned mediator.

When is the best time to use a mediator? Although mediators can be helpful in the early and middle phases of negotiations, they may be most valuable during the end game but only when you are deadlocked and having difficulty speaking face to face. Otherwise, a mediator's separate meetings with each side may slow the process. Face to face direct contact should normally be the preferred method of dealing with the other side. Without it, you will be unable to read the fine nuances of signals, including body language, and you cannot be absolutely certain that your mediator is not filtering and distorting information. You may use a mediator to convey information to the other side, either by direct proposals or by managing the mediator's perceptions of your positions.

XYZ Corporation wants to make clear to the ABC Workers Union that it is completely serious about a major restructuring of the employer's pension plan for union represented employees. It has conveyed this message across the table, but the union does not seem to have yet accepted that the company is fully committed to its pension proposals. XYZ calls in a mediator and, in a private meeting, members of the XYZ team, in a planned move, surround the mediator and "vent their frustrations" with the union's failure to recognize that pensions are a strike issue for the employer. All management team members come across as being emotionally and intellectually committed. The mediator leaves the meeting with the management team somewhat shaken and personally convinced the company is quite serious. She moves on to a separate meeting with the union team. During this meeting, she advises the union team that the company is quite serious about pension reform and is unlikely to budge. Coming from a third party, the union credits this position more than it has when hearing it directly from management.

Keep in mind that if a mediator goes outside the parameters allowed by either side, the mediator may be told to leave the negotiations. Other third parties, such as political figures, may be difficult to have at a negotiating table. They may well have agendas of their own. However, ignoring these powerful people may have significant public relations and political consequences.

⚘ TIP

If you have a choice of mediators, research the mediators' backgrounds before selecting and agreeing to a mediator's participation. If you want only a facilitator, make this clear to the selected mediator before a formal appointment is made and accepted. If your selection of a mediator turns out to have been an unfortunate one, consider withdrawing from cooperation with that mediator and asking the mediator to leave. Mediation is supposed to be confidential, but the wiser course is to assume that anything you say to the mediator could be leaked accidentally, or on purpose, to the other side.

Arbitration is a different form of alternative dispute resolution (ADR) than mediation. An arbitrator is a third party neutral who is empowered by the parties to make a decision regarding a dispute, which is binding on all concerned. When the dispute concerns the making of a negotiated agreement itself, rather than its interpretation or application, this form of arbitration is known as "interest arbitration," and is fairly unusual. Under the Federal Arbitration Act, agreements to arbitrate are valid, irrevocable, and enforceable. Most states have parallel general arbitration statutes. The question of the applicability of the Federal Arbitration Act to collectively bargained labor contracts is too complex for discussion in this book. For a full discussion of alternative dispute resolution, including its use in court annexed processes, see Kramer, *Alternative Dispute Resolution in the Work Place*, published by American Law Media, Law Journal Press.

The most important thing to remember about the use of mediators and other neutral third parties is that they participate in a negotiation on sufferance of both sides. Either side may dispense with a mediator's or third party neutral's services at any time. The use of arbitration in a negotiation is optional. However, once an arbitrator is given jurisdiction, the arbitrator may only be removed by the mutual agreement of both sides.

FIRST OFFER

"He has half the deed done who has made a beginning." [Horace] Suppose the time has come for you to make your first economic offer to the other side. How do you construct a first offer? How much of your final offer do you show in your initial proposal? Some offers are for a single period of time at a fixed level, while others cover multiple time periods and multiple wage or price items. For example, an automobile dealer will structure a sales offer based on a price for the new car, a value for the trade in, the cost of optional extras agreed upon, and the financing terms. The dealer may couple a high value on the trade in with a low discount on the new car price. It is the total package that matters, not the specific items. With credit cards, some programs offer a "low ball" initial interest rate with fuzzy, but potent, escalator clauses.

Some offers are front end loaded, while some are back end loaded. Front end loaded means that the largest benefits are offered in the first period of a multi-period agreement. Back end loaded agreements shift the best benefits for the other side to the later periods of the proposed agreement. Keep in mind that if you are paying out money, doing so as late as possible offers cash flow advantages, provided that interest is earned during the delay. Later payments will be made in dollars that inflation has usually eroded in value. In that sense, inflation is a friend of the debtor classes and an enemy of the creditor classes. If you are receiving money, barring tax consequences, the sooner the better is a good rule. Consider which of the following two offers is more advantageous for each side in a labor negotiation:

White Knight Corporation has placed a first economic offer on the bargaining table. It provides for a three year contract. The immediate (first year) increase is offered at 3%, the second year increase at 2%, and the third year increase at 1%, across the board.

Black Knight Corporation has placed a first economic offer on the bargaining table. It provides for a three year contract. The immediate (first year) increase is offered at 1%, the second year increase at 2%, and the third year increase at 3%, across the board.

The first offer is more favorable to the union, since the represented employees will be getting a larger increase for more of the contract term, but it is more costly to the employer for the same reason. The second offer delays the increases for the union represented employees, which is less costly for the employer which will have the use of its money for a longer period.

There are two ways in which a first offer may be improved. More may be added to the offer or the offer on the table may be modified by moving some of the items forward to earlier periods. In that sense, Black Knight has the advantage. It could end up in the same place as White Knight, but could show more movement in working its way there. Multiple item and multi-year agreements allow progress to be made by moving items forward.

✐ TIP

In a first offer, show some items only in the later periods. These items will indicate to the other side that they are available. Then, as you make subsequent offers, you may move these items to earlier periods to show flexibility, while showing additional items in the later periods.

A negotiating team that has followed the preparation and approval process outlined in this book will know what its final offer will look like long before it makes its first offer. This enables the use of backwards planning, as described in chapter 9. To formulate its initial offer, the negotiating team may use the authorized final offer and take a percentage of that offer to put on the table. There is no hard and fast rule as to the percentage of the authorized amount that should be chosen for a first offer. This is variable and may depend on the time frame remaining, the opportunity to make a number of economic offers, and the negotiating team's sense of what is necessary. The first offer should be generous enough to avoid being objectively insulting, but should still leave plenty of room for movement as an economic negotiation progresses. The receiving side's demands are far less important than the giving side's ultimate bottom line—its ultimate willingness to pay, whether voluntarily or under pressure.

⚡ TRAP

In a labor-management negotiation, the law requires that an employer who pleads inability to pay open its books on demand. An employer who is able to pay, but is unwilling, should be careful not to claim poverty or inability to pay. A large employer may be losing money in one part of its operation and making money in others. The fact that one site within a corporation is losing money does not mean the organization as a whole lacks the ability to pay. Union negotiators should seek a statement from the employer's negotiators that they are "unable to pay." Employer negotiators may speak of competitive pressures or of a facility that is losing money without opening their books, if they claim unwillingness to pay rather than poverty.

⚡ TIP

Consider as a basic starting point an initial economic offer at about sixty percent (60%) to seventy-five percent (75%) of the final authorization. If, however, you engage in a series of negotiations with the same people over time, or with people who may share information (such as labor unions), do not follow an invariable rule. If you do, and this becomes known, the other side will also be able to "reverse engineer" their way to your final position and will maximize their gains.

⚡ TIP

Never apologize for a first offer, but do not expect gratitude. No matter how reasonable your first offer is, objectively measured, the other side knows that there is likely to be more. After all, your first offer may well be labeled as such. They will be in no rush to accept this offer, or to compliment you for it. One possible speech accompanying a first offer might state, "This is our first offer to you. We believe it is a fair and generous offer in light of market forces. But, we still need to talk about economics with you. We want to understand your needs. We do have more to offer, provided we make progress and there is a sense of give and take on both sides." This speech makes explicit that the offer is not a "take it or leave it" one. It also makes clear that for there to be more money on the table, the other side must first make concessions.

INTERMEDIATE OFFERS

"A horse is dangerous at both ends and uncomfortable in the middle." [Ian Fleming] Intermediate offers come in the middle of the end game, paced to match the other side's response. As offers are made, the open issues on the table should be reduced in number. If there is no response to an offer, be very careful about offering additional concessions or you will be negotiating against yourself.

✐ TIP

The number of offers you make will vary. If progress is slow, make numerous offers, but keep the increments small and proportional to the rate of progress. If progress is good, be prepared to show more economic flexibility as the other side works toward resolution. If there is no progress at all, don't be afraid to hold your opening position and to demand that the other side respond to your offer by showing some movement.

Assuming progress is being made, the size of the increment in each subsequent offer should diminish from the prior offer. So, if your first offer was at sixty percent of your authorized final package, the second offer might be at eighty percent, an increment of twenty percent of final, the third at ninety percent, an increment of ten percent, the fourth at ninety-five percent of final, an increment of five percent, and the fifth and last offer at one hundred percent of final. The reason for the diminishing increments is to signal the other side that the well is gradually running dry and that further offers, if any (up to the final offer), will yield increasingly smaller concessions. Whenever possible, try to adhere to this decreasing increment pattern, whether the subject is wages, prices, what you will pay for a car, or a house or some other issue.

✐ TIP

Under time pressure, if you have prepared offers in advance (a good idea when the clock is a factor), avoid the ultimate mistake of handing the other side the wrong economic package. Color code your offers in a pattern that you clearly understand: for example, white paper for a first offer, pink for a second, blue for a third, light yellow for a fourth, and gold for a final. Take to the table with you only the offer you intend to distribute.

✐ TIP

If there are conditions or clarifications on your economic offer, be sure they are expressly listed in writing on the offer sheet. Differences over the meaning of an accepted offer may demolish trust. Consider the following:

Foreign Banknote Printers and the Money Printers Union are in negotiations for a successor labor agreement. Foreign Banknote hands across the table a final economic offer which states:

Across the board increases for all classifications:

FIRST YEAR	SECOND YEAR	THIRD YEAR
2.0%	1.5%	1.75%

The Money Printers accept. The contract is signed. At the beginning of the second year, the employer processes a wage increase of 1.5% not of the wages then in effect, but rather of the wages in effect a year earlier when the prior contract expired. "Oh, didn't you understand," Foreign Banknote Printers' Vice President of Labor Relations says, "the percentages on the chart are non-compound; that is they apply to the wages last in effect under the old contract, not each year's current wages under the new agreement. I think we said something about that." The union feels cheated. If the remark was actually made, it was forgotten. If it wasn't, the employer is stretching ambiguity and acting unethi-

> *cally. To prevent this type of problem, any qualifications or terms which could be read in multiple ways should be explained, in writing, in the offer. Had Foreign Banknote stated on the offer in writing, "all percentages will be computed on today's wages and are non-compound," there would be no real room for argument.*

Why would you choose non-compound percentages when you are making an offer which benefits the other side? The answer is that the use of non-compound numbers slightly increases the percentages in an offer, making it look better. When percentage increases are large, the distinctions between non-compound and compound increases are also large.

🖝 TRAP

Accepting figures without asking questions and seeking examples of how proposals work is an invitation to an eventual misunderstanding. **Even if the other side is not trying to deceive you, it is to no one's advantage to have misunderstandings about economic terms.** Don't be afraid to ask even if a question seems basic.

🖝 TIP

If you are offering money, do it in defined dollars, not in percentages which are subject to variance. Conversely, if you are receiving benefits, your interests will be best served by using percentage formulas. Consider the difference between an insurance policy that pays your actual loss up to $100,000 when your home burns and an insurance policy that pays the replacement value of that home. Replacement value is a moving target, while a capped actual loss can never be in excess of the cap. Also, for an employee who makes $40,000 per year, employer paid group life insurance equal to one hundred percent of a year's salary is better than flat rate life insurance of $40,000. If the employee gets a raise, the multiplication factor, or percentage, formula increases insurance, while the flat rate remains static.

BEST, LAST, AND FINAL OFFERS; THROW-INS; AND, "KICKERS"

"In my end is my beginning." [Mary Stuart] You are now nearing the end of the negotiation game. A match victory is almost in hand. You have only to make your final economic moves. To the non-professional negotiator, there may seem little difference between someone's best, last, and final offers, but to professionals, particularly those who work in labor-management relations, these terms have meaning. A best offer is a kind of stage setter, a signal that economic offers are drawing closer to the maximum. A last offer is a way of doing better than one's best offer, while still avoiding the word "final." **Do not use the label final on an offer unless you mean it. With the limited exceptions of throw-ins and "kickers," as explained below, once a final offer is made it should remain final.** Your final offer may be accompanied by a speech such as, "This is our final offer. There is no more. We are willing to explain any items and to clarify. We may consider shifting some items around. But, we do not intend to add any more economic value to this offer. The bank is now empty." Once you say something similar to this, be prepared to adhere firmly to it.

What is a "kicker" or a "throw-in?" In labor-management negotiations, when ratification by the body of represented employees is required for a final contract, an exception to the general rule of not adding to a final offer is to throw-in a selected benefit, or to add something desirable to the other side, *expressly in return for the other side's negotiators' commitment, in good faith, to unanimously (or less desirably, by a majority) promote the package for ratification.* If the other side does not accept the condition requiring a recommendation for ratification, the extra item is withdrawn. Because commercial business to business negotiations do not usually require ratification, the kicker concept is generally not applicable to them. In automobile negotiations, the dealer will frequently throw-in something minor on request, such as floor mats, when closing the deal.

Why should a final offer be cast in concrete? If you modify a final offer, your use of the word "final" will not be taken seriously in future negotiations. The other side will always assume there is still more to be had. In labor-management negotiations, this may cause a future strike.

You recently joined the Sluggish Slag Company as its chief negotiator and spokesperson. At your first negotiation for Slag, you put a final offer on the table, stating, "There isn't any more." The union spurns the package and demands another nickel be added to the wage rates as the price of settlement. You are surprised and call the Vice President of Operations for the Division and report the impending labor dispute. "I don't understand why they would strike over a nickel," you tell her. There is a silence on the other end of the phone. Subsequently, you find out that at the last negotiation the union tried the same ploy. This very same Vice President, in a state of panic over the possibility of a strike, ordered the company negotiating team to give the union an added nickel. The union's behavior is now perfectly explicable. They got more after the final offer last time, so it is not at all unreasonable for them to expect to get more again.

If negotiations break down or circumstances change, it is not always possible to adhere to the principle of refusing to modify your final offer. Your first effort should be to redistribute the same economic package in other ways that might be more acceptable in bringing both sides together, without adding to the package's economic value.

A word about "stopping the clock." Negotiators do sometimes "stop the clock" at the deadline hour in order to preserve the fiction that they are settling on time. Generally, this will be accompanied by an agreement that the status quo will prevail during the clock stopping period, or both sides will sign a written extension of an existing agreement for a set number of minutes or hours. In labor-management negotiations, employees may continue to work during the clock stopping period. This could be accomplished by either working without a contract (with the employer not locking employees out), or by extending the existing agreement (an extended contract period). The significance of a contact extension in relation to working without a contract is that in the former all of the terms of the contract are extended including a no strike pledge, but in the latter only the terms and conditions of employment are maintained from moment to moment and a strike is possible at any time.

TIP

Stopping the clock is not necessarily a problem, provided you are extremely close to agreement and simply need another hour or two to finish the details. However, if you are far apart, stopping the clock will probably serve no useful purpose. Stopping the clock is a technique that should be used sparingly.

THE END GAME AND NEGOTIATION POWER

"Power tends to corrupt, and absolute power corrupts absolutely." [Lord Acton] While it is dangerous to generalize, in the end stages of a negotiation issues are usually resolved in proportion to each side's relative bargaining power. If an issue cannot be settled, you or the other side will either have to give way, or in commercial negotiations walk away, or in labor-management situations risk a labor dispute. Walk away endings in commercial negotiations and labor disputes in labor-management bargaining often result from incompatible primary objectives or from political needs that cannot be sufficiently satisfied through compromise. Some negotiations have no settlement window. These negotiations are doomed to inevitable failure, no matter how professional the negotiators.

To the extent that resolution is possible but could not be obtained by negotiators' best efforts at problem solving and mutual involvement, power is the major determinant of final results. But, it is not the sheer extent of power one side has and that the other lacks that determines the actual outcome. It is the understanding of the sources of power and the knowledge of how to apply pressure that leads one party to prevail in those negotiations that ultimately come down to who blinks first. In end game negotiations, it is essential to apply sufficient pressure on the other side to cause it to yield on points that your side must have and which the other side is very resistant to giving away. **Applying pressure and exerting power does not mean that you should turn nasty or fail to be civil. Separate the other side's representatives personally from their positions. You are doing your job and they are doing their job. If it comes down to only one side perceiving itself as winning, although this is not a preferred outcome, you will want your side to be the winner. If you have dominant negotiating power, try not to blink first.**

It is an interesting phenomenon in labor-management negotiations that while except for national bargaining units in heavy manufacturing the employer usually has the bargaining power advantage, it is also far more likely that management negotiators will not understand the extent of that power or know how to use it. Union spokespersons frequently are professional negotiators. In relative terms, they are often better able to use the power they have, although since the PATCO strike during the Reagan administration, unions should no longer assume that strikes will always be successful.

A final word about negotiating power. Many negotiators quit taking gains when they are ahead and thereby yield advantages that are theirs to win. At the end of the Gulf War when General Schwartzkopf was negotiating a cease fire, he let the Iraqis have generous terms. He could have driven a much harder bargain. The Iraqis were defeated and could have been forced to make more concessions, but the war had been won and pressure was not fully applied. Conversely, what may have brought about the final end of the Cold War was the unremitting pressure that President Reagan kept on the Soviet Union, never letting up as they showed signs of collapse. Baseball teams know you can never have a large enough lead to ensure victory. **Don't end the negotiating game prematurely because you have "won enough for today." Just because you have achieved your primary objectives does not mean that you should not try to win your secondary goals and some of your smoke screens. When you have the advantage carry it to the point where you have gained as much as possible, consistent with good faith, a long term relationship, and ethical and legal constraints.**

WRAPPING UP THE FINAL PACKAGE

"There's a six-word formula for success: Think things through, then follow through." [Edward Rickenbacker] Assume that you've followed the principles in this text and you have just reached complete agreement with the other side, both in principle and with detailed language. Congratulations are in order, but you will need to follow through with some last minute details before breaking open the champagne.

What do you need to do after the handshake that marks final agreement? Make sure that nothing has been overlooked, that all the tentative agreements that comprise the full package have been initialed, and that no agreement in principle lacks necessary detailed implementing language. In some organizations, those who commissioned the negotiations may almost instantly demand a "cost of settlement" or "terms of the agreement" summary report. Once these things are completed, a brief rest and champagne are in order. In commercial and personal negotiations, you should be able to get signatures on your agreement quickly and the process is then complete. You need merely forward copies of the agreements to the appropriate people for action.

In the world of labor-management negotiations, the completion of negotiations at the bargaining table results in a complete "tentative agreement." This is not the end of the process, because the tentative agreement normally must be ratified by the union body. Until there is a formal ratification, there is no new agreement, although it is conventional to extend existing agreements for a short period to allow time for the ratification process. A word of caution. Most agreements recommended by union negotiators are ratified by the union body, but not all of them. Ratification meetings may slip out of the union leadership's control, particularly if they do not plan properly for the discussion and voting.

✐ TIP

Once a union and management have reached tentative agreement on a complete contract, it is usually to their mutual advantage to have that contract ratified. Hence, they have a common interest. If you are representing management, consider lending the union assistance with packaging the settlement for ratification and suggesting ways to present it, with due concern for the union's sensitivities since the presentation is an internal union matter. Most experienced union bargainers are very familiar with the things that enhance ratification, such as packing the meeting with supporters, recognizing the right people for pre-planned questions, and timing the ratification meeting properly. **Set a time limit by which you must be notified of the outcome of the ratification vote and after which your tentative agreement is either automatically withdrawn or subject to withdrawal at your discretion if it has not been ratified.**

Suppose that the union body rejects a tentative labor agreement. You will need to go back to the table. If the failure was in the ratification presentation, cosmetic changes may lead to another vote. If rejection was based on something substantive, the employer may consider ways to repackage the same level of economics for another vote. However, if the rejection was over an issue on which the employer cannot compromise, then it will be as if the tentative agreement had not been reached and all matters will once again be at least theoretically open for negotiation. If the old contract has expired without a written extension that is still effective, a labor dispute may occur.

DEADLOCK AND IMPASSE

"Crises and deadlocks when they occur have at least this advantage, that they force us to think." [Jawaharlal Nehru] Not all negotiations end in success stories. In commercial and personal negotiations either side may break off negotiations, permanently or temporarily. If the two side's primary objectives are in irreconcilable conflict, a deadlock will result. Except in labor-management negotiations, you may then turn to others and seek to open new lines of negotiation in the hope of finding a more congenial partner. Remember, you have not failed when you walk away from a negotiation in which it is not possible to obtain your side's primary objectives. Were you to reach agreement by compromising your primary objectives and going outside your authorized instructions, you would have failed. It is in this scenario that a fortune teller may suggest that you will soon be making a series of visits to the unemployment insurance office.

Jim Jordan and Michael Bird are the chief spokespersons for Endless Malls and Vast Acres, respectively. They have been negotiating a contract under which Endless Malls would purchase a large tract of land from Vast Acres for a shopping center. After weeks of negotiating with the help of a mediator, they settled all the major and minor points, with the exception of a final price. Jordan's negotiating instructions contain the primary objective of obtaining suitable land, at a cost not to exceed $1,000,000. Jordan makes a final offer at the $1,000,000 level. Bird rejects it, demanding $1,250,000. What Jordan cannot know is that Bird's negotiating instructions contain the primary objective of obtaining no less than $1,250,000 for the land. The mediator suggests to Jordan and Bird that they settle at $1,125,000, splitting the difference. Both decline. Jordan goes on to find other suitable land at an agreed upon price of $900,000. Suppose, however, that Jordan and Bird were so anxious to settle that they agreed to the mediator's "split the difference" proposal. Both would have exceeded their negotiating authority and have compromised their respective primary objectives. Both may now be looking for new jobs. Many non-professional negotiators, faced with being very close to settlement but unable to get there, will violate their instructions in order to settle. Negotiators do this at their peril.

Labor negotiations differ from commercial ones when a deadlock is reached. If you are bargaining in a personal or commercial negotiation, you may choose to travel an alternative path. If you are negotiating a labor agreement, you are not free to substitute a different negotiating partner. You must continue to bargain with the other side, even after deadlock. A deadlock, accompanied by a labor dispute, constitutes what may be characterized as "war by other means." Each side is now attempting to use its perceived relative power to hurt the other until the other side blinks. Private sector labor law does give employers (except those under the Railway Labor Act) one advantage—the right to implement their last proposal, at "impasse." An impasse is a technical legal term which means that a moment is occurring when neither side has any positional movement to offer the other. When this happens and the previous contract has expired without being extended, the employer may implement the last offer it has on the table. Impasse law is very complex and labor counsel should always be consulted.

DRIVING TOO HARD A BARGAIN MAY HAUNT YOU LATER

"The humble and the meek are thirsting for blood." [Joe Orton] Is it possible to win too much in a negotiation? The answer is a definite, "Yes." If you push the other side in a mandated continuing relationship too far, you will create resentments that will come home to roost when conditions change. After World War I, the Entente Powers imposed the harsh treaty of Versailles on Germany. The treaty was so severe that it gave a platform to German nationalists and helped create the climate that led to Hitler's Third Reich. A Lincoln-like "let 'em up easy" policy might have been a better long term approach.

Suppose you are a manufacturer who drives a great price bargain with a sole source supplier for whom you are the dominant customer. If the price is very low, it may seem you have a wonderful deal. But, should your sole source supplier be forced to lose money on every transaction with you and be unable to make up the losses with its other customers due to price competition, your sole source might fail, go into bankruptcy, or close altogether. Similarly, if you negotiate a wage level that is too low in relation to area labor markets, you may find that while your wage costs are modest, you are unable to compete in the labor markets for replacements for employees who leave as part of ordinary attrition or in response to higher wages elsewhere.

Assume that three years ago, during a time when the economy of his area was depressed and labor plentiful, Ebenezer Scrooge, the chief spokesperson for Luxury Industries, negotiated a contract with the Hard Laborers Union. Scrooge forced the union to accept a three year contract with wage rates at rock bottom minimums. By the beginning of the second year, the economy improved and labor went into short supply. Because its wage rates remained low and its competitors were both paying considerable higher rates and recruiting labor, Luxury Industries experienced very high turnover. The employees who left could not easily be replaced for few potential employees were willing to accept Luxury Industries pay rates. Responding to high turnover and the disruption caused by personnel movement became quite expensive. Luxury Industries terminated Scrooge's services and hired Linus Van Pelt as its new chief negotiator. Now, to bring Luxury Industries wages into line with its labor market competitors, Van Pelt must put one large wage offer after another on the bargaining table. The rank and file union members are bewildered. They are more than ready to accept each new offer as incredibly generous. The union's international representative, an experienced negotiator, tells the rank and file what has happened and persists in demanding more. Finally, when wages have "caught up" with market forces, the union accepts an economic offer. The Company's excessive "win" three years previously has forced it into playing catch up. As an additional problem, three years hence, no matter what the labor market does, the employees are likely to again expect big increases.

The problem of winning too much is primarily applicable to negotiations when you need to have an ongoing relationship with the other side. If you achieve a terrific buy on a Persian rug in Turkey and are not likely to return to that shop ever again, you need not worry about driving too hard a bargain (unless of course, the low price suggests that the goods are stolen property). In business to business negotiations, you will often be negotiating with people you will want to negotiate with repeatedly and with whom you need to maintain an ongoing relationship based on trust. Going too far, even if legal and ethical, may be counterproductive in the long run under these circumstances. Successful, winning negotiations should be pushed no further than the point at which you will do yourself long term harm by going still further.

In the next chapter, we will look at some of the chores that may still remain in the wake of your negotiation. If the negotiation was between labor and management, both sides will have to worry about getting a successful ratification vote from the union represented employees. In any form of business negotiation, a "cost of settlement" report may be required. You will need to follow up to enforce your negotiated agreement and, in long term relationships, you will need to set the stage for the next negotiation. So, although you may have won your match, we are not quite finished.

CHAPTER 14

FOLLOWING UP
ON YOUR RESULTS

"Begin at the beginning and go on until you come to the end: then stop." [Lewis Carroll] If you have been conducting an actual negotiation and have worked your way chronologically to this point with a successful negotiation outcome, congratulations. Your task is almost, but not quite, over. You have achieved your bargain at the table but there is still some important follow up work which may be required. Don't assume that the handshake across the table that marks a completed deal means it is time to celebrate. You've done well and you deserve a respite, but only briefly.

SELLING YOUR PACKAGE TO GET NECESSARY RATIFICATIONS

If your negotiation was commercial and you did not formalize any ratification requirements, you can sit back, relax, and skip this issue. If your negotiation was personal, perhaps for a car, the sales representative's deal with you may have to be approved by a sales manager, a form of ratification. Otherwise, in the private sector, ratification is usually only necessary in labor-management negotiations. There, management does not need to ratify. Ratification (if required) is only by the union side.

In the last chapter, we took a brief look at the role of ratification in the context of the end game. Now, we will look at ratification process in greater depth and consider what to do if ratification fails. Once a complete agreement is reached, management and the union may begin working together for ratification. Don't be surprised if a union, for political or face saving reasons, rejects management's offer of help. The importance of the ratification requirement should not be underestimated. If ratification fails, both sides' laboriously worked out complete labor agreement may be gone with the wind or it may require several additional bargaining sessions to recast the original agreement for another vote. There may be a long labor dispute before another tentative contract is reached. Make no mistake, ratification is not always a "slam-dunk."

Clark Kent Enterprises and the Kryptonite Workers Union have reached a complete tentative agreement across the bargaining table and the union team has agreed to unanimously recommend the package to the union body for ratification. The union negotiators, communicating with the represented employees to obtain ratification, try to characterize the settlement as large, while the management negotiators, communicating with their superiors, try to characterize the same settlement as modest. Both sides will use statistical and presentation tools to put the right "spin" on the outcome. The union, which criticized the company's proposals for benefit improvements at the table as "too cheap," in its ratification document to the employees stresses the number of improvements it won, ignoring their small value to each employee. The employer's negotiators, when reporting on the cost of settlement internally, naturally emphasize the low cost of the benefit changes. In making its wage offers during negotiations, company negotiators stated the percentage increases over a three year term based on today's wages (non-compound increases), which made the increases look slightly larger. To win the ratification it now also wants, the union, which was demanding compound values from the employer during negotiations, now happily uses the employer's non-compound numbers. At the ratification meeting, the union also uses a number of charts and tables provided by the employer during negotiations, about which they were previously skeptical. To assist the union, the employer has its graphic arts department make up some new colorful charts and graphs which show the settlement in the most favorable light. Whatever they are reporting internally to minimize concessions, management's negotiation team members assist the union to characterize the union's gains in the best possible light for the represented employ-

ees. There are limits. Private sector federal labor law makes it unlawful for an employer to provide a union with "anything of value." Support services of this type are generally ignored, but money must not be given to the union. During this period, management says little about the settlement to the public or to employees. When ratification is complete, management's negotiators then make a more detailed statement to supervisors and managers about the terms of the settlement.

🖉 TIP

If the employer wants a high turnout for the ratification election, it may offer to permit the union to hold the ratification vote on company premises. A high turnout is not always desirable and may run counter to a union's ratification strategy of holding a quick meeting with only a core group of supporters attending. The question of turn out may influence each side's ratification strategy.

🖉 TRAP

A final negotiation package which runs contra to bargaining unit demographics will be far less likely to be ratified. If, for example, the work force is mostly nearing retirement age and is very interested in pensions, putting all the available economic increases into wages may be rejected, while if the work force is mostly young, large pension increases at the cost of small wage improvements may prevent ratification.

🖉 TRICK

A ratification that is achieved by a narrow majority may be read by management's negotiators as an indicia of their success. An overwhelming ratification generally indicates that the employer, when it drew up its negotiation plan and put money on the table, placed more there than was necessary for settlement. A close positive vote is feedback demonstrating a correct estimate of what was required to settle.

Suppose that ratification fails. Under the National Labor Relations Act, the parties continue to have a duty to meet and bargain in good faith. The first post-ratification failure meeting should be about why ratification failed. If the defect was in the way in which the package was presented or was due to a failure of the union leadership to control the meeting, it may only be necessary to make cosmetic changes and then to resubmit the "revised" agreement for a new ratification vote. If the problem is more fundamental, you will need to discuss what the problem was and whether management is willing to make any changes to address it. Sometimes, these situations may be resolved by redistribution of the available economic resources in a different package, but one which has the same overall cost to the employer.

Ratification failures followed by demands for greater economic concessions are a big problem for employer negotiation teams. Any upward movement after the rejection of a final offer package through ratification failure sets the stage for future ratification failure. Refusal to add money may lead to a lengthy labor dispute. These same scenarios are also very difficult for a union. Failure of the union body to consent to the package recommended by their negotiators leaves union representatives looking weak and unable to confirm the commitments they made to management and which they might make in the future. Management may also complicate the union's task by offering the union choices about the redistribution of an economic package. Choices tend to cause enormous political infighting within the union over the division of the resources.

BigOne and the Omni Workers Union reached a full tentative labor agreement. The union negotiating team agreed to unanimously recommend the package to the employees. However, the one hundred employee bargaining unit rejected ratification by a vote of fifty-five to forty-five. The bargaining unit has interesting demographics. Forty-five percent of the unit is between fifty-five and sixty-five years of age and most of its members have many years of plant seniority. This group is very interested in pension improvements and considers pension gains far more important than wage gains. This group also provides most of the members of the union bargaining team. Because of a hiring gap, the other fifty-five percent of the work force is between eighteen and thirty-five years of age (no one is between thirty-six and fifty-four). This lower seniority group has very little interest in pension improvements and considers wage gains to be far more important. To satisfy bargaining committee members, most of whom are older and who stressed the union principle of seniority, management structured the origi-

nal package to modestly favor pensions over wages. At the first meeting after the failure to ratify, BigOne tossed the distribution of economics between wages and pensions back to the union. Giving them charts of the relative costs of pension improvements and wage improvements, the company declared, "We don't care how you do this, as long as we don't spend more on the redistribution than we had on the table at the time we settled. We leave it to you to work this out." Company and union representatives then went into separate caucuses. Despite considerable room separation, company team members heard the union team members arguing with each other loudly about what to do with the money. In the end, the union team deadlocked and asked the employer to do the job. They rebalanced the package to slightly favor the less senior but more numerous group. The union bargaining committee felt compelled to accept the changes and the revised package was ratified by a fifty-seven to forty-three vote margin.

✐ TIP

If you are a management negotiator, you should generally avoid giving the union choices and options for the redistribution of economics unless you wish to cause internal problems within the union caucus or you have no other recourse. Choices pit one union group against another but a "divide and conquer" strategy also runs the risk of "dividing and destroying" those who could bring about ratification.

COST OF SETTLEMENT REPORTS

"As we read the school reports on our children, we realize a sense of relief that can rise to delight that thank Heaven nobody is reporting in this fashion on us." [J. B. Priestley] Many organizations have a thirst for reports and data. Suppose you've had a long commercial or labor negotiation and reached a final agreement. You are celebrating in the bar of the hotel where you negotiated. The telephone rings and you make the mistake of answering. One of your internal people demands that you submit a "cost of settlement (or agreement) report" immediately. If this happens, don't be surprised. Sophisticated modern organizations tend to want cost data very quickly after a negotiation. Personal negotiators will want to figure out later how well they did in a negotiation but at least they don't have to face the demand for these reports.

If your negotiation utilized computerized costing systems a cost of settlement report may be easy to generate. One of the purposes of a cost of settlement report is to be sure that you, as a seemingly successful negotiator, did not achieve settlement by going outside your authorization. A professional negotiator might have a cost of settlement report ready to send before being asked to generate one.

✍ TRAP

A flag may be raised when you turn in a cost of settlement report that comes in well under your authorized budget. First, it may indicate that the negotiation plan you devised and the authorization you requested allowed for far more money than necessary. This means you did not accurately predict what was required for settlement and might be prone to the same failure in the future. Second, it raises the question of whether you may have risked a disastrous negotiation outcome in order to achieve a "below budget" settlement. This is particularly true if the below budget savings that were obtained were not large and (in labor negotiations) the ratification vote shows that the package came close to failure. In short, if you save too much of your authorization you will be suspect. If you spend it all and get a lopsided favorable ratification vote, you will also be suspect. Your personal objective is to have spent just the right amount of resources to get a favorable outcome. If you happen to be a union negotiator, a large ratification majority may be viewed an indicator of your success. There are so many ways to lose. This is not an easy game!

MAKING SURE YOU GET WHAT YOU BARGAINED FOR

"I have a habit of comparing the phraseology of communiqués. . . noting a certain similarity of words, a certain similarity of optimism. . . and a certain similarity in the lack of practical results during the ensuing years." [Margaret Thatcher] The success of your negotiation cannot be measured entirely by the agreement that you secure today. To really determine how well you've done, you must follow up, look at the practical results over the agreement's term, and make sure that the bargain is being carried out by both sides. Post-negotiation failures generally result from either poor estimates of the value of the provisions that were sought and won or from failures of the organizational bureaucracy to make the mandated changes. Negotiation failures are learning points for future bargaining.

You may need to establish some base line benchmarks to measure the value of what you've won in negotiations. These benchmarks might include the cost to produce or purchase a unit, the number of items produced per work hour, or reductions in the costs of carrying out certain operations. What is important is to revisit these benchmarks from time to time after the completion of your negotiation. Almost all negotiation plans include some estimate of predicted results. Determining the reality of these projected outcomes requires follow up.

✒ TIP

In multiple year agreements, annually review the actual progress toward your projected goals and toward any gains you claimed in your post-settlement report. When slippage occurs, find out why and move to correct the problem. If you are managing negotiations, require these annual reports from those who negotiated agreements and reported successes.

Another problem in monitoring compliance with negotiated agreements with ongoing terms is administrative inertia and passive (or active) resistance to change. The fact is that people often find it difficult to accept change, particularly change they may view as retrogressive. Resistance will not be confined to the other side. Your own people may not want to make the changes that you have won in negotiations. There are several "enemies" to compliance with ongoing negotiated agreements:

* "The computer isn't set up to do that";
* "We'll get to it when we can (passive resistance)"; and
* "But, we've never done it that way."

Blaming the computer is convenient. While you should keep in mind the problems of altering existing computerized systems when making changes in negotiated agreements, you may need to remind people that an organization's goals are not set for the convenience of the systems analysts and the programmers. Computers do what programmers tell them to do. Certainly, a change in a contractual provision may require some work from your systems people. But, that is part of what they get paid to do. There are magnetic stickers that say, "When all else fails, blame the computer."

✒ TIP

Don't assume that the computer support group in your organization will automatically make the necessary changes to carry out the terms of your negotiated agreement. Follow up as soon as the agreement is reached to be sure that computerized systems will be altered as necessary. Then, check again frequently until it is done.

Passive resistance to changes in renegotiated agreements is a definite danger, particularly toward alterations in provisions beloved of the day to day administrators of the agreement or enforcing changes they perceive as "unfair." If you do not follow up to insure compliance by these people you will risk losing the fruits of your negotiation in the bureaucratic maze. If you challenge them, these obstructers may tell you they don't have time to make the changes or that the changes are just "wrong." Remember that many negotiated agreements are evidenced by legally binding contracts. If the changes you make are unpopular, expect active or passive resistance to implementation. Overcoming this requires you to follow up.

Passionetta Advocate, a plaintiff's attorney, negotiated a settlement of her client's employment discrimination claim against Puppy Biscuit Industries. Under the settlement, Puppy Biscuit was required to pay the plaintiff a lump sum in damages and to consider her for certain future openings. The lump sum was paid. At that point, Advocate moved on to other cases with pressing deadlines. Six months later, the plaintiff was back in Advocate's office. "I don't think they have been giving me the consideration for openings they promised," she told Advocate. Advocate telephoned Puppy Biscuit and only after a number of calls went unreturned was she able to speak with their attorney. The result was a series of excuses and half explanations. Ongoing settlement terms require monitoring. There should be no expectation of automatic compliance.

✒ TIP

Legal counsel negotiating settlement arrangements with ongoing terms should establish a compliance reporting system which utilizes the recipient of the negotiated benefit to moni-

CHAPTER 14—FOLLOWING UP ON YOUR RESULTS

tor compliance and report back. A responsible individual on the other side should be named in the settlement as responsible to insure the other side's compliance.

Another form of passive resistance to negotiated changes is the "but, we've always done it that way, so that's the right way" syndrome. During a negotiation, you may trade away an existing right or benefit in return for something else. There are always individuals who are devoted to the "time tested" extant practices. When changes are made, these individuals may seek to nullify them by not carrying them out.

Tight and Pinch Shoe Manufacturers has engaged in a prolonged labor contract negotiation with the Shod Workers United union for a successor agreement at its Blister City plant. The negotiations featured "win-win" bargaining. The union won unusually large base wage increases in relation to similar companies in the region, but in return it gave the employer a number of work rule and payroll changes. The union agreed to an employer proposal eliminating the prior pay practice of paying time and one half for all work on Saturdays and double time for all work on Sundays. This payment system was not in the contract, but existed only as a result of a long established payroll practice. Both teams were well pleased with the outcome and believed they had struck a just bargain. Six months later, the chief negotiator for Tight and Pinch, who is based at distant corporate headquarters, visited the Blister City plant. She was surprised to find that the payroll department at the plant had continued to pay employees time and half for all Saturday work and double time for all Sunday work. When she confronted the payroll manager, he said, "But, we've paid it that way since the time my grandfather ran this department. Saturday work should be paid at time and a half and Sunday work at double time. That's fair." The spokesperson, invoking corporate authority and explaining the nature of the bargain, insisted on immediate compliance with the changed payroll terms. She informed the payroll manager he did not have the authority to ignore a negotiated agreement. The payroll manager grudgingly complied. Five days later, an employee filed a grievance alleging that by continuing to pay Saturday and Sunday premiums, the company's payroll department had reestablished the past practice of paying time and a half and double time for Saturday and Sunday work. Eventually an arbitrator ruled that Tight and Pinch had reverted to the prior payroll practice and was bound to observe it for at least the term of the current three year agreement. The result is that the union continues to enjoy the benefits of the negotiated bargain, but the employer loses the value of the pay practice supposedly eliminated as part of that bargain. Failure to follow up and insure that payroll made the negotiated changes has made Tight and Pinch's negotiation achievement worthless. If Tight and Pinch still wants that benefit, they will have to negotiate for it a second time in the next negotiation and probably will have to pay for it a second time by making additional concessions.

⚡ TIP

Never assume that administrative personnel will carry out changes in a negotiated agreement as a matter of routine. The negotiator should always check to be sure that the organization is implementing negotiated changes.

⚡ TRAP

In labor agreements, the principle of past practice makes it difficult for an employer to make unilateral changes during the term of an agreement. In the case of pay practices, they may be discontinued only by negotiating an express provision permitting the change or by unilaterally announcing an intent to change the payroll practice during the negotiations preceding the start of a successor agreement (giving the union the opportunity to try to negotiate the practice into contract language). Failure to carry through on a proper change in a pay practice may vitiate a negotiated gain.

SETTING THE STAGE FOR THE NEXT NEGOTIATION

"By failing to prepare, you are preparing to fail." [Benjamin Franklin] The match is over and you have done a complete follow up. Your tasks are not finished if your negotiation formed part of an ongoing series in which a new agreement will be sought with the same party when the current agreement is nearing expiration. What is required now is for you to set the stage for the next negotiation match. This is a long, slow, continuous process.

Negotiators and organizations which have long term negotiation goals are far more likely to achieve successes than those that operate only with a short term horizon. There are changes in negotiated agreements that are too drastic to be achievable in one negotiation, but which require spreading the change out over a period of years and a series of agreements. Under these conditions, the best negotiation plan is not only a blueprint for the current negotiation, but a long range plan as well.

At First Equality Space Shuttle Products, production, maintenance, and technical employees are represented by the Space Workers Union. The company produces a wide range of complex and highly technical products built to exacting specifications. The Space Workers Union was built on the slogan "a loaf of bread costs the same for all of us." As a result of the union's orientation and management's need to avoid labor disputes, the pay structure at First Equality provides virtually the same rate of pay for all union represented workers from the plant custodian to the plant electrician and computer-aided designer. Because of its almost flat wage rate, the company has an overabundance of applicants for custodial positions but finds it almost impossible to find qualified electricians or computer-aided design technicians. The company decides, as a primary objective, that it must begin to drive a wage spread between the least and most skilled classifications. Because the spread needs to be wide and is now so flat and because the union is likely to resist heavily, the company decides that the wage spread must be developed not in a single three year contract but over a period of three contracts (normally nine years, based on past history). This long term objective becomes part of the company's negotiating plan.

There is a short story about a person who commits what he thinks is the perfect murder of his wife on her birthday. However, when he brings the body into his home and opens the door, the lights come on and there is a great shout from a crowd yelling, "surprise." Whatever you may do in negotiating a series of agreements with the same party, one of the most important things to avoid is strategic surprise. New or important issues should be foreshadowed long before negotiations begin and not be raised for the first time at the bargaining table. Psychology teaches that it is easier to introduce change to people who are prepared for it than it is to those who are surprised and have to rapidly assimilate the need for strategic change. Tactical moves are another matter. There, surprise may be useful at times. But, each side's major goals and needs are more likely to be met when the other side understands the driving motivations before negotiations ever begin.

🖋 TIP

In an ongoing relationship, in which both sides are in constant communication, you should (in a planned way) let the other side know what concerns you have. For example, a company which is under cost pressure from foreign competition should be sure and talk about this often during its contacts with another party which is one of its contractual suppliers. At the next negotiation, when the company with the foreign pressures stresses that it needs price relief because its own market has become more competitive, this will no longer come as a surprise to its negotiating partner. A company wanting to make reductions in its health care plan should share newspaper articles and stories related to the high cost of health insurance with its employees and union well in advance of negotiations, so there will be no surprise when the company presses for changes. A shocked, surprised negotiating opponent will prove to be a difficult one.

CONCLUSION

"O! that a man might know the end of this day's business ere it come." [William Shakespeare] Game, Set, Match. Follow up and preparation for the next match, done. The techniques outlined in this book have taken you step by step from initial planning to the end of your negotiation, and a bit beyond. Because negotiations are an unavoidable part of life, you will be repeating this cycle over and over, consciously or unconsciously. Once you become used to applying the techniques, they will serve you in good stead in all sorts and varieties of negotiations. Of course, you won't be carrying out all the steps for all the negotiations. But, when you do need to negotiate, familiarity with the techniques in this book should help you deal with professional, as well as inexperienced, negotiators. If you feel a bit more confident, you can and you will do better, achieve more success, and you will win the negotiations game. Good planning and good luck!

ABOUT THE AUTHOR

Henry S. Kramer is a Professor at the New York State School of Industrial and Labor Relations, Cornell University, where he teaches a negotiations simulation program. He is the former Corporate Manager of Labor Relations and Legal Services for BASF Corporation, serving there as chief spokesperson in negotiations, and was previously Director of Employee Relations for Cornell University. He is a consultant and trainer in negotiations techniques. Mr. Kramer has also authored two successful desk reference texts for attorneys, human resource managers, and others: *Alternative Dispute Resolution in the Work Place* and *Sex Discrimination and Sexual Harassment in the Work Place* (co-authored), both published by Law Journal Press.